THE BIG BOOK OF
BACKYARD COOKING

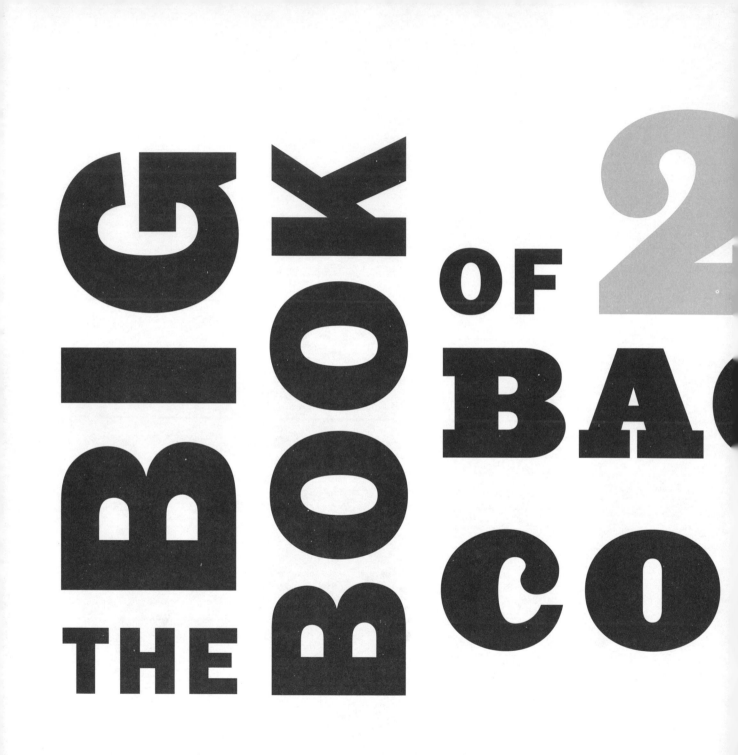

50

FAVORITE RECIPES FOR ENJOYING THE GREAT OUTDOORS

KYARD

BY BETTY ROSBOTTOM

oking

CHRONICLE BOOKS

SAN FRANCISCO

TEXT COPYRIGHT © 2004 BY
BETTY ROSBOTTOM.
COVER PHOTOGRAPH COPYRIGHT © 2004 BY
RITA MAAS.

LIBRARY OF CONGRESS CATALOGING-IN-PUBLICATION
DATA AVAILABLE.

ISBN **0-8118-3604-5**

MANUFACTURED IN
CANADA

DESIGN AND ILLUSTRATION
AISHA BURNES/ gogotumbleweed.com

DISTRIBUTED IN CANADA BY
RAINCOAST BOOKS
9050 SHAUGHNESSY STREET
VANCOUVER, BRITISH COLUMBIA V6P 6E5

10   9   8   7   6   5   4   3   2   1

CHRONICLE BOOKS LLC
85 SECOND STREET
SAN FRANCISCO, CALIFORNIA 94105

www.chroniclebooks.com

DEDICATION

This book, which is designed to bring family and friends together, is dedicated to my own family:

To Ronny, my husband and my best recipe-tester, who samples both my successes and disasters with equal enthusiasm, and who is the most efficient dish-washer I could ever hope for;

To Michael, my son, who has turned into a talented cook himself, both to my surprise and his, and some of whose ideas can be found on the following pages;

To Heidi, my daughter-in-law, who married into a family of serious eaters and loves good food and entertaining as much as we do;

And, finally, and with great expectations, to Edie, my granddaughter, who now dines on baby food, but whose DNA is primed for her to have an adventurous palate, too!

ACKNOWLEDGMENTS

No cookbook, especially one like this with 250 recipes, is ever the effort of a single person. Students, assistants, professional colleagues, neighbors, friends, and family all helped me in various ways to bring this book to fruition.

My longtime cooking associates, Emily Bell and Sheri Lisak, came on board early in the planning stages and offered creative and practical advice every step of the way. Deb Brown, Jane Giat, and Ellen Wilkins Ellis helped create and test recipes in my kitchen for months on end. Lesley Abrams-Schwartz traveled from Boston to my home in western Massachusetts weekly to cook with me. And more than a dozen generous friends and cooking students all over the country volunteered to make and critique the finished recipes. Thank you Marilyn Dougherty, Ann Ryan Small, Jackie Murrill, Cindy Pizzanelli, Sara Evans, Suzanne Goldberg, Marilyn Cozad, Cheryl Brooks, Mark Zacek, Brenda McDowell, Barbara Morse, and Gerry and Gavin Spence.

Elinor Lipman and Ellen Wilkins Ellis offered invaluable suggestions when it came time to write the text for this book.

The inspiration for some of the recipes in this collection came from my weekly column, "That's Entertaining," published by The Los Angeles Times Syndicate, and from articles I authored in *Bon Appétit* magazine. I would like to thank my editors, Connie Pollack at the Syndicate and Kristine Kidd, and Barbara Fairchild at *Bon Appétit*, for giving me the opportunity to write about food.

My longtime agent, Judith Weber, found a perfect home for this book at Chronicle Books, where Bill LeBlond, editor *extraordinaire*, welcomed it. Thanks also to book designer Aisha Burnes.

And, although I've come a long way in tapping out the pages of a manuscript on my laptop, this project never would have been completed without the help of computer whiz Nicholas Dahlman.

Last I would like to thank my family, especially my husband, for all their love and support.

Americans began their love affair with backyard cooking over fifty years ago, after World War II. Across the country during the late 1940s and early 1950s, there was a burst of suburban development in the United States. It was the era when ranch homes surrounded by grassy yards were sprouting up outside the country's metropolises. The economy was flourishing, and many growing families moved from cities to these out-lying areas. Gradually, America's suburban landscape became defined by quiet streets lined with neat rows of houses, each with its own patch of green.

Two things influenced these new suburbanites to start cooking outdoors. Leisure time was one of them. Many had 9-to-5 jobs with weekends free. Individuals could finally relax after the manic war years, and slowed their pace. The second influence was their new habitat. A huge number of Americans now lived in houses surrounded by a yard—a public one in the front and a more private one in the back. It didn't take long for people to discover that the backyard, sheltered from the street, was an invit-ing setting for friends and family to gather. The welcoming breezes on warm days and nights were an enticement as well, because most homes, post World War II, were not air-conditioned.

Gradually, the yard evolved into another room—an outdoor dining room—and eating there was a natural but exciting development. Eventually, cooking began to take place outside, too. The appearance of the famous Weber kettle grill, invented in 1951 and first sold in 1952, made cooking over an open fire an easy enterprise. The rest is history. Backyard cooking quickly became a national trend, one that has not

INTRO

waned over the years. Decades later, cooking and eating outdoors are both firmly ensconced as a defining part of American culture.

Through the decades many foods have become mainstays of backyard menus. Of course, there's that trio of grill favorites—steaks, burgers, and hot dogs—as popular today as in the early days of backyard cooking. But, now we cook all manner of meats, fish, and fowl, as well as vegetables, over searing flames. Then there are the backyard classics—dishes that are not grilled but still beloved outdoor fare: boiled lobsters, steamed mussels, fried chicken, or baked ham served cool, and sandwiches. Slaws and salads, and soothing drinks to quench a warm day's thirst, are other perennials. No alfresco meal would be complete without a sweet conclusion. An A-list of desserts would include fruit and icebox pies; pound, layer, or short cakes; crisps and crumbles; brownies; cookies; and ice creams.

Just thinking about these foods makes my mouth water. Creating a collection of recipes for backyard cooking has been a truly delicious project. You'll find many familiar recipes on the following pages. In each case I looked for the best version of such dishes. Try, for example, Old-Fashioned Potato Salad with mashed hard-boiled eggs in the mayonnaise dressing, or the easy baked beans recipe called A Mixed Bag of Beans, or Burnt-Sugar Vanilla Ice Cream, made with caramelized sugar. Other entries are popular dishes with updates. Grilled Caesar Salad has the usual ingredients, but the lettuce is grilled in this version. And, instead of standard coleslaw, you can choose from Parmesan Black Pepper Coleslaw, Red and Yellow Pepper Coleslaw, and Coleslaw with Spanish Olives.

America's culinary borders extend far beyond our Atlantic and Pacific coastlines and past our neighbors Canada and Mexico, so many recipes in this book have international touches. Brazil's celebrated parsley sauce, chimichurri, is perfectly gorgeous spooned over lightly charred steaks. Gremolata, the famous Italian herb garnish, embellishes grilled veal chops, while wasabi powder, fiery ground horseradish root from Japan, adds pizzazz to mayonnaise. From southern France, there's a Provençal-inspired vegetable tart. Sutrisno's Chicken Satay is an authentic dish from Indonesia, and Zucchini, Potatoes, and Tomatoes, Cooked Greek-Style found its way to me via a Greek friend. Countries with warm climates seem to have an inexhaustible repertoire of cooling drinks to stave off the heat, so there are mojitos from Cuba, caipirinhas from Brazil, and sangria from Spain.

Having taught cooking for well over two decades, I've noticed how much my students appreciate extra information—those little tips and hints that aren't usually written into a recipe. So, sprinkled throughout this book, you'll find notes on marketing for new or unusual ingredients. You'll discover that there is a lot of descriptive detail in the steps of each recipe to ensure that you make these dishes successfully. Finally, since every home cook I have ever encountered always asks me if a dish can be prepared in advance, you'll see many make-ahead suggestions.

This is the cookbook for those who love to eat and entertain outside. Whether you have a huge expanse of green lawn, a porch, a patio, or a city rooftop, food just seems to taste better when sampled under the stars or the sun's warming rays. The dishes in this collection are not fancy, but rather down-to-earth fare brimming with flavor, to enjoy leisurely with family, friends, and neighbors. I hope they will be an inspiration for you to dine out—in your backyard!

BASICS:
TIPS AND HELPFUL HINTS, TECHNIQUES, AND SOME BASIC RECIPES

TIPS AND HELPFUL HINTS

ABOUT GRILLING

Whether you use a charcoal or a gas grill, make a mental note of how long it takes you to grill foods to the desired degree of doneness. Grills (even different makes of charcoal or gas grills) work differently. **Some grills cook faster than others, so cooking times can vary widely depending on the type of grill used and the intensity of the heat. Being familiar with your own grill will help you calculate cooking times accurately.**

✳ If you are using a charcoal grill, you can avoid using starter fluids by investing in a metal chimney stack. You fill the bottom of this cylinder with crushed newspaper and mound charcoal briquets on top. After lighting the paper you simply wait for the fire to turn the coals gray. Then the chimney is removed and the hot coals are scattered.

✳ Always be sure the grill rack is clean and oiled before grilling.

✳ A grill basket or grate is helpful when cooking fish or other items likely to stick on a grill rack.

✳ An instant-read thermometer is an inexpensive and helpful tool for checking the internal temperature of meats and poultry.

✳ When grilling skewered foods, you can use either metal or wooden skewers. When using the latter, soak them for 30 minutes in water to cover to avoid burning.

✳ The degree of doneness of grilled foods is one of choice. My own opinion is that beef and lamb are best when rosy pink inside, although an exception to this is beef burgers. Recent recommendations are to cook them to medium (160 degrees F) for safety reasons. Poultry is done when the juices run clear when the meatiest (usually the thigh) area is pierced with a knife. Fish fillets are done when the flesh is opaque and flakes easily. Grilled vegetables should retain just a slight degree of crispness when cooked.

When smoking food on the grill, be prepared to start a charcoal fire a second time. Smoking is often a slow process. To keep the food moist, it's smart to nestle a small flameproof bowl of water among the coals.

ABOUT BUYING FISH

Buy the freshest fish available, and use it that day or as soon as possible after purchase. Fish should smell fresh; if you detect a "fishy" scent, don't buy it. And, it's never a bad idea to ask the fishmonger when the fish arrived in the store. That way you'll know exactly how old your seafood is. Oysters, mussels, and lobsters should be kept alive until cooking, so do not refrigerate them in a plastic bag, which would cause them to suffocate.

ABOUT VEGETABLES AND SALADS

It goes without saying that buying the freshest and best produce available, an easy task in warm-weather months when farmers' markets abound, is a golden rule. Look for tender young green beans; for peppers, summer squash, and eggplants without blemishes; and for lettuces picked that very day. If you have local farms in your area that allow berry picking, take advantage of this opportunity. Strawberries and raspberries that are handpicked are far superior to the cellophane-wrapped packages in the supermarket.

ABOUT FRESH HERBS

Nothing adds more flavor or color to a dish than fresh herbs, and today they are readily available in our supermarkets. However, if a recipe calls for a fresh herb that you can't find, you can substitute dried, using a third of the fresh amount specified, since dried herbs are more concentrated in taste.

ABOUT SALTS

Table salt, fine-grained with additives, is an all-purpose salt. It can be used to season savory dishes and is always used in baking. Kosher salt, which is coarse-grained and additive free, is often preferable to table salt because its texture and flavor are more appealing. Coarse kosher salt crystals are particularly good to use in rubs for steaks and other meats. Sea salt, which I think of as a "finishing" salt because it is best when used to season a finished dish, is another choice. It is more costly than table and kosher salt, since it is harvested from sea water, sometimes by hand. Sea salts contain trace minerals and are incredible flavor boosters. A few grains of sea salt sprinkled over a bowl of blanched green beans or a platter of grilled potatoes will enhance these dishes immeasurably. One of the best-known sea salts is fleur de sel, which comes from France. For the recipes in this collection, count on using table salt unless otherwise indicated.

ABOUT ICE-CREAM MAKING

An electric ice-cream machine is a good investment for fans of homemade ice cream. You simply assemble the ice-cream base, pour it in the freezer bowl of the machine, turn on the power, and let it churn away. No more salt or mess. Professional machines are quite costly, but the new home models are modestly priced and readily available. Many of these have a 1½-quart-capacity freezer, ideal for home cooks.

SOME BASIC TECHNIQUES

TOASTING NUTS, SEEDS, OR COCONUT FLAKES

ALMONDS, PECANS, AND WALNUTS Arrange an oven shelf at center position and preheat oven to 350 degrees F. Spread nuts on a rimmed baking sheet and bake until lightly browned. Almonds will take 6 to 8 minutes, pecans 5 to 6 minutes, and walnuts 5 to 8 minutes. Watch carefully so nuts do not burn. Remove and cool.

SESAME SEEDS Place seeds in a medium skillet over medium heat, and stir until golden brown, 3 to 5 minutes. Remove and cool.

SWEETENED COCONUT FLAKES Arrange an oven shelf at center position and preheat oven to 350 degrees F. Spread coconut flakes on a rimmed baking sheet, and bake about 5 minutes until flakes just start to brown. Watch carefully, as coconut flakes brown very quickly. Remove, transfer to a plate, and cool.

CRUSHING FENNEL, CARAWAY, OR ROSEMARY SEEDS

Crushing seeds releases more of their flavor. There are several ways to do this. Crush them in a mortar with a pestle. Or, place the seeds in a small plastic bag, and using a meat pounder or rolling pin, crush them until they resemble a very coarse powder. You can also grind them in a small electric mini-grinder. Just make certain you clean this machine thoroughly after each use so that the taste of the just-ground seeds is completely removed.

"PERFECT" HARD-BOILED EGGS

Place eggs in a saucepan in a single layer and add enough water to cover by 1 inch. Bring water to a boil over medium-high heat. Then, lower the heat to a gentle simmer and cook for 12 minutes for large eggs. Drain eggs, then plunge eggs into a bowl of cold water for 2 to 3 minutes. Remove from water, and if still warm to the touch, place under cold running water until cool. Crack and remove shells.

CLEANING LEEKS

Since leeks grow in sandy soil, they are often filled with dirt or grit. To clean them, cut off the root ends, then split the leeks lengthwise. Rinse thoroughly under cold running water to remove all particles. Then dry and use as needed. Some recipes will call for just the white parts of leeks, while others will ask for the white and light green parts. Most times the dark green stems are cut off and not used.

PEELING GARLIC CLOVES

The easiest way I've found to separate a whole head of garlic into cloves is to wrap a clean kitchen towel around a head and then with the handle of a chef's knife, firmly but gently hit the head until the cloves are released. To peel individual cloves, lay them flat on a work surface and lightly crush them with the flat side of a knife to loosen the thin paper coating. A new kitchen tool, a small rubber tube called the E-Z-Rol garlic peeler, makes this task even simpler. A clove is put into the rubber tube and rolled back and forth. Because the interior surface of these rolls is made of a sticky substance, the papery coating of a garlic clove is immediately loosened.

PEELING AND CHOPPING TOMATOES

Using a sharp knife, cut a shallow X on the bottom of each tomato. Drop 2 to 3 tomatoes at a time into a large pot of boiling water and leave about 5 seconds for very ripe tomatoes and about 10 seconds for firmer ones. Remove with a slotted spoon and plunge into a bowl of cold water for 1 minute. Remove from water, and using a sharp paring knife, peel off the skins. To chop peeled tomatoes, cut them in half horizontally, squeeze out seeds and juices, then chop.

SEEDING AND CHOPPING HOT PEPPERS

The tissues around your mouth, nose, and eyes are very sensitive to the oils of hot peppers, so if you touch any of these areas with pepper-coated fingers, you will feel an unpleasant burning sensation! Wearing rubbing gloves when seeding and chopping peppers will prevent this problem. Remove the gloves and wash your hands as soon as you are finished.

ZESTING OR REMOVING THE PEEL FROM CITRUS FRUIT

The zest of a citrus fruit is the thin colored outer layer. Because this skin contains the oils of the fruit and is packed with flavor, many recipes call for grated peel or zest. You want to be careful to remove only the colored portion of the skin, and not the white pith beneath, which is bitter. You can use a vegetable peeler or sharp paring knife to remove long ribbons of the skin, then chop them. Or, you can use a citrus zester, a kitchen tool that you scrape across the fruit to remove fine threads of skin. But, by far, the easiest way is to use a Microplane grater, a long rectangular metal grater, which is extremely efficient in removing small bits of the skin without any white pith.

A FEW BASIC RECIPES

BUTTER-RICH SAVORY PIE DOUGH

1½ cups all-purpose flour

½ teaspoon salt

6 tablespoons (¾ stick) unsalted butter, chilled and diced

3 tablespoons solid vegetable shortening, chilled and diced

About 4 tablespoons ice water

MAKES ENOUGH DOUGH FOR A **9-To10-** INCH PIE OR TART CRUST

FOR FOOD PROCESSOR METHOD: Combine dry ingredients in a food processor, and add butter and shortening. Process, pulsing machine, until mixture resembles coarse meal. With machine running, slowly add water just until moist clumps form. Remove dough and gather into a ball; flatten into a disk.

FOR HAND METHOD: Combine dry ingredients in a mixing bowl. Cut in butter and shortening with a pastry blender or 2 knives until mixture resembles oatmeal flakes. Gradually add water, mixing just until dough holds together. Gather into a ball. To ensure even blending of the flour and fat, pull off about ¼ of the dough and place on a floured work surface. Smear the dough across the work surface and repeat with remaining dough. Then gather into a ball again and flatten into a disk.

Wrap dough in plastic wrap and refrigerate 30 minutes before using. (Dough can be made 1 day ahead; soften slightly at room temperature before using.)

BUTTER-RICH SWEET PIE DOUGH

1½ cups all-purpose flour

2 tablespoons confectioners' sugar

Pinch of salt

5 tablespoons unsalted butter, chilled and diced

2½ tablespoons solid vegetable shortening, chilled and diced

About 4 tablespoons ice water

9-TO10-

MAKES ENOUGH DOUGH FOR A   INCH PIE OR TART CRUST

FOR FOOD PROCESSOR METHOD: Combine dry ingredients in a food processor, and add butter and shortening. Process, pulsing machine, until mixture resembles coarse meal. With machine running, slowly add water just until moist clumps form. Remove dough and gather into a ball; flatten into a disk.

FOR HAND METHOD: Combine dry ingredients in a mixing bowl. Cut in butter and shortening with a pastry blender or 2 knives until mixture resembles oatmeal flakes. Gradually add water, mixing just until dough holds together. Gather into a ball. To ensure even blending of the flour and fat, pull off about ¼ of the dough and place on a floured work surface. Smear the dough across the work surface and repeat with remaining dough. Then gather into a ball again and flatten into a disk.

Wrap dough in plastic wrap and refrigerate 30 minutes before using. (Dough can be made 1 day ahead; soften slightly at room temperature before using.)

CRÈME FRAÎCHE

MAKES ABOUT **1 1/3** CUPS

1 cup heavy cream

1/3 cup sour cream

Whisk cream and sour cream together in a medium nonreactive bowl. Let stand at room temperature until thickened, 6 hours or longer. Cover and refrigerate. (Crème fraîche can be stored up to 1 week, covered, in refrigerator.)

HERBES DE PROVENCE

MAKES ABOUT **6** TABLESPOONS

3 tablespoons dried thyme

1 tablespoon dried oregano

1½ teaspoons dried summer savory

1½ teaspoons dried marjoram

In a small bowl, mix together thyme, oregano, summer savory, and marjoram to blend. (The herb mixture can be stored in an airtight container for 2 to 3 months.)

NOTE: Herbs de Provence, a mixture of dried herbs used in southern France, can be used to season meat, poultry, and vegatables. This homemade version takes only a minute to assemble and is an especially nice blend. Also available at specialty food stores and at some supermarkets, common ingredients include basil, fennel seed, lavender, marjoram, rosemary, sage, summer savory, and thyme.

EASY SAFFRON RICE

1½ tablespoons olive oil

1½ cups long-grain white rice, preferably basmati rice

Salt

3 cups chicken stock

2 generous pinches (⅛ teaspoon total) crushed saffron threads

SERVES 4

Heat oil in a medium, heavy saucepan over medium heat. When hot, add rice and cook, stirring, until grains are coated with oil, 1 minute or less. Add ¼ teaspoon salt, the stock, and saffron, and bring mixture to a simmer. Reduce heat to low and cover. Cook until all liquid has been absorbed, 15 to 20 minutes. Taste and season with more salt if needed. Rice can be used immediately or kept covered off the heat for up to 45 minutes.

GRILL FAVORITES

CHAPTER 1

STEAKS, BURGERS, AND HOTDOGS

Mention grilling, and the vision that comes to mind is of thick steaks, juicy burgers, and spicy hot dogs. This threesome is just as popular today as it was a half century ago. But what a long way we've come in how we prepare these foods! Steaks used to be served plain or with the standard, store-bought garnishes of ketchup and mustard. Today we season sirloins, porterhouses, or rib-eyes with aromatic rubs, serve them with bracing salsas, or top them with pats of flavored butters. Our burger repertoire has expanded exponentially. Beef burgers share billing with those made with turkey, chicken, lamb, salmon, and tuna, and for vegetarians there are enticing meatless variations. Ball-park hot dogs will always have a special place on the grill, but equally tempting are Italian sausages, bratwursts, and kielbasa cooked until lightly charred, then garnished with simple homemade condiments.

This chapter offers many variations of these all-time favorites. From Chili-Rubbed Sirloins with Guacamole Salsa, or Salmon Burgers with Cucumbers and Sesame Mayo, to Italian Sausages on Toasted Rolls with Sweet Pepper and Onion Sauté, there's a bounty of up-dated tried-and-true favorites to sample.

CHILI-RUBBED SIRLOINS WITH GUACAMOLE SALSA

Hot, juicy sirloin steaks and homemade guacamole salsa are a match made in heaven. These boneless steaks, coated with a cumin and chili dry rub, are grilled until lightly charred, but still pink inside, then garnished with a mound of chunky guacamole. Grilled Corn on the Cob with Lime Butter (page 136) and Sweet Potato Chips (page 160) would make delicious side dishes.

1   tablespoon ground cumin

2   teaspoons chili powder

½   teaspoon kosher salt

⅛   teaspoon freshly ground black pepper

3   1-pound boneless sirloins, 1 inch thick, trimmed of excess fat

Vegetable oil for oiling grill rack

Chunky Guacamole Salsa (page 306)

SERVES 6

Mix together cumin, chili powder, salt, and pepper in a small bowl. Rub both sides of each steak with this mixture. Let stand at cool room temperature 15 minutes.

When ready to cook, oil a grill rack and arrange 4 to 5 inches from heat source. Prepare grill for a hot fire (high temperature). Grill steaks until charred outside and pink inside, 4 to 6 minutes per side for medium-rare. (Internal temperature should be 145 degrees F.) Halve each steak and mound each portion with a generous serving of Guacamole Salsa. Pass extra salsa in a bowl.

George Stephen, who worked for Weber Brothers Metal Works in Chicago, invented the first kettle-style grill in 1951.

GARLIC-SCENTED SIRLOINS WITH RED AND YELLOW PEPPER RELISH

⅓ cup olive oil, plus extra for oiling grill rack

4 large cloves garlic, peeled

4½ teaspoons chopped fresh thyme

4½ teaspoons chopped fresh rosemary

3 1-pound boneless sirloins, 1 inch thick, trimmed of excess fat

Salt

Freshly ground black pepper

Red and Yellow Pepper Relish (page 311)

A trio of complementary flavors—garlic, thyme, and rosemary—are puréed with olive oil to produce a quick marinade for these boneless sirloins. The steaks are grilled, then served with a colorful sweet pepper relish. For side dishes, try the Scalloped Potatoes with Crème Fraîche and Gruyère (page 158) and the Green Beans Tossed with Olive Oil and Chives (page 147).

SERVES 6

Combine ⅓ cup of olive oil, garlic, thyme, and rosemary in a food processor or blender and process, pulsing several times, until garlic and herbs are finely minced. Brush this mixture on both sides of each steak. Salt and pepper steaks and let stand at cool room temperature 15 to 20 minutes.

Oil a grill rack and arrange 4 to 5 inches from heat source. Prepare grill for a hot fire (high temperature). Grill steaks 4 to 6 minutes per side or until rosy pink inside for medium-rare. (Internal temperature should be 145 degrees F.) Halve each steak and top each portion with a mound of Red and Yellow Pepper Relish. Pass extra relish in a small bowl.

SIRLOIN STEAKS WITH BLUE CHEESE WALNUT BUTTER

6 large cloves garlic, peeled

1 tablespoon crushed, dried rosemary

1½ teaspoons salt

1½ teaspoons freshly ground black pepper

3 1-pound boneless sirloin steaks, 1 inch thick, trimmed of excess fat

Vegetable oil for oiling grill rack

Blue Cheese Walnut Butter (page 325)

This is a recipe for those who love strong, assertive tastes. The steaks, enhanced by a fresh rosemary and garlic rub, are grilled, then topped with pats of Blue Cheese Walnut Butter. When the seasoned butter is spooned over the piping hot grilled steaks, it starts to melt and forms a delicious sauce for the meat.

SERVES **6**

Combine garlic, rosemary, salt, and pepper in a food processor or blender and process several seconds until mixture resembles a coarse paste. Pat steaks dry and rub each side with some of the garlic paste. Place steaks on a platter and let stand at cool room temperature for 30 minutes.

When ready to grill steaks, oil a grill rack and arrange 4 to 5 inches from heat source. Prepare grill for a hot fire (high temperature). Grill steaks 4 to 6 minutes per side for medium-rare. (Internal temperature should be 145 degrees F.) Remove and let stand for 3 minutes.

Halve each steak and top each portion with some Blue Cheese Walnut Butter.

CHARRED T-BONE OR PORTERHOUSE STEAKS WITH CHIMICHURRI SAUCE

The Argentines, creators of the vibrant green condiment known as chimichurri, serve this parsley, vinegar, and olive oil sauce with grilled beef. In the following recipe, the quick and simple sauce makes an excellent accompaniment to grilled T-bone or porterhouse steaks.

Kosher salt

Freshly ground black pepper

4 1-pound T-bone or porterhouse steaks, 1 inch thick, trimmed of excess fat

Vegetable oil for oiling grill rack

Chimichurri Sauce (page 320)

Salt and pepper the steaks on both sides and set aside.

Oil a grill rack and arrange 4 to 5 inches from heat source. Prepare grill for a hot fire (high temperature). Grill steaks until lightly charred on the outside and rosy pink inside, about 4 to 6 minutes per side. (Internal temperature should be 145 degrees F.)

Serve steaks with a bowl of Chimichurri Sauce. Ladle a generous amount of sauce over each steak.

SERVES 4

Porterhouse steaks got their name from 19th-century "porter houses" where steak and ale were served. Around 1814, a New York City porter house keeper started serving the cut we know as a porterhouse.

BACON-WRAPPED FILET STEAKS
TOPPED WITH ROASTED GARLIC BUTTER

These incredibly tender, bacon-wrapped filet steaks are grilled, then topped with decadent pats of Roasted Garlic Butter. The topping, a combination of roasted garlic cloves blended with butter and thyme, can be made ahead so at serving time you will simply need to grill the steaks, then spread this special butter over them. The Roasted Garlic Butter can be used with other cuts of beef and also makes a good garnish for baked potatoes or a tempting spread for grilled slices of country or peasant bread.

12 large (not jumbo) cloves garlic, peeled

¼ cup olive oil plus extra for oiling
grill rack

3 tablespoons unsalted butter, diced
Kosher salt

3½ teaspoons chopped fresh chives or
flat-leaf parsley, divided

½ teaspoon coarsely ground black pepper

½ teaspoon dried thyme

4 6- to 7-ounce filet steaks, 1 inch
thick, trimmed of excess fat

4 very thin slices lean bacon (see note)
6-inch wooden skewers or toothpicks
(which have been soaked in water
for 30 minutes before using and
patted dry)

Arrange an oven rack at center position and preheat oven to 400 degrees F. Place garlic in a 1-cup, ovenproof ramekin, soufflé dish, or custard cup, and add ¼ cup olive oil. Cover dish tightly with aluminum foil and place in oven. Start checking cloves after 20 minutes and check every 5 minutes until done. Roast until garlic cloves are golden and soft when pierced with a knife, about 30 minutes. Remove from oven.

TO MAKE ROASTED GARLIC BUTTER: With a slotted spoon, remove garlic cloves from bowl and reserve oil. Combine garlic, ½ tablespoon of the reserved oil, the butter, and ⅛ teaspoon salt in a food processor or blender and process, pulsing machine on and off for 30 seconds or less, until garlic is coarsely chopped and blended with butter and oil. Remove garlic butter to a small bowl and stir in 2 teaspoons of the chives. If the butter melts during this process, do not worry. Just refrigerate until firm again. (Garlic butter can be prepared a day ahead. Cover with plastic wrap and refrigerate. Bring to room temperature 30 minutes before ready to use.)

When ready to cook steaks, oil a grill rack and arrange 4 to 5 inches from heat source. Prepare grill for a hot fire (high temperature). In a small bowl, stir together 1 teaspoon salt, the black pepper, and thyme. Rub both sides of each filet with some of this seasoning. Then wrap each steak around its sides with a slice of bacon. Secure bacon in place with a wooden skewer or with 2 to 3 toothpicks. Grill steaks until lightly charred on the outside and until bacon is cooked, 4 to 6 minutes per side for medium-rare. (Internal temperature should be 145 degrees F.) Watch carefully to prevent overcooking.

Place steaks on a serving plate. Top each steak with a generous pat of Roasted Garlic Butter and sprinkle with some of the remaining chives. Serve immediately. The butter will start to melt and season the steaks.

NOTE: The bacon provides a robust smoky accent to the beef, but if you prefer, you can omit it, and the steaks will still be well-flavored with just the Roasted Garlic Butter.

TENDERLOIN STEAKS WITH HOT SPICY TOMATO RELISH

¾ teaspoon dried rosemary, crushed

¾ teaspoon coarsely ground black pepper

½ teaspoon Kosher salt

4 6- to 7-ounce tenderloin steaks, 1 inch thick, trimmed of excess fat

Vegetable oil for oiling grill rack

Hot Spicy Tomato Relish (page 314)

4 fresh rosemary sprigs for garnish (optional)

For special occasions I like to serve these grilled tenderloin steaks, rubbed with crushed rosemary, with a colorful mélange of cooked tomatoes and leeks. The steaks, seared for only a few minutes until dark and crusted with bits of aromatic rosemary, are delicious paired with the Spicy Tomato Relish.

SERVES 4

Mix together rosemary, pepper, and salt in a small bowl. Pat meat dry and rub both sides of each steak with the seasoning mixture.

Oil a grill rack and arrange 4 to 5 inches from heat source. Prepare grill for a hot fire (high temperature). Grill steaks until lightly charred on the outside and pink inside, 4 to 6 minutes per side for medium-rare. (Internal temperature should be 145 degrees F.)

To serve, arrange steaks on a serving platter and top each with Hot Spicy Tomato Relish. Garnish each steak with a rosemary sprig, if desired.

RIB-EYE STEAKS WITH WHIPPED HORSERADISH CREAM

Rib-eye steaks, tender and flavorful with their pearly white marbling, are seasoned simply with kosher salt and cracked black pepper in this recipe. It's the Whipped Horseradish Cream, a satisfying condiment that takes only minutes to assemble, that makes the dish special. The piquant, snowy white sauce, sprinkled with chives and served cold, is spooned atop the hot grilled meat at serving time.

Vegetable oil for oiling grill rack

6 8- to 10-ounce boneless rib-eye steaks, 1 inch thick, trimmed of excess fat

Kosher salt

Coarsely ground black pepper

Whipped Horseradish Cream (page 321)

SERVES

When ready to grill steaks, oil a grill rack and arrange 4 to 5 inches from heat. Prepare grill for a hot fire (high temperature). Season steaks generously on both sides with salt and pepper. Grill steaks 4 to 6 minutes per side for medium-rare. (Internal temperature should be 145 degrees F.)

Serve steaks on a platter along with a bowl of the Whipped Horseradish Cream.

Automobile mogul Henry Ford invented charcoal briquets in the early 1920s.

RIB-EYE STEAKS WITH SMOKY CHILE TOMATO SAUCE

Lightly charred rib-eye steaks seasoned with ground cumin are partnered with a smoky tomato sauce made with chipotle peppers. The chipotles, which are smoked jalapeño peppers, contribute a distinctive rich undertone to the sauce. Red and Yellow Pepper Coleslaw (page 179) and corn on the cob would make fine accompaniments to the rib-eyes.

2   small dried chipotle peppers, 2 ½ to 3 inches long (see note)

1   cup boiling water

2   tablespoons olive oil, plus extra for oiling grill rack

¾   cup chopped yellow onion

1   teaspoon chopped garlic

1   14-ounce can Italian-style tomatoes, drained and chopped

Kosher salt

2   teaspoons ground cumin

¼   teaspoon coarsely ground black pepper

4   8- to 10-ounce boneless rib-eye steaks, 1 inch thick, trimmed of excess fat

4   teaspoons chopped fresh cilantro

Thomas Edison designed the first charcoal briquet plant for his friend Henry Ford.

SERVES

Place chipotle peppers in a small bowl and cover with boiling water. Soak until softened, 30 minutes or longer. Strain peppers, reserving water for making sauce. Wearing rubber gloves, halve peppers lengthwise and scrape out and discard all seeds. (The seeds are what make these peppers so hot; removing them will result in a spicy rather than a fiery hot dish.) Chop seeded peppers finely and measure out 2 teaspoons; you can save any extra peppers for another use.

Heat 2 tablespoons oil in a medium, heavy skillet over medium heat. Cook onion, stirring 2 minutes. Add garlic and 2 teaspoons chopped chipotles, and cook and stir 1 minute more. Add tomatoes, reserved soaking water, and ¼ teaspoon salt. Bring mixture to a simmer and lower heat. Cook, uncovered, until most, but not quite all, of liquid has evaporated, about 10 minutes more. Taste and season with more salt if needed. (Sauce can be prepared 1 day ahead; cool, cover, and refrigerate. Reheat, stirring, just to warm when ready to use.) Makes 1½ cups sauce.

Thirty minutes before you plan to cook steaks, combine cumin, ½ teaspoon salt, and pepper in a small bowl. Rub both sides of each steak lightly with seasonings and let stand at cool room temperature while you prepare the grill.

Oil a grill rack and arrange 4 to 5 inches from heat source. Prepare grill for a hot fire (high temperature). Grill steaks 4 to 6 minutes per side for medium-rare. (Internal temperature should be 145 degrees F.)

Arrange steaks on a serving plate and top each with some sauce. Sprinkle steaks with chopped cilantro.

NOTE: Chipotle peppers are sold both dried and in sauce and are available in specialty food stores and some groceries. Buy the dried ones for this recipe.

GINGER AND GARLIC FLANK STEAKS

1   1½-inch piece of ginger

4   medium cloves garlic, peeled

2   1½-pound flank steaks, about
    ½ inch thick, trimmed of excess fat

3   tablespoons red wine vinegar

2   teaspoons coarsely ground black
    pepper

1½ teaspoons Dijon mustard

¾ teaspoon salt

6   tablespoons olive oil, plus extra for
    oiling grill rack

1   bunch watercress, cleaned and
    dried (optional)

These grilled steaks, studded with slivers of ginger and garlic, then marinated in wine vinegar and olive oil, are low in fat but high in flavor. The taste of ginger and garlic comes through with each bite of the tender meat. The steaks would be good served with Sesame and Ginger Coleslaw (page 178) and with Green Beans Tossed with Olive Oil and Chives (page 147).

SERVES 6

Peel ginger and cut into thin slices, then cut slices into thin slivers. Measure 2 tablespoons and save extra for another use. Cut garlic into thin slivers. With a sharp paring knife, make small slits over both top and bottom surface of steaks and insert ginger and garlic slivers in slits.

Place the steaks in a shallow nonreactive dish, which will hold them comfortably in a single layer. In a small bowl, whisk together vinegar, pepper, mustard, and salt to blend. Whisk in 6 tablespoons olive oil. Pour this mixture over the steaks. Cover the meat with plastic wrap, refrigerate, and marinate, turning several times, at least 2 hours or overnight. Bring to room temperature 30 minutes before grilling.

When ready to cook, oil a grill rack and arrange 4 to 5 inches from heat source. Prepare grill for a hot fire (high temperature). Grill steaks 6 to 7 minutes per side or until rosy inside when pierced with a knife. (Internal temperature should be 145 degrees F.)

When done, remove meat to a chopping board. Let rest 5 minutes. Cut meat on the diagonal against the grain into ¼-inch-thick slices. Arrange overlapping slices on a platter and garnish with several bouquets of watercress arranged around the border of the platter, if desired.

SESAME FLANK STEAKS WITH GRILLED GREEN ONIONS

2 1 ½-pound flank steaks, about ½ inch thick, trimmed of excess fat

½ cup soy sauce

8 tablespoons sesame oil, divided

6 tablespoons rice wine vinegar

Vegetable oil for oiling grill rack

2 bunches green onions

Sea salt or kosher salt (see page 14)

3 tablespoons sesame seeds, toasted (see page 15)

Flank steaks, marinated in rice wine vinegar, sesame oil, and soy sauce, are grilled along with whole green onions for this easy main course. The grilled steaks, sliced and arranged with charred scallions on a serving platter, are sprinkled with toasted sesame seeds and sea salt for a glorious finish.

SERVES 6

Place steaks in a shallow nonreactive dish, which will hold them comfortably in a single layer. In a small bowl, whisk together soy sauce, 6 tablespoons of the sesame oil, and vinegar. Pour marinade over the meat and marinate 6 hours or overnight, turning several times.

When ready to cook meat, oil a grill rack and arrange 4 to 5 inches from heat source. Prepare a grill for a hot fire (high temperature).

Cut off root ends of green onions, then trim stems, leaving 4 inches of the green. Place the onions in a shallow dish or pan and brush all over with remaining 2 tablespoons of sesame oil. Set aside.

When grill is hot, remove steaks from marinade. Pat dry lightly with paper towels, then grill 6 to 7 minutes per side for medium-rare. (Internal temperature should be 145 degrees F.) Remove to a platter and cover loosely with aluminum foil to keep warm.

Grill green onions, turning occasionally, until slightly charred, 3 to 5 minutes. Remove to a side dish.

To serve, slice the meat diagonally, across the grain, into ¼-inch-thick slices. Arrange slices on a serving platter. Garnish platter with grilled onions. Season meat and onions with salt, then sprinkle with sesame seeds.

GRILLED LEMON PARSLEY VEAL CHOPS

What makes these veal chops unique is the delicious garnish of chopped parsley, rosemary, and garlic, mixed with grated lemon zest. Known as gremolata, this herb topping (usually made without the rosemary) is typically sprinkled over braised veal shanks in the classic Italian dish called osso buco. In this recipe, the bright green herb mixture makes a striking accompaniment to succulent grilled veal chops.

2 large thick-skinned lemons

1 bunch fresh flat-leaf parsley

1 bunch fresh rosemary

4 to 5 medium cloves garlic, peeled

½ cup olive oil, plus extra for oiling grill rack

6 8- to 10-ounce veal loin chops, trimmed of excess fat

Kosher salt

Freshly ground black pepper

Using a citrus zester or grater, grate enough peel from the lemons to make 1 tablespoon. Place in a small bowl and cover with a paper towel that has been dampened with water and folded several times so it fits in the bowl. Wrap bowl tightly in plastic and refrigerate for up to 1 day. (Stored this way the lemon peel will stay moist so that it can be used later for the garnish.)

To make the marinade, juice the lemons to yield 6 tablespoons and put juice in a medium nonreactive bowl. Chop enough parsley to yield ⅓ cup and enough rosemary to yield 1 tablespoon; add to mixing bowl. Crush 3 garlic cloves and add to bowl. Save the remaining parsley, rosemary, and garlic cloves for the garnish. Whisk ½ cup olive oil into the mixing bowl.

Place the veal chops in a large, shallow nonreactive pan and pour marinade over them. Cover and refrigerate. Marinate 6 hours or overnight, turning several times.

Thirty minutes before you are ready to grill chops, prepare the garnish. Chop 3 tablespoons parsley, 1½ teaspoons rosemary, and 1 teaspoon garlic. Add to the small bowl with the reserved lemon peel and mix well.

Oil a grill rack and arrange 4 to 5 inches from heat source. Prepare grill for a hot fire (high temperature). Remove chops from marinade and salt and pepper them generously on both sides. Grill chops until rosy pink inside when pierced with a knife, 4 to 6 minutes per side. (Internal temperature should be between 145 and 150 degrees F.)

Arrange chops on a serving platter and top each with a generous amount of the parsley-lemon garnish.

HAMBURGERS WITH CHUNKY GUACAMOLE SALSA AND SMOKED BACON

Grilled burgers topped with homemade, spicy guacamole salsa and crispy bacon are an irresistible combination. Pepper Jack Corn Pudding (page 140) and Sweet Potato Chips (page 160) would be colorful side dishes to serve with the burgers.

6 thick slices (about 6 ounces) bacon

1½ pounds 80% lean ground beef

Vegetable oil for oiling grill rack

6 good-quality hamburger buns, lightly toasted

Salt

Chunky Guacamole Salsa (page 306)

SERVES

Fry bacon in a medium, heavy skillet over medium heat until crisp and golden. Remove and drain on paper towels. Break each slice in half and set aside for up to 2 hours until needed.

Shape ground beef into 6 patties, each about ½ inch thick. Cover with plastic wrap and refrigerate until needed.

When ready to cook, oil a grill rack and arrange 4 to 5 inches from heat source. Prepare grill for a hot fire (high temperature). Grill burgers 4 to 5 minutes per side until cooked through. (Internal temperature should be 160 degrees F.)

Place burgers on bottoms of toasted buns. Salt burgers very lightly, then top each with 2 halves of bacon. Mound burgers with a generous amount of Chunky Guacamole Salsa. (You may not need to use all the salsa; save extra for another use.) Cover with tops of buns.

Hamburgers were introduced to Americans at the St. Louis World's Fair in 1904. Their name is derived from the German city of Hamburg.

"TRUE BLUES" HAMBURGERS

1½ pounds 80% lean ground beef

1 tablespoon crushed dried rosemary

1 teaspoon salt

¼ teaspoon freshly ground black pepper

Olive oil for brushing on onions and oiling grill rack

1 large red onion, cut into six ¼-inch-thick round slices

1 6- to 8-ounce piece of Saga blue cheese (or another creamy-style blue cheese), cut into 6 slices

6 good-quality hamburger buns, lightly toasted

6 leaves red leaf lettuce or other crispy lettuce

Creamy blue cheese and robust rosemary are the flavorings that make these burgers so tempting. Red, Yellow, Orange, and Green Heirloom Tomato Salad (page 190) and grilled or boiled corn on the cob would make fine side dishes.

6

SERVES

Combine ground beef, rosemary, salt, and pepper in a medium bowl and mix well to combine. Shape into six ½-inch-thick patties. (Patties can be prepared 1 day ahead. Cover with plastic wrap and refrigerate.)

When ready to cook burgers, oil a grill rack and arrange 4 to 5 inches from heat source. Prepare a grill for a hot fire (high temperature). Brush onion slices on both sides with some oil. Grill burgers and onions about 4 to 5 minutes per side, using a metal spatula to turn them. (Internal temperature of burgers should be 160 degrees F.) When burgers are almost done, cover with some sliced Saga blue and continue to cook until cheese melts. Onions are done when slightly charred and soft when pierced with a knife.

To serve, arrange burgers on bottoms of toasted buns and top with onion slices and lettuce. Cover with tops of buns and serve immediately.

BBQ BURGERS

1 pound 80% lean ground beef

½ cup Deep South Barbecue Sauce, divided (page 322)

Vegetable oil for oiling grill rack

Kosher salt

Freshly ground black pepper

About 4 ounces sliced sharp white Cheddar cheese

4 good-quality hamburger buns, lightly toasted

½ cup finely chopped red onion

These beef burgers, made with ground beef mixed with homemade barbecue sauce, are a personal favorite. Grilled, then topped with sliced white Cheddar, chopped onions, and more barbecue sauce, they are manna for barbecue fans. Old-Fashioned Potato Salad (page 172) and A Mixed Bag of Beans (page 162) are all-time favorites that would complement the burgers.

SERVES 4

Combine ground beef and ¼ cup of the barbecue sauce in a mixing bowl. Mix well with a fork to combine meat and sauce. Shape into 4 patties about ½ inch thick. Cover with plastic wrap and refrigerate to firm, 30 to 45 minutes.

When ready to cook burgers, oil a grill rack and arrange 4 to 5 inches from heat source. Prepare grill for a hot fire (high temperature). Season burgers with salt and pepper. Grill until burgers are cooked through, 4 to 5 minutes per side. (Internal temperature should be 160 degrees F.) Top each burger with some sliced cheese and cook 1 minute more, or until cheese melts.

To serve, place burgers on bottoms of toasted buns and garnish each with some chopped onions and additional sauce. Cover with tops of buns.

Seymour, Wisconsin, has a Hamburger Hall of Fame. In 2001 the town made the Guinness Book of World Records *by producing the world's largest hamburger, which weighed 8,266 pounds and fed close to 8,500 people.*

LAMB BURGERS with ROASTED RED PEPPER RELISH

SERVES **6**

Seasoned ground lamb replaces beef in these savory burgers. Quick Roasted Red Pepper Relish is the only garnish needed. Serve these distinctive burgers with Extra-Special Tabbouleh with Avocado and Feta (page 204).

1½ pounds ground lamb (see note)

⅔ cup minced yellow onion

2 tablespoons chopped fresh flat-leaf parsley

2 teaspoons ground cumin

1 teaspoon salt

½ teaspoon freshly ground black pepper

¼ teaspoon paprika, preferably Hungarian paprika

Vegetable oil for oiling grill rack

6 good-quality hamburger buns, lightly toasted

½ recipe Quick Roasted Red Pepper Relish (page 310)

Combine lamb, onion, parsley, cumin, salt, pepper, and paprika in a bowl and stir well to mix. Shape into 4 patties about ½ inch thick. Cover with plastic wrap, and refrigerate to firm, 1 hour or longer.

When ready to cook burgers, oil a grill rack and arrange 4 to 5 inches from heat source. Prepare grill for a hot fire (high temperature). Grill burgers until cooked through, 4 to 5 minutes per side. (Internal temperature should be 160 degrees F.)

Place burgers on bottoms of toasted buns. Top burgers with some Quick Roasted Red Pepper Relish. Cover with tops of buns and serve immediately.

NOTE: If you have trouble finding ground lamb, ask your butcher to grind lamb shoulder for this recipe.

LEMON DILL CHICKEN BURGERS

1 pound ground chicken or turkey (preferably both white and dark meat, which will keep the burgers moist during grilling)

½ cup finely chopped yellow onion

2 tablespoons chopped fresh dill

1½ tablespoons fresh lemon juice

1½ teaspoons grated lemon zest

¾ teaspoon salt

¼ teaspoon freshly ground black pepper

Vegetable oil for oiling grill rack

4 ounces thinly sliced plain Havarti cheese

4 good-quality hamburger buns, lightly toasted

1 large ripe medium tomato, cut into 4 slices

Red leaf or romaine lettuce for garnish

Lemon and dill add a clean, refreshing note to these ground chicken burgers. Although lower in fat than those made with ground beef, these burgers are certainly not lacking in flavor. Havarti cheese added in the final minutes of grilling melts to make a delectable topping and pairs well with a garnish of juicy tomato slices and crunchy romaine lettuce.

SERVES 4

Combine ground chicken, onion, dill, lemon juice and zest, salt, and pepper in a large bowl, and mix well with a spoon. Divide into 4 equal portions and shape into patties about ½ inch thick. Cover with plastic wrap and refrigerate to firm, at least 1 hour.

When ready to cook, oil a grill rack and arrange 4 to 5 inches from heat source. Prepare grill for a hot fire (high temperature). Grill burgers until completely cooked through and juices run clear when pierced with a sharp knife, about 5 minutes per side. (Internal temperature should be 165 degrees F.) Top each burger with a slice of cheese and cook 1 minute more, or until cheese melts.

Arrange burgers on bottoms of toasted buns, and top with sliced tomatoes and lettuce. Cover with tops of buns and serve immediately.

TURKEY BURGERS WITH HONEY MUSTARD, WHITE CHEDDAR, AND CRISP APPLE SLICES

1 pound ground turkey (preferably both white and dark meat, which will keep the burgers moist during grilling)

2 tablespoons honey Dijon mustard, plus extra for spreading on the buns

½ tablespoon finely minced yellow onion

½ teaspoon grated orange zest

½ teaspoon salt

½ teaspoon freshly ground black pepper

1 large Fuji apple, unpeeled

Vegetable oil for oiling grill rack

2 ounces sharp Cheddar cheese, grated

4 good quality hamburger buns, lightly toasted

1 small bunch watercress, cleaned and stemmed

These moist, juicy burgers, flavored with a hint of orange, grated apple, and honey mustard, could easily rival those made with beef for great taste. Try them with Grilled Asparagus Spears (page 134) and Creamy Caraway Coleslaw (page 182).

Combine turkey, 2 tablespoons mustard, onion, orange zest, salt, and pepper in a bowl. Using a coarse grater, grate enough apple to yield 1½ tablespoons. Add grated apple to turkey mixture and mix well to blend. Cover remaining apple with plastic wrap and refrigerate to use later. Shape turkey mixture into 4 patties about ½ inch thick. Cover with plastic wrap and refrigerate to firm, at least 1 hour.

When ready to cook, oil a grill rack and arrange 4 to 5 inches from heat source. Prepare grill for a hot fire (high temperature). While grill is heating, slice remaining apple into very thin ⅛-inch-thick wedges. Grill turkey burgers until completely cooked through, about 5 minutes per side. (Internal temperature should be 165 degrees F.) When almost done, top each burger with 3 to 4 apple slices and some grated cheese. Cook 1 minute more, until cheese starts to melt, then remove from heat.

To assemble, spread honey Dijon mustard generously on both sides of buns. Arrange burgers on bottoms of toasted buns, add a few sprigs of watercress, and cover with tops of buns. Serve hot.

TURKEY BURGERS WITH BALSAMIC ONION MARMALADE

1 pound ground turkey (preferably both white and dark meat, which will keep the burgers moist during grilling)

1 teaspoon curry powder

Salt

Freshly ground black pepper

Vegetable oil for oiling grill rack

3 to 4 ounces thinly sliced plain Havarti cheese (see note)

4 good-quality whole-wheat hamburger buns, lightly toasted

Balsamic Onion Marmalade (page 319)

4 crisp red leaf lettuce leaves

These turkey burgers, seasoned with a hint of curry, are grilled, then topped with slices of creamy Havarti cheese and generous dollops of a homemade onion marmalade. Crisp red leaf lettuce leaves add texture to the burgers, which are served on whole-wheat buns. The onion marmalade, which is simple to prepare and will hold up well for several days in the refrigerator, is what makes these sandwiches so special.

SERVES 4

Combine turkey, curry, ½ teaspoon salt, and ⅛ teaspoon pepper in a medium bowl and mix well. Shape into 4 patties about ½ inch thick.

Oil a grill rack and arrange 4 to 5 inches from heat source. Prepare grill for a hot fire (high temperature). Grill burgers until they are completely cooked through, about 5 minutes per side. (Internal temperature should be 165 degrees F.) When almost done, top burgers with several thin slices of cheese and cook 1 minute more, or until cheese melts.

Place burgers on bottoms of toasted buns. Divide onion marmalade evenly among burgers, then top each with a lettuce leaf. Cover with tops of buns.

NOTE: Use plain Havarti cheese (not one with caraway seeds or herbs) or another mild cheese such as Monterey Jack.

GOAT CHEESE–STUFFED TURKEY BURGERS WITH ROASTED RED PEPPER RELISH

1½ pounds ground turkey (preferably both white and dark meat, which will keep the burgers moist during grilling)

6 tablespoons fresh bread crumbs

3 tablespoons fresh lemon juice

2 teaspoons grated lemon zest

2 teaspoons dried thyme

1⅛ teaspoons salt

½ teaspoon freshly ground black pepper

6 tablespoons soft creamy goat cheese (such as Montrachet)

Vegetable oil for oiling grill rack

6 good-quality whole-wheat hamburger buns, lightly toasted

½ recipe Quick Roasted Red Pepper Relish (page 310)

Creamy goat cheese enclosed in the centers of these turkey patties keeps these burgers extra moist. Quick Roasted Red Pepper Relish makes a colorful garnish. Corn and Tomato Pudding with Basil (page 141) and a mixed green salad tossed in a vinaigrette dressing would make good accompaniments.

SERVES

Combine turkey, bread crumbs, lemon juice and zest, thyme, salt, and pepper in a large bowl. Mix well. Divide turkey mixture into 6 equal portions. Form each portion into two 4-inch-diameter patties. Place 1 tablespoon of goat cheese atop 1 turkey patty; place second patty atop cheese. Seal patties at edges to enclose cheese. Repeat with remaining 5 portions. Cover with plastic wrap and refrigerate burgers at least 2 hours.

Oil a grill rack and arrange 4 to 5 inches from heat. Prepare grill for a hot fire (high temperature). Grill burgers until cooked through, about 5 minutes per side. (Internal temperature should be 165 degrees F.)

Place turkey burgers on bottoms of toasted buns. Top burgers with some Quick Roasted Red Pepper Relish, then cover with tops of buns.

SALMON BURGERS WITH CUCUMBERS AND SESAME MAYO

For those who have given up red meat burgers, these salmon burgers are a delectable alternative. They are made with salmon fillet tails in place of the usual chopped salmon. The tails are marinated for a couple of hours in a mixture of fresh ginger, soy sauce, and rice wine vinegar, then grilled and placed on buns spread with delicious sesame-scented mayonnaise. Thinly sliced strips of cucumber and watercress make fine garnishes.

4 4- to 5-ounce salmon fillet tails, ½ inch thick (see note)

3 tablespoons vegetable oil, plus extra for oiling grill rack

1½ tablespoons soy sauce

1½ tablespoons minced peeled fresh ginger

1½ teaspoons unflavored rice wine vinegar

⅛ teaspoon salt

⅛ teaspoon cayenne pepper

1 seedless cucumber (about 12 ounces), peeled

½ recipe Sesame Orange Mayo (page 329)

4 good-quality hamburger buns, lightly toasted

1 small bunch watercress, cleaned and stemmed

Place salmon fillets, flesh-side down, in a shallow nonreactive pan that will hold them comfortably in a single layer. In a small bowl, whisk together 3 tablespoons oil, soy sauce, ginger, vinegar, salt, and cayenne. Pour the marinade over the fish, cover, and refrigerate for 2 hours. Bring to room temperature 30 minutes before grilling.

Use a vegetable peeler to shave thin, ribbon-like strips from the cucumber. You will need about 3 to 4 strips for each sandwich. You may not need all of the cucumber; save any extra for another use. Cover cucumber strips with plastic wrap and leave at room temperature.

Oil a grill rack generously, and arrange 4 to 5 inches from heat source. Prepare grill for a hot fire (high temperature). Grill salmon fillets, flesh-side down, 3 minutes, then turn over and cook another 2 to 3 minutes until flesh is opaque and flakes easily when pierced with a knife.

Remove salmon and place on a platter. Slide a knife between the flesh and skin to loosen the skin, then remove and discard skin from each fillet. Cover the fillets loosely with foil while you prepare the buns. Spread both sides of each bun generously with Sesame Orange Mayo. Place salmon fillets on bottoms of toasted buns, top with 3 to 4 folded cucumber strips, and finally with several watercress sprigs. Cover with tops of buns and serve immediately.

NOTE: Choose salmon tails that fit well on hamburger buns.

TUNA BURGERS with PICKLED GINGER and WASABI MAYO

1 pound fresh tuna, preferably yellow fin or blue fin

1 tablespoon soy sauce

¼ teaspoon freshly ground black pepper

Vegetable oil for oiling grill rack

4 good-quality hamburger buns, lightly toasted

Wasabi Mayonnaise (page 330)

1 to **2** ounces pickled ginger

Several sprigs watercress

Grilled tuna burgers are delicious when topped with pickled ginger, then placed on buns spread with peppery Wasabi Mayonnaise. Try them with Watercress, Cucumber, and Belgian Endive Salad with Mustard Seed Dressing (page 194).

SERVES 4

Cut tuna into chunks and place in a food processor fitted with a metal blade. Pulse several times, just until tuna is coarsely ground. Remove tuna to a mixing bowl and add soy sauce and pepper. Mix well. Divide the mixture into 4 even portions and shape into patties about ¼ inch thick. Cover with plastic wrap and refrigerate at least 1 hour.

When ready to cook, oil a grill rack and arrange 4 to 5 inches from heat source. Prepare grill for a hot fire (high temperature). Grill burgers 2 to 3 minutes per side. The tuna should be slightly pink in the center so that the burgers are not dried out.

Place burgers on bottoms of toasted buns and spread each generously with some Wasabi Mayonnaise. Top each burger with some pickled ginger, then with several watercress sprigs. Cover with tops of buns and serve immediately.

PORTOBELLO MUSHROOM BURGERS WITH PEPPER BOURSIN AND MIXED GREENS

These burgers are so satisfying and rich in flavor that both vegetarians and meat eaters will find them appealing. Large portobello mushrooms, brushed with a balsamic vinaigrette sauce and grilled until fork tender, replace ground beef. The cavities of the mushrooms are filled with peppered Boursin cheese, then the mushrooms are topped with a small mound of mixed greens. Served on lightly toasted buns, the burgers could be accompanied by Tomato and Fennel Salad with Fennel Seed Dressing (page 191) and with Grilled Asparagus Spears (page 134).

3 tablespoons balsamic vinegar

1½ teaspoons Dijon mustard

¾ teaspoon minced garlic

Kosher salt

Freshly ground black pepper

6 tablespoons olive oil, plus extra for oiling grill rack and brushing mushrooms

6 large (4-inch) portobello mushrooms

1 5-ounce package Pepper Boursin cheese

3 cups (3 to 4 ounces) loosely packed mixed greens such as mesclun

6 good-quality whole-wheat or regular hamburger buns, lightly toasted

Whisk together vinegar, mustard, garlic, ¼ teaspoon salt, and ⅛ teaspoon pepper in a small bowl. Whisk in 6 tablespoons olive oil.

Remove and discard stems from mushrooms. Clean mushrooms by wiping with a damp paper towel. Brush mushrooms on all surfaces with about half of the vinaigrette dressing. Set aside.

On a plate, divide the Boursin into 6 equal portions. With a small spatula, flatten each portion into a thin disk and set aside.

When ready to grill, oil a grill rack and arrange 4 to 5 inches from heat source. Prepare grill for a hot fire (high temperature). Brush the mushrooms with a little olive oil, and place stem-side down on grill. Grill 4 minutes, then turn and place a disk of cheese into each cavity. Grill for another 4 minutes, or until mushrooms are very tender when pierced with a knife. Season with salt and pepper.

Toss greens with just enough of the remaining dressing to coat lightly. (You may have a little dressing left over.) Arrange mushrooms, cheese-side up, on bottoms of toasted buns. Sprinkle lightly with salt and pepper. Mound with a little salad and cover with tops of buns.

BRATWURSTS ON TOASTED ROLLS WITH CARAMELIZED ONIONS AND CREAMY HORSERADISH SAUCE

These hearty sausages, served on toasted rolls, are topped with a mound of caramelized onions and a splash of Creamy Horseradish Sauce. The onions and the sauce can be assembled well in advance so that at serving time all that is necessary is to grill the bratwursts and toast the buns. You could serve the grilled brats with A Mixed Bag of Beans (page 162) and Roasted Potato Salad with Dill and Mint Dressing (page 174).

3 tablespoons unsalted butter

1 pound yellow onions, thinly sliced

½ teaspoon sugar

6 3- to 4-ounce bratwursts (see note)

Vegetable oil for oiling grill rack

6 good-quality hot dog buns, lightly toasted

Creamy Horseradish Sauce (page 320)

SERVES

To caramelize onions, heat butter in a large, heavy skillet over medium-high heat. When melted and hot, add onion slices and cook until golden brown, stirring occasionally, 10 to 15 minutes. Add sugar and cook until onions are deep golden brown, stirring frequently, about 5 minutes more. Remove onions from heat and set aside. (Onions can be prepared 3 hours ahead. Cover and leave at cool room temperature. Reheat, stirring, just to warm when needed.)

When ready to cook bratwursts, oil a grill rack and arrange 4 to 5 inches from heat source. Prepare grill for a hot fire (high temperature). Grill bratwursts, turning several times until lightly charred and cooked completely through, 10 minutes or longer. (Internal temperature should be 160 degrees F.) Remove from heat.

Spread 1 side of each bun with some Creamy Horseradish Sauce, then place bratwursts in toasted buns, and finally garnish with some caramelized onions. Serve immediately.

NOTE: Bratwursts tend to be quite thick sausages. If you like, you can halve them lengthwise and use a half in place of a whole sausage. Like most sausages, traditional bratwursts are high in fat, but there are some excellent reduced-fat varieties available, which you can substitute in this recipe.

SAUSAGES on TOASTED ROLLS with TOMATO MUSTARD RELISH

1	large yellow onion
	Metal or wooden skewers (which have been soaked in water for 30 minutes before using and patted dry)
	Vegetable oil for brushing onions and oiling grill rack
4	4-ounce bratwursts or other sausages such as knockwurst or cooked kielbasa
4	good quality hot dog buns, lightly toasted
	Tomato Mustard Relish (page 313)

Grilled bratwursts and onion wedges, tucked into lightly toasted buns and garnished with a warm tomato mustard relish, take hot dogs to new heights. The easy homemade relish can be prepared several days ahead and reheated at serving time.

SERVES

Halve the unpeeled onion lengthwise through the root end. Peel the onion, leaving the root end intact, and slice each half lengthwise through the root end into ¾-inch wedges. (Leaving the root end intact will prevent onion wedges from separating.) Skewer onion wedges through their centers. Brush onions with oil. Set aside.

Oil a grill rack and arrange 4 to 5 inches from heat source. Prepare grill for a hot fire (high temperature). Grill bratwursts and skewered onions, turning often, until sausages are lightly charred on the outside and fully cooked inside, and onions are lightly charred and soft when pierced with a knife. (Internal temperature for the sausages should be 160 degrees F for bratwurst and knockwurst and 165 degrees F for cooked kielbasa.) Onions usually take about 12 minutes and uncooked sausages a little longer.

Arrange a sausage and some onions on each toasted bun. Spoon some Tomato Mustard Relish on each. (You may have some relish left over; save for another use.)

The Bratwurst Capital of the World is Sheboygan, Wisconsin, where National Bratwurst Day is observed in August—bratwurst pizzas, bratwurst Reubens, and bratwursts on sticks are served at the celebration.

ITALIAN SAUSAGES ON TOASTED ROLLS WITH SWEET PEPPER AND ONION SAUTÉ

1 medium red bell pepper

1 medium yellow bell pepper

½ pound yellow onions

1½ tablespoons olive oil, plus extra for oiling grill rack

1 tablespoon balsamic vinegar

Kosher salt

6 4-ounce sweet Italian sausages (either traditional pork or a reduced-fat variety made with poultry)

6 ounces grated Italian fontina cheese (optional)

6 good-quality long, narrow rolls, lightly toasted

Exchanging childhood memories of backyard meals with an Italian-American friend, I was struck by the differences in our recollections of family food mainstays. While my mouth watered at the thought of barbecued ribs or chicken, he was equally rhapsodic about the grilled Italian sausages, peppers, and onions his family served on crusty rolls. Inspired by his enthusiasm, I sautéed sweet peppers and onions, seasoned them with balsamic vinegar, and used the vegetables to garnish grilled Italian links.

SERVES 6

Cut bell peppers into ¼-inch-wide julienne strips. Halve onions lengthwise, then cut into ¼-inch-wide julienne strips.

Heat 1½ teaspoons oil until hot in a large, heavy skillet over medium-high heat. Sauté bell peppers, stirring often, for 5 minutes. Add onions and cook and stir until all vegetables are softened and lightly browned, 8 to 10 minutes. Add vinegar and cook, stirring 1 to 2 minutes more until all vinegar has evaporated. Season with salt. (The pepper and onion sauté can be prepared 1 day ahead. Cover and refrigerate. Bring to room temperature or reheat in a skillet over medium heat, stirring, before using.)

Oil a grill rack and arrange 4 to 5 inches from heat source. Prepare grill for a hot fire (high temperature). Grill sausages, turning several times, until browned well, 6 to 8 minutes. Then with a sharp knife, split sausages lengthwise, without cutting all the way through, and cook sausages, cut-side down, until they are fully cooked, 2 to 3 minutes more or longer. (Internal temperature should be 160 degrees F.) With cut sides up, sprinkle sausages with some grated cheese, if desired, and cook 1 to 2 minutes more until cheese melts.

Place sausages in toasted buns and garnish generously with the pepper and onion sauté. Serve warm.

KIELBASA ON TOASTED BUNS WITH HOT APRICOT MUSTARD

The robust taste of kielbasa cooked over a hot grill is complemented by a simple mustard sauce flavored with apricot preserves and rosemary. Served on toasted buns, the sausages would be especially good with Creamy Caraway Coleslaw (page 182).

Vegetable oil for oiling grill rack

1 1-pound regular or light cooked kielbasa sausage

8 good-quality hot dogs buns or long rolls, lightly toasted

2 recipes Hot Apricot Mustard (page 326)

1 cup finely chopped yellow onion (optional)

SERVES 8

Oil a grill rack and arrange 4 to 5 inches from heat source. Prepare grill for a hot fire (high temperature).

While grill is heating, cut the kielbasa into 4 equal links. Cut each link in half lengthwise, so that you have 8 pieces. Grill kielbasa until hot and lightly browned, about 5 to 6 minutes per side. (Internal temperature should be 165 degrees F.)

Place each kielbasa link in a toasted bun. Brush the links generously with some Hot Apricot Mustard, and garnish, if desired, with some chopped onion. You may have some mustard left over; save for another use.

Frankfurters take their name from the German city of Frankfurt, while the word "wieners" is derived from wien, which is German for Vienna.

CHAPTER 2
LAMB, PORK, BIRDS, AND FISH

COOKED OVER AN OPEN FIRE

You don't have to limit your barbecue repertory to the bovine family. There's a world of other foods that are not only worthy of the grill, but are markedly enhanced by its smoky goodness. Lamb, cut into chops or prepared as a butterflied leg, is a glorious sight when cooked until slightly charred on the outside but still rosy pink within. Pork, mildly sweet, pairs well with fruits, herbs, and spices, and can be carved into chops, slabs, or roasts for grilling. And feathered fowl might just be the most versatile of all. Chickens or turkeys, whole, quartered, divided into individual pieces, or cubed and skewered, take on extra flavor when prepared over an open fire. All manner of fish, including fin fish and shellfish, make excellent grill candidates and typically cook in a matter of minutes.

This chapter is filled with recipes that star grilled lamb, pork, fish, and fowl. You might be tempted by lamb chops that are cooked quickly, then topped with a delectable mixture of crumbled Roquefort, figs, and rosemary. There's a succulent pork tenderloin served with an unusual fresh peach sauce, and a pork loin that is wrapped in a "rosemary jacket" before being set over hot coals. You'll find directions for smoking a stuffed, rolled turkey breast over hickory chips, and discover how practical it is to grill oysters and shrimp in their shells. Lightly charred salmon, tuna, and swordfish are paired with colorful garnishes, including a fresh mango lime salsa and a tomato-orange salsa. And, for indulgent occasions, there are lobster tails cooked on the grill with a citrus butter sauce for dipping.

LAMB CHOPS WITH ROQUEFORT, FIGS, AND ROSEMARY

This main course was a last-minute inspiration. For a small supper for friends, I had decided to grill lamb chops and serve them plain. But, while at the supermarket, I came across some glorious Roquefort and then spotted some Black Mission figs. At home I soaked the dried figs in warm red wine, then combined them with bits of cheese and chopped rosemary. The slightly charred meat topped with the mixture of salty cheese, sweet fruit, and robust rosemary turned out to be a stellar combination.

LAMB CHOPS

½ cup dry red wine

3 tablespoons olive oil, plus extra for oiling grill rack

¾ teaspoon chopped fresh rosemary or ¼ teaspoon dried

¾ teaspoon chopped fresh thyme or ¼ teaspoon dried

Scant ½ teaspoon salt

Scant ½ teaspoon freshly ground black pepper

12 3- to 4-ounce rib lamb chops, about ¾ inch thick, trimmed of excess fat

TOPPING

½ cup dry red wine

12 dried Black Mission figs

4 ounces Roquefort cheese, crumbled

½ teaspoon chopped fresh rosemary, plus fresh rosemary sprigs for garnish

SERVES **4** WITH 3 CHOPS PER SERVING OR 6 WITH 2 CHOPS PER SERVING

TO PREPARE THE LAMB CHOPS: Combine wine, 3 tablespoons olive oil, rosemary, thyme, salt, and pepper in a bowl. Place chops in a shallow nonreactive dish. Pour marinade over them, cover, and refrigerate. Marinate 2 hours or longer. Bring to room temperature 30 minutes before ready to grill.

TO MAKE THE TOPPING: In a small saucepan, heat wine until hot. Place figs in small bowl and pour wine over them. Soak until softened, about 15 minutes. Remove, pat dry, then cut figs lengthwise into thin slivers. In another bowl, combine figs, cheese, and ½ teaspoon fresh rosemary. Set aside.

When ready to cook lamb, oil a grill rack and arrange 4 to 5 inches from heat source. Prepare grill for a hot fire (high temperature). Remove meat from marinade and lightly pat dry with paper towels. Grill chops about 3 minutes per side or until browned on the outside and just pink in center. (Internal temperature for medium-rare is 145 degrees F.)

Remove chops to a serving platter and top each with a generous tablespoon of the cheese/fig mixture. Garnish each chop with a rosemary sprig.

GRILLED LAMB CHOPS WITH ORANGE AND MINT COUSCOUS

This main course requires only a modest effort on the cook's part, yet the results are impressive. Rib lamb chops are covered with a flavorful marinade, then grilled and served with quick-cooking couscous flavored with orange and raisins. For serving, the golden couscous grains are mounded in the center of a platter, sprinkled with fresh mint and surrounded by the crusty chops.

LAMB CHOPS

- **8**   3- to 4-ounce rib lamb chops, about ¾ inch thick, trimmed of excess fat
- **4**   cloves garlic, minced
- **2**   teaspoons ground cumin
- Kosher salt
- ½   teaspoon cayenne pepper
- **3**   tablespoons olive oil plus extra for oiling grill rack

ORANGE AND MINT COUSCOUS

- **1**   large navel orange
- **3**   tablespoons golden raisins
- **1½** cups chicken stock
- **1½** tablespoons unsalted butter
- **1**   cup quick-cooking couscous
- **2**   tablespoons chopped fresh mint plus several mint sprigs for garnish

TO PREPARE THE LAMB CHOPS: Place the lamb chops in a shallow nonreactive pan. Crush minced garlic along with cumin, 1 teaspoon salt, and cayenne in a mortar with a pestle, or place in a small bowl and crush with a teaspoon. Stir in 3 tablespoons olive oil. Brush both sides of each of the lamb chops with some of the seasoning mixture; cover and refrigerate. Marinate 45 to 60 minutes or longer. Bring to room temperature 30 minutes before grilling.

TO MAKE THE COUSCOUS: Grate enough peel from the orange to make 2 teaspoons zest. Place in a small bowl and add the raisins. Juice the orange to get ½ cup. Heat the juice in a small saucepan set over high heat until hot. Pour juice over the raisins in the bowl and marinate 20 to 30 minutes to soften.

When ready to cook, oil grill rack and arrange 4 to 5 inches from heat source. Prepare grill for a hot fire (high temperature). Grill chops 3 minutes per side, until rosy pink inside. (Internal temperature should be 145 degrees F for medium-rare.) Remove to a large plate and cover loosely with foil.

To finish couscous, heat stock and butter in a medium, heavy saucepan (with a lid) over high heat until simmering. Remove from heat and stir in couscous. Cover and let rest for 5 minutes. Then stir in orange zest, raisins, and orange juice. Season couscous to taste with salt.

To serve, mound couscous in the center of a platter and surround with a border of chops. Sprinkle chopped mint over the couscous and garnish the dish with several bouquets of fresh mint sprigs. Serve hot.

PROVENÇAL LAMB CHOPS AND SUMMER VEGETABLES

Brushed with olive oil, then rubbed with a quickly made mixture of herbes de Provence, these lamb chops are grilled along with skewers of little red-skin potatoes, zucchini, and grape tomatoes. For serving, the vegetables are mounded in the center of a platter surrounded by the succulent chops. This colorful dish is a meal in itself and needs only a salad and some crusty French bread as accompaniments.

12 3- to 4-ounce rib lamb chops, about ¾ inch thick, trimmed of excess fat

¼ cup olive oil, divided, plus extra for oiling grill rack

6 tablespoons herbes de Provence (page 20)

Salt

Freshly ground black pepper

1½ pounds very small red-skin potatoes, about 1 to 1½ inches in diameter, unpeeled

3 small zucchini, about 1 inch in diameter, cut into ½-inch-thick rounds

12 ounces grape or cherry tomatoes

Metal or wooden skewers (which have been soaked in water for 30 minutes before using and patted dry)

4

Brush chops with olive oil on both sides, using half of the oil. Sprinkle both sides of each chop with ½ teaspoon of the herbes de Provence. Salt and pepper chops generously and refrigerate, covered, for at least 3 hours. Bring to room temperature 30 minutes before grilling.

Bring a large pot of water to a boil and add 1 tablespoon of salt and the potatoes. Boil until potatoes are tender when pierced with a sharp knife, about 15 minutes. Remove with a slotted spoon, halve potatoes, and set aside. To the same boiling water add zucchini and cook for 2 minutes. Remove zucchini with a slotted spoon and rinse under cold running water to cool so that color stays bright green. Pat dry and set aside.

Thread potatoes, zucchini, and grape tomatoes on separate skewers. Skewer potatoes and zucchini with cut sides exposed. (Vegetables can be prepared 2 hours ahead.)

To cook, oil a grill rack and arrange 4 to 5 inches from heat. Prepare grill for a hot fire (high temperature). Grill skewered potatoes 7 minutes, turning occasionally. Then add skewered zucchini and tomatoes and grill 5 minutes, turning several times, until all vegetables are hot and have started to char slightly. Remove, season vegetables with salt and pepper, and sprinkle with remaining herbes de Provence. Cover vegetables loosely with foil to keep warm.

Grill chops 3 per side, until just pink inside. (Internal temperature should be 145 degrees F for medium-rare.)

To serve, remove vegetables from skewers and mound in the center of a serving platter. Arrange chops as a border around the vegetables. Serve warm.

BUTTERFLIED LEG OF LAMB WITH GARLIC, MINT, AND LEMON

Copious amounts of garlic and fresh mint are the keys to the allure of this dish. The simple preparation includes puréeing those two ingredients along with lemon juice, olive oil, and spicy pepper flakes to make a paste, which is then rubbed over a butterflied leg of lamb. The grilled leg looks attractive sliced and arranged on a platter garnished with fresh mint and lemon wedges. Roasted Tomato Slices with Olives and Herbs (page 163) and Skewered Rosemary Red Skins (page 154) would make fine accompaniments. If you have any leftovers, you could fill pita pockets with lamb, sliced tomatoes, crumbled feta, and shredded romaine, and serve the sandwiches at another meal.

1½ cups loosely packed fresh mint leaves, plus 8 sprigs for garnish

⅔ cup olive oil, plus extra for oiling grill rack

12 medium cloves garlic, peeled

2 tablespoons fresh lemon juice

1 teaspoon salt

½ teaspoon red pepper flakes

1 4½-pound boneless leg of lamb, butterflied (see note)

1 lemon cut into 8 wedges for garnish

Gilroy, California, claims to be the Garlic Capital of the World.

Combine mint leaves, ⅔ cup oil, garlic, lemon juice, salt, and red pepper flakes in a food processor fitted with metal blade or in a blender, and process about 30 seconds or until the herbs and garlic are finely minced and mixture has a pesto-like consistency.

Rub garlic/mint mixture over all surfaces of butterflied lamb and place meat in a shallow nonreactive dish. Cover with plastic wrap and refrigerate for at least 6 hours or up to 24 hours. Bring to room temperature 30 minutes before grilling.

When ready to cook meat, oil a grill rack and arrange 4 to 5 inches from heat source. Prepare grill for a medium fire (medium temperature). Grill meat, fat-side down, until well seared on that side, 12 to 15 minutes. Turn and cook until seared well on other side. When done, an instant-read meat thermometer inserted into center of lamb should register 145 degrees F for medium-rare. You can also check lamb by making a slit with a sharp knife in center; meat should be juicy and rosy pink when done.

Remove and let rest 5 minutes. Cut meat into ½-inch-thick slices. Arrange overlapping slices on a serving platter and garnish with lemon wedges and mint sprigs. Serve immediately, garnishing each portion with a mint sprig and a lemon wedge.

NOTE: Have the butcher butterfly the leg of lamb and remove all but a thin layer of fat from the skin side of the meat. Ask that the lamb be trimmed to a thickness of about 2 inches to ensure that it will cook evenly.

LAMB CHOPS WITH CRUSHED GARLIC, ROSEMARY, AND RED PEPPER FLAKES

A recipe tester for this book described these chops by saying that they were "easy, foolproof, and made a sophisticated statement." She summed them up well, for only a handful of ingredients are needed, and the prep work and grilling take only minutes. My own experience has proven that these garlic-flavored, crusty chops with their rosy pink interiors seem to please even the most discriminating palates.

3 tablespoons olive oil, plus extra for oiling grill rack

2 tablespoons minced garlic

1½ tablespoons chopped fresh rosemary or 2 teaspoons crushed, dried rosemary, plus fresh rosemary sprigs for garnish (optional)

1 teaspoon crushed red pepper flakes

12 3- to 4-ounce rib lamb chops, about ¾ inch thick, trimmed of excess fat

Kosher salt

SERVES **4** WITH 3 CHOPS PER SERVING OR 6 WITH 2 CHOPS PER SERVING

Combine 3 tablespoons oil, garlic, chopped rosemary, and red pepper flakes in a small bowl. Brush some of this mixture on both sides of each chop. Sprinkle chops lightly with salt on both sides, and place them on a large platter. Cover with plastic wrap and refrigerate at least an hour or up to 4 hours. Bring to room temperature 30 minutes before ready to grill.

When ready to cook, oil a grill rack and arrange 4 to 5 inches from heat source. Prepare grill for a hot fire (high temperature). Grill chops until rosy pink inside, about 3 minutes per side. (Internal temperature should be 145 degrees F for medium-rare.) Arrange chops on a platter. Garnish chops, if desired, with a bouquet of fresh rosemary sprigs.

BUTTERFLIED PORK CHOPS BRUSHED WITH **TARRAGON MUSTARD BUTTER**

3 tablespoons unsalted butter at room temperature

1½ tablespoons chopped fresh tarragon, plus 6 sprigs for garnish

2 teaspoons, plus 2 tablespoons tarragon vinegar

1½ teaspoons Dijon mustard

6 5- to 6-ounce butterflied boneless pork chops, trimmed of excess fat (see note)

Kosher salt

Freshly ground black pepper

Vegetable oil for oiling grill rack

The inspiration for this dish came from a small Parisian Left Bank restaurant called L'Epi Dupin, where I tasted succulent roasted pork tenderloins with tarragon butter. This version calls for grilled butterflied pork chops, but as in the French original, it is the creamy butter, scented with Dijon mustard and both tarragon vinegar and fresh tarragon, that makes the dish so special. The herbed butter, which takes only minutes to assemble, complements the pork with its distinctive flavor and also adds visual appeal.

SERVES 6

Combine butter, chopped tarragon, 2 teaspoons of the vinegar, and mustard in a small bowl, and stir well to blend. Do not worry if all of the vinegar is not completely absorbed in the butter. (Butter can be prepared 1 day ahead; cover with plastic wrap and refrigerate.)

Bring pork chops to room temperature 30 minutes before grilling and place them in a shallow nonreactive pan. Using about 2 tablespoons of tarragon vinegar, sprinkle chops generously on both sides. Salt and pepper both sides of pork chops generously. Cover with plastic wrap and leave at cool room temperature.

Oil a grill rack and arrange 4 to 5 inches from heat source. Prepare grill for a hot fire (high temperature). Grill chops 3 to 4 minutes per side or until cooked through and flesh is white. (Internal temperature should be 160 degrees F.)

Arrange chops on a serving platter and place a dollop of the seasoned butter on top of each. The butter will start to melt and cover the meat with its delicious flavors. Garnish each chop with a tarragon sprig. Serve immediately.

NOTE: When buying pork chops for this recipe, ask the butcher to use 1-inch-thick chops, each about 5 to 6 ounces, and to butterfly them so that they are ½ inch thick.

PORK TENDERLOINS WITH PEACH GINGER SAUCE

Sautéed sweet Vidalia onions, fresh ginger, balsamic vinegar, red wine, soy sauce, and generous hints of cinnamon and black pepper are the unusual combination of ingredients used for both the marinade and the sauce for these succulent pork tenderloins. At serving time, ripe peaches are diced and added to the warm sauce. Sesame and Ginger Coleslaw (page 178) and Green Beans Tossed with Olive Oil and Chives (page 147) are good side dishes to go with the pork.

1 tablespoon vegetable oil, plus extra for oiling grill rack

1 cup chopped Vidalia onion

5 tablespoons sugar

1½ cups dry red wine

¾ cup reduced-sodium soy sauce

¼ cup balsamic vinegar

2½ tablespoons minced peeled fresh ginger

1½ teaspoons ground cinnamon

½ teaspoon coarsely ground black pepper

3 12-ounce pork tenderloins, trimmed of excess fat

1½ cups diced fresh peaches (3 to 4 peaches cut into ½-inch dice)

2 tablespoons chopped fresh chives

6 TO 8

SERVES

Heat 1 tablespoon oil in a medium, heavy nonreactive saucepan over medium-high heat. When hot, add the onion and sugar and cook, stirring constantly, until onion is golden brown, 5 to 8 minutes. Add the wine, soy sauce, vinegar, ginger, cinnamon, and pepper, and cook for 1 minute, stirring just to combine. Remove from heat and cool mixture completely.

Place pork tenderloins in a large, self-sealing plastic bag or in a shallow nonreactive pan. Pour 1 cup of the sauce over the meat and seal the bag or cover pan with plastic wrap. Marinate at least 6 hours or overnight, turning meat several times. Cover and refrigerate remaining sauce mixture. Bring pork to room temperature 30 minutes before grilling.

When ready to cook, oil a grill rack and arrange 4 to 5 inches from heat source. Prepare grill for a medium fire (medium temperature). Grill pork, turning several times, until a meat thermometer registers 160 degrees F, 35 to 45 minutes. Remove meat and let rest for 5 to 10 minutes.

Heat reserved sauce in a medium saucepan over high heat until it has reduced slightly. Stir in diced peaches and cook until peaches are warmed, about 1 minute more.

To serve, slice tenderloins on the diagonal into ½-inch-thick slices. Arrange on a serving plate and coat lightly with sauce. Sprinkle chives over meat. Pass extra sauce in a small bowl.

NOTE: You can replace peaches with nectarines in this recipe.

PORK LOIN IN A ROSEMARY JACKET

A creative assistant suggested the idea of a grilled pork loin wrapped in fresh herbs. After trying many versions, the best turned out to be one in which a boneless loin is split and filled with chopped herbs, orange peel, and garlic. The pork is then brushed with mustard, covered with rosemary and thyme sprigs, and tied. During the grilling the herb jacket slowly becomes charred, producing a pleasant fragrance, while keeping the meat beneath from drying out. For serving, the sprigs are removed and the meat carved. The pale white slices, with distinctive lines of filling running through the centers, are exceptionally moist and tender. This roast is delicious served warm or cold.

1   2-pound boneless center-cut pork loin, about 8 inches long and 4 inches in diameter (see note)

3   large navel oranges

1   tablespoon chopped garlic

1½ teaspoons chopped fresh rosemary, plus 10 to 12 long sprigs

1   teaspoon chopped fresh thyme, plus 10 to 12 long sprigs

Kosher salt

Coarsely ground black pepper

¼   cup whole-grain Dijon mustard

Cotton kitchen twine

Vegetable oil for oiling grill rack

Place the roast on a work surface, and with a sharp knife held parallel to the work surface, make a slit ¾ of the way through the center of the roast. Do not cut all the way through. Open the meat out like it was a book and set aside.

Grate enough zest from the oranges to yield 1 tablespoon and place in a small bowl. Juice the oranges.

Add the garlic, chopped rosemary, chopped thyme, ¼ teaspoon salt, and several grinds of black pepper to the bowl with the orange zest. Mix well. Spread the mixture on one side of the opened meat and then close. Brush the entire outside surface (top, bottoms, sides, and ends) of meat with mustard. Encase the roast alternately with rosemary and thyme sprigs, leaving the short rounded ends uncovered. (The mustard will help the herbs adhere to the meat.)

Tie the roast with twine at 1-inch intervals. Place the roast in a large self-sealing plastic bag and add the reserved orange juice. Refrigerate, turning several times while marinating, 6 hours or overnight.

An hour before grilling, remove meat from the refrigerator and bring to room temperature. Pour marinade into a small saucepan and boil over high heat for 5 minutes. Set aside for basting roast.

Oil a grill rack and arrange 4 to 5 inches from heat source. Prepare grill for a medium fire (medium temperature). Grill roast, covered with the lid of grill. Turn and baste the roast often with the reserved marinade as this will keep the herbs and the string from burning. Grill until an instant-read thermometer registers 160 degrees F when stuck into the thickest part of the roast. Grilling time should be 55 to 70 minutes or longer. (You may need to start the fire a second time if using a charcoal grill.)

Remove pork loin and let rest 10 minutes. Then cut string and remove herbs. Slice into ¼- to ½-inch-thick slices. Arrange overlapping slices on a platter and salt lightly.

NOTE: Pork loins of similar weights can vary in shape. For this recipe a single loin that is long and slender is the best choice.

PORK AND PRUNE BROCHETTES

Tender morsels of pork skewered with prunes are a simple but distinctive main course to cook on the grill. The prunes are first simmered in wine, brandy, honey, and spices, then removed so that the liquids can be reduced to form a glaze to brush on the grilled pork and prunes. A sprinkling of orange peel adds flavor as well as color to the finished dish. Sesame-Scented Sugar Snaps (page 161) and Watercress, Cucumber, and Belgian Endive Salad (page 194) would make fine accompaniments.

40 large (about 14 ounces) pitted prunes

2¼ cups dry red wine

6 tablespoons brandy

4½ tablespoons honey

3 3-inch sticks cinnamon, broken in half

¼ teaspoon ground cloves

Coarsely ground black pepper

6 metal or wooden skewers (which have been soaked in water for 30 minutes before using and patted dry)

2 12- to 14-ounce pork tenderloins, trimmed of excess fat and cut into 1-inch cubes

Vegetable oil for oiling grill rack and brushing prunes and pork

Salt

2 large navel oranges

Place prunes in a medium, heavy saucepan and add wine, ¾ cup water, brandy, honey, cinnamon, cloves, and ¼ teaspoon pepper. Stir to combine, place over medium-high heat, and bring to a simmer. Lower heat and simmer for 5 minutes, stirring occasionally. Remove saucepan from heat. Using a slotted spoon, remove prunes and cinnamon. Set prunes aside and discard cinnamon.

Return the saucepan to high heat and cook until mixture becomes syrupy and has reduced to about ⅓ cup. This will take several minutes; watch carefully. Remove from heat and set aside. When prunes have cooled to room temperature, skewer them alternately with pork cubes. (The brochettes can be prepared 4 to 5 hours ahead. Place on a platter, cover with plastic wrap, and refrigerate. Bring to room temperature 30 minutes before grilling.)

When ready to grill, oil a grill rack and arrange 4 to 5 inches from heat source. Prepare grill for a hot fire (high temperature). Brush prunes and pork with vegetable oil, then salt and pepper them generously. Grill skewered pork 10 to 12 minutes, turning frequently. If you have a lid, cover the grill with it, leaving the vents open. When done, the pork cubes should be browned and the meat cooked through so that a meat thermometer inserted into several cubes registers 160 degrees F.

While the pork is cooking, use a citrus stripper to remove the rind from the oranges in long strips. If you don't have a citrus stripper, use a sharp paring knife to remove just the colored portion of the skin in long peels. Cut the peels into very thin matchstick strips.

Arrange the cooked pork and prune brochettes on a serving platter and brush on all sides with some of the reduced wine mixture. Sprinkle with orange strips.

Shish kebab originates from the Turkish words sis *(skewer) and* kebabiu *(meat grilled in small chunks).*

LIME PORK CHOPS WITH TOMATO SOUR CREAM GARNISH

6 5-ounce boneless center-cut pork loin chops, ¾ to 1 inch thick, trimmed of excess fat

¼ cup olive oil, plus extra for oiling grill rack

3 serrano peppers, about 3 inches long, seeded and minced (see page 17)

2½ tablespoons fresh lime juice (2 to 3 limes)

1½ teaspoons ground cumin

Kosher salt

¾ teaspoon red pepper flakes

GARNISH

¾ cup regular or reduced-fat (not nonfat) sour cream

12 small grape or cherry tomatoes, quartered and seeded

3 green onions including 3 inches of green stems, finely sliced

Kosher salt

3 tablespoons chopped fresh cilantro

These succulent chops, flavored with robust spices, are well balanced by a bracing accompaniment of sour cream combined with sliced grape tomatoes and chopped green onions. Try them with the Roasted Sweet Potato Salad with Lime and Honey (page 176) and Grilled Corn on the Cob (page 136).

SERVES 6

Place pork chops in a shallow nonreactive dish that will hold them comfortably in a single layer. Whisk together ¼ cup oil, minced serranos, lime juice, cumin, 1 teaspoon salt, and red pepper flakes. Pour over pork. Cover and refrigerate. Marinate 6 hours or overnight, turning several times. Bring to room temperature 30 minutes before grilling.

Thirty minutes before you are ready to cook the pork chops, prepare the garnish. In a small bowl, mix together sour cream, tomatoes, green onions, ½ teaspoon salt, and cilantro. Set aside at room temperature.

When ready to cook, oil a grill rack and arrange 4 to 5 inches from heat source. Prepare grill for a hot fire (high temperature). Remove pork from marinade and pat dry. Grill chops until cooked all the way through, 6 minutes or longer per side. The flesh should be white when done. (Internal temperature should be 160 degrees F.) Arrange chops on a platter. Garnish each chop with a dollop of sauce and pass extra sauce separately.

CHICKEN WITH MANGO, TOMATO, AND KIWI SALSA

4 tablespoons fresh lime juice

4 tablespoons olive oil, plus extra for oiling grill rack

Kosher salt

½ teaspoon ground cumin

½ teaspoon red pepper flakes

8 5- to 6-ounce boneless, skinless chicken breast halves, trimmed of excess fat, or 16 four-ounce skinless chicken thighs, trimmed of excess fat

Mango, Tomato, and Kiwi Salsa (page 309)

This simple marinated grilled chicken served with a bracing salsa was one of the most popular recipes I taught in a series of cooking classes one summer. The tri-color salsa can be made several hours ahead so that all that is necessary at serving time is to fire the grill and quickly cook the chicken.

SERVES

Three hours ahead, prepare marinade for chicken. Combine lime juice, 4 tablespoons oil, ½ teaspoon salt, cumin, and red pepper flakes in a small bowl and whisk well. Remove the small strip of meat called the fillet from the underside of each chicken breast and save for another use. Place chicken in a shallow nonreactive pan and pour marinade over. Cover and refrigerate, 2 to 3 hours, turning several times.

Oil a grill rack and arrange 4 to 5 inches from heat source. Prepare grill for a hot fire (high temperature). Remove chicken from marinade. Grill until chicken springs back when touched with your fingers and juices run clear when chicken is pierced with a sharp knife, 4 to 5 minutes per side for breasts and slightly longer for thighs. (Internal temperature should be 170 degrees F for breasts and 180 degrees F for thighs.)

Arrange cooked chicken on a serving platter. Season with salt, and garnish generously with Mango, Tomato, and Kiwi Salsa. Pass any remaining salsa separately.

FENNEL AND ROSEMARY–COATED CHICKEN

A distinctive trio of strong flavors—crushed rosemary, fennel seeds, and lemon juice—give these boneless chicken breasts their robust taste. Much to my delight, I've discovered that this main course is not very demanding of my time. I place the chicken pieces in the marinade in the morning and forget about them while they marinate all day. Then at serving time I rub dry seasonings on the breasts and quickly grill them.

MARINADE

- **3** tablespoons olive oil
- **3** tablespoons fresh lemon juice
- **3** medium cloves garlic, peeled and smashed
- **3** bay leaves, broken in half
- **¾** teaspoon kosher salt
- **½** teaspoon coarsely ground black pepper
- **6** 6- to 7-ounce boneless, skinless chicken breast halves, trimmed of excess fat

SEASONING RUB

- **2** teaspoons dried rosemary leaves, crushed (see page 15)
- **2** teaspoons fennel seeds, crushed (see page 15)
- **1¼** teaspoons coarsely ground black pepper
- **1** teaspoon kosher salt

  Vegetable oil for oiling grill rack
- **6** fresh rosemary sprigs for garnish (optional)
- **6** thick lemon wedges for garnish (optional)

TO MAKE THE MARINADE: Combine oil, lemon juice, garlic, bay leaves, salt, and pepper in a shallow nonreactive pan, and whisk well. Remove the small strip of meat called the fillet from the underside of each breast and save for another use. Add chicken to marinade and cover with plastic wrap. Refrigerate at least 2 hours or overnight, turning several times.

TO MAKE THE RUB: Mix together dried rosemary, fennel seeds, pepper, and salt in a small bowl. Remove chicken from marinade and pat dry with paper towels. Rub about ½ teaspoon seasoning on each side of each breast.

Oil a grill rack and arrange 4 to 5 inches from heat source. Prepare grill for a hot fire (high temperature). Grill until chicken springs back when touched with your fingers and juices run clear when pierced with a sharp knife, 4 to 5 minutes per side. (Internal temperature should be 170 degrees F.)

To serve, arrange chicken on a platter and garnish breasts with rosemary sprigs and lemon wedges, if desired. Squeeze a lemon wedge over each serving before eating.

HONEY CITRUS CHICKEN

Although the list of ingredients for this refreshing chicken entrée with peppery accents seems long, the dish is not difficult to assemble, and the breasts can be marinated a day ahead. The pineapple, orange, and lime-scented marinade, seasoned with both jalapeño and black pepper, does triple duty in this recipe. First it is used to marinate the poultry, next some is combined with honey to be slathered on the breasts as they grill, and the remainder is reduced to make a sauce. Try this with Orzo Salad with Vegetables and Herbs (page 206) and with blanched tender green beans.

3 large oranges

2 to 3 limes

2 cups diced pineapple (or 1 medium pineapple, peeled, cored, and diced)

1 3-inch jalapeño pepper, seeds and membranes removed, chopped (see page 17)

1 teaspoon minced garlic

3 tablespoons soy sauce

2 tablespoons chopped fresh cilantro, plus extra sprigs for garnish

2 tablespoons chopped fresh basil, plus extra sprigs for garnish

Freshly ground black pepper

2 tablespoons honey

8 6- to 7-ounce boneless, skinless chicken breast halves, trimmed of excess fat

3 tablespoons unsalted butter

Kosher salt (optional)

Vegetable oil for oiling grill rack and for brushing chicken

Grate enough orange peel from the oranges to yield 1 teaspoon and then juice them to yield 1 cup. Grate enough lime peel from the limes to yield 1 teaspoon and then juice them to yield ½ cup. Set aside both zests and juices.

Combine diced pineapple, jalapeño, and garlic in a food processor or blender and process until mixture is almost smooth. Pour marinade into a large, nonreactive shallow dish (a 9-x-13-inch Pyrex baking dish works well), and add orange and lime zests and juices, soy sauce, chopped cilantro, chopped basil, and 1 tablespoon black pepper. Stir to blend. Remove ⅓ cup of the marinade to a small nonreactive bowl and whisk in honey. (Cover and refrigerate the honey mixture until ready to grill chicken.) Add chicken to dish and turn to coat in marinade. Cover and refrigerate 4 to 5 hours, turning several times.

Remove chicken from marinade and using a rubber spatula, scrape excess marinade from breasts. Strain marinade into a heavy, medium saucepan. To make sauce, boil marinade in saucepan until reduced to 1½ cups, about 15 minutes. Whisk in butter and season with additional pepper and salt if desired.

Oil a grill rack and arrange 4 to 5 inches from heat source. Prepare grill for a hot fire (high temperature). Brush chicken with oil and grill, turning several times and basting with reserved honey mixture, until chicken springs back when touched with your fingers and juices run clear when chicken is pierced with a sharp knife, 4 to 5 minutes per side. (Internal temperature should be 170 degrees F.)

Arrange breasts on a serving platter and garnish with cilantro and basil sprigs. Serve with sauce.

CHICKEN "SCALLOPS" TOPPED with TOMATOES, BLACK OLIVES, and FETA

Typically, when boneless chicken breasts are pounded into thin scallops, they are then sautéed. In this recipe, they are grilled, then topped with a distinctive garnish of quartered grape tomatoes, slivered kalamata olives, and crumbled feta. The tomatoes add a sweet note while the olives and cheese provide salty undertones. Good accompaniments would be the Easy Saffron Rice (page 21 in Basics) and grilled zucchini halves.

8   6- to 7-ounce boneless, skinless chicken breast halves, trimmed of excess fat

⅓   cup olive oil, plus extra for oiling grill rack

¼   cup fresh lemon juice

2   tablespoons, plus 2 teaspoons chopped fresh oregano, divided (see notes), plus 8 sprigs of oregano for garnish (optional)

2   medium cloves garlic, peeled and smashed

Kosher salt

Freshly ground black pepper

20   pitted kalamata olives, cut lengthwise into slivers

10   sweet grape tomatoes, stemmed and quartered lengthwise (see notes)

3   to 4 ounces feta cheese, crumbled

SERVES **8**

Remove the small strip of meat called the fillet from the underside of each chicken breast and save for another use. Place a chicken breast between 2 sheets of waxed paper and using a meat pounder or rolling pin, pound until between ¼ and ½ inch thick. Continue, using more waxed paper as needed, until all chicken has been pounded. Place chicken in a large, shallow nonreactive dish. With a sharp knife, score the top of the chicken breasts.

Combine ½ cup oil, lemon juice, 2 tablespoons chopped oregano, garlic, ½ teaspoon salt, and several grinds of black pepper in a small bowl and whisk well to blend. Pour over chicken. Cover chicken with plastic wrap and refrigerate, turning several times, for at least 2 hours or up to 6 hours.

Thirty minutes before you are ready to grill chicken, combine olives, tomatoes, cheese, and remaining 2 teaspoons chopped oregano in a small bowl and mix well. Set aside.

When ready to grill chicken, oil a grill rack and arrange 4 to 5 inches from heat source. Prepare grill for a hot fire (high temperature). Pat chicken dry and grill until chicken springs back when touched with your fingers and juices run clear when flesh is pierced with a sharp knife, about 3 minutes per side. (Internal temperature should be 170 degrees F.) Do not overcook or chicken will be dry.

Remove to a platter and salt and pepper chicken lightly. Garnish each chicken breast with a generous topping of tomato garnish and then with a sprig of oregano, if desired.

NOTES: This dish is best made with fresh oregano, but if it is unavailable substitute 2 teaspoons dried oregano for the fresh herb in the marinade and use a scant teaspoon dried oregano in the tomato/olive/feta garnish.

: Grape tomatoes, a variety of tomatoes slightly smaller and sweeter than traditional cherry tomatoes, are available in most supermarkets. If you can't find them, substitute 8 cherry tomatoes.

HICKORY-SMOKED TURKEY BREAST WITH HERB STUFFING

1 2-pound (with bone) turkey breast half, butterflied (see notes)

2 cups loosely packed fresh bread crumbs

2 cups loosely packed fresh flat-leaf parsley

4 medium cloves garlic, minced

2 green onions with 2 inches green tops included, chopped

½ tablespoon minced fresh chives

1 teaspoon grated lemon zest

1 egg

4 ounces prosciutto, sliced paper-thin

Cotton kitchen twine

Olive oil for brushing turkey and for oiling grill rack

10 to **12** large hickory chunks

This is a striking make-ahead dish worthy of a little extra effort. A boned butterflied turkey breast is topped with thin slices of prosciutto and a fresh bread and herb stuffing scented with lemon. The breast is rolled into a cylinder, tied, and smoked slowly over hickory chips. Then the breast is chilled, and carved into slices that reveal a colorful mosaic. Grilled Asparagus Spears (page 134) and Orzo Salad with Vegetables and Herbs (page 206) would make attractive side dishes.

Pound the butterflied turkey with a meat pounder to an even thickness of about ½ inch.

Combine bread crumbs, parsley, garlic, green onions, chives, lemon zest, and egg in a medium bowl, and toss to combine. Arrange prosciutto over entire surface of turkey breast. Spread the stuffing evenly over the prosciutto slices. Starting with the longest side, roll the meat into a cylinder. Tie at 1-inch intervals with twine and brush with olive oil. (Turkey can be prepared 3 hours ahead; cover and keep refrigerated until ready to smoke.)

Soak hickory chunks in water to cover while you prepare the grill.

SERVES **4 TO 5**

For a charcoal grill, open all vents in bottom and top. Place a small fireproof pan filled with water in the center of the grill's bottom grate. Surround the pan generously with charcoal. Ignite, and when the coals become gray and hot, scatter the hickory chunks over them. Oil the top grate and arrange 4 to 5 inches from coals. Place the turkey on the grill and cover with the lid with vents open. Grill, brushing the turkey roll with olive oil about every 20 minutes and turning the meat. Cooking time should be 1½ to 2 hours. (You may need to start a charcoal fire a second time if it goes out before the turkey is done.) Roast is done when the skin becomes a rich mahogany brown and juices run clear when flesh is pierced with a sharp knife. (Internal temperature should be 170 degrees F for the turkey and 165 degrees F for the stuffing.)

Remove from grill and cool to room temperature. Refrigerate 1 hour or overnight to chill. Slice roast into ¼-inch-thick slices and arrange overlapping on a serving platter. Serve cold or at room temperature.

NOTES: Ask the butcher to remove the bone but leave the skin intact, and then to butterfly the turkey breast to yield more surface for stuffing. Have the strip of meat called the fillet removed from the underside of the turkey breast and save for another use. A boneless breast will weigh about 1½ pounds.

: You can smoke this turkey breast using a gas grill. If your gas grill has a smoker box and water chamber, place the soaked hickory chunks in the box and fill the water chamber with water, then proceed with the manufacturer's directions. If your grill doesn't have these features, barbecuing and smoking expert Cheryl Alters Jamisan suggests that the wood chunk be soaked in water, then wrapped in a foil packet. Holes should be poked in the packet and then it should be placed on the cooking grate opposite the meat being cooked. Some gas grills cook more quickly than charcoal ones, so check often for doneness. This breast could cook in an hour or less.

OLD-FASHIONED BARBECUED CHICKEN

The quintessentials—ketchup, brown sugar, vinegar, and mustard—that characterize classic American barbecue sauce can be found in this dish. Whole chickens are cut into serving pieces, then marinated in the spicy sauce before being popped on the grill. When done, the lightly charred chicken with its moist flesh is served on a bed of watercress. Roasted Potato Salad with Dill and Mint Dressing (page 174) and grilled or boiled corn on the cob would make excellent sides.

1½ cups ketchup

1 cup light brown sugar

½ cup red wine vinegar

¼ cup Worcestershire sauce

2½ tablespoons dry mustard, preferably English mustard sauce, such as Coleman's, sifted to remove any lumps

2 teaspoons paprika, preferably Hungarian

2 teaspoons Tabasco sauce

2 teaspoons salt

1½ teaspoons freshly ground black pepper

2 3½-pound broiler-fryer chickens, each cut into 2 wings, 2 breasts, 2 thighs, 2 legs (save extra parts for another use)

Vegetable oil for oiling grill rack

1 bunch watercress for garnish (optional)

"Barbecue," "barbeque," "Bar-B-Cue," "Bar-B-Q," and "BBQ" are all common spellings for one of America's favorite foods and/or social gatherings. The word "barbecue" is said to originate from the Spanish word barbacoa, *which in turn came from a similar word with early Native Caribbean roots.*

SERVES

In a medium bowl, whisk together ketchup, sugar, vinegar, ½ cup water, Worcestershire sauce, mustard, paprika, Tabasco sauce, salt, and pepper until well blended. Remove 1½ cups of this mixture, and cover and refrigerate it. (This reserved marinade will be used later as a sauce for the grilled chicken.) Place the chicken pieces in a large, shallow non-reactive dish or in extra-large self-sealing plastic bags. Add the remaining marinade and mix well to coat each piece. Refrigerate 6 hours or overnight, turning several times.

When ready to grill chicken, oil a grill rack and arrange 4 to 5 inches from heat source. Prepare grill for a medium fire (medium temperature). Place thighs and legs on grill and cook 10 minutes, then add breasts and wings. Cover grill (leaving any vents open) and cook, turning chicken pieces often, until skin is charred lightly and flesh is cooked through, about 30 to 35 minutes more. Watch carefully, and if chicken pieces start to char and burn, move to a cooler part of the grill to finish cooking. When done, juices should run clear when chicken pieces are pierced with a sharp knife. (Internal temperature for breasts should be 170 degrees F and 100 degrees F for thighs, legs, and wings.) Place cooked chicken on a large serving plate and cover loosely with foil.

Heat the reserved marinade in a small saucepan over medium heat until hot. Remove foil from chicken and brush each piece generously with some of the sauce. Transfer remaining sauce to a small serving bowl.

Garnish the chicken with several bouquets of watercress, if desired, and serve with additional sauce.

SUTRISNO'S CHICKEN SATAY

Although I have never been to Indonesia, I love the alluring blend of flavors found in many of their dishes. Satay, one of the country's celebrated culinary creations, consists of marinated cubes or strips of meat, fish, or poultry that are skewered and grilled. The following recipe for chicken satay was given to me by a friend who, while living in Indonesia, learned how to make this version from a native named Sutrisno.

CHICKEN

6 medium cloves garlic, minced

4 teaspoons dried leaf coriander (see notes)

4 teaspoons light brown sugar

1 tablespoon ground black pepper

1 teaspoon salt

2½ to 2¾ pounds boneless skinless chicken breast halves, cut into 1½- to 2-inch cubes

½ cup soy sauce

6 tablespoons vegetable oil, plus extra for oiling grill rack

2 tablespoons fresh lime juice

4 teaspoons minced peeled fresh ginger

PEANUT SAUCE

1 cup smooth peanut butter

½ cup peanut oil, plus more if needed

6 tablespoons fresh lime juice

3 tablespoons honey

2 tablespoons soy sauce

1 teaspoon hot chili sauce, plus extra if desired (see notes)

1 teaspoon cayenne pepper

2 medium cloves garlic, peeled and crushed

8 long metal or wooden skewers (which have been soaked in water for 30 minutes before using, then patted dry)

¼ cup chopped fresh cilantro for garnish

SERVES

TO PREPARE THE CHICKEN: Combine garlic, coriander, sugar, pepper, and salt in a small bowl. Toss the chicken pieces with this mixture and place on a platter; cover and refrigerate. Marinate for 45 minutes.

Combine soy sauce, 6 tablespoons oil, lime juice, and ginger in a shallow nonreactive pan. Add the chicken pieces, cover, and refrigerate for 6 hours more or overnight. Turn several times while marinating.

TO MAKE THE PEANUT SAUCE: Combine all ingredients in a food processor and process until smooth. Taste and, if desired, add additional hot chili sauce to make sauce more piquant. If you want a thinner sauce, add an additional 1 to 2 tablespoons peanut oil. (Sauce can be made 1 day ahead. Cover and refrigerate but bring to room temperature before serving.)

When ready to cook chicken, oil a grill rack and arrange 4 to 5 inches from heat source. Prepare grill for a hot fire (high temperature). Remove chicken from marinade and divide evenly among skewers. Grill chicken, turning frequently, until chicken springs back when touched with your fingers and juices run clear when chicken is pierced with a sharp knife, 8 to 10 minutes. (Internal temperature should be 170 degrees F.)

To serve, arrange skewers on a serving platter and sprinkle with chopped cilantro. Serve skewers with 8 small individual bowls of the Peanut Sauce for dipping.

NOTES: Dried leaf coriander or cilantro (not ground coriander seeds) is available in many groceries; however, if you can't find it you can substitute ¼ cup chopped fresh cilantro.

: Either hot chili sauce or hot chili sauce with garlic, which are available in the Asian section of some groceries and in Asian markets, can be used in this recipe.

BARBECUED SALMON
WITH A MAHOGANY GLAZE

A simple marinade made with only four ingredients—dark molasses, soy sauce, fresh chopped ginger, and lime juice—turns a salmon fillet into something memorable. While the fillet is marinated for an hour or more, some of the marinade is reduced to a rich, dark syrupy glaze. Then the salmon is grilled and brushed with the delicious dark sauce. When done, the fish, moist and juicy, is a rich mahogany color. This salmon is delicious served with Coleslaw with Spanish Olives (page 177) and with corn on the cob.

6 tablespoons soy sauce

¼ cup molasses, preferably unsulfured (see note)

4 teaspoons minced peeled fresh ginger

1 tablespoon fresh lime juice

1 2- to 2½-pound salmon fillet

Vegetable oil for oiling grill rack

Thin lime slices for garnish

SERVES 4

Combine soy sauce, molasses, ginger, and lime juice in a small nonreactive bowl and whisk to blend. Reserve ⅓ cup of this mixture for glaze and pour the rest in a shallow nonreactive dish. Place the salmon on a work surface, run your fingers over flesh against the grain, and remove, with clean tweezers, any bones you feel. Place salmon skin-side up in marinade, cover with plastic wrap, and refrigerate. Marinate at least 1 hour or up to 2 hours.

While salmon is marinating, place reserved ⅓ cup marinade in a small, heavy saucepan over medium-high heat. Cook, stirring, until mixture has reduced to a syrupy glaze, 2 to 3 minutes. Remove and set aside at room temperature. (The sauce can be prepared 2 hours ahead; leave at room temperature.)

When ready to cook salmon, oil a grill rack and arrange 4 to 5 inches from heat source. Prepare grill for a hot fire (high temperature). Grill salmon, skin-side down, 10 minutes. Cover grill with lid (with all vents open) or tent salmon loosely with foil. Continue to cook until flesh is opaque and flakes easily when pierced with a sharp knife and edges of salmon are browned, 10 to 15 minutes more depending on the thickness of the fish. Remove salmon from grill and with a sharp knife cut off and discard skin.

Arrange salmon on a serving platter and brush top of fish with glaze. Garnish top of salmon with lime slices. Cut into 4 portions.

NOTE: Both sulfured and unsulfured molasses are available. The latter is lighter and has a cleaner flavor.

SALMON FILLETS WITH FRESH TARRAGON AND CRUSHED FENNEL

6	tablespoons unsalted butter, cut into small chunks	**1**	tablespoon grated lemon zest
2	tablespoons chopped fresh tarragon, plus 6 sprigs fresh tarragon for garnish (optional)	**1**	tablespoon fresh lemon juice
		1	teaspoon kosher salt
		¾	teaspoon coarsely ground black pepper
4	teaspoons fennel seeds, crushed (see page 15)	**6**	6- to 8-ounce salmon fillets, about ¾ inch thick
			Vegetable oil for oiling grill rack and salmon
			Thin lemon slices for garnish (optional)
			Cucumber Watercress Relish (optional, page 312)

Fresh tarragon and crushed fennel seeds are a winning flavor combination and are even better when blended with butter and lemon as a topping for succulent grilled salmon fillets. A Cucumber Watercress Relish (page 312) makes a fine garnish for the fish, as would Sesame-Scented Sugar Snaps (page 161).

SERVES

Combine butter, chopped tarragon, fennel seeds, lemon zest and juice, salt, and pepper in a small bowl and stir well to blend. (If not using immediately, cover with plastic wrap and refrigerate up to 1 day. Bring to room temperature before using.)

Run your fingers over salmon against the grain, and remove, with clean tweezers, any bones you feel.

When ready to grill salmon, oil a grill rack generously and arrange 4 to 5 inches from heat source. Prepare grill for a hot fire (high temperature). Brush both the flesh and skin sides of the salmon lightly with oil. Place on grill and cook, flesh-side down, 3 to 5 minutes, then turn over and cook until the flesh is opaque and salmon flakes easily when pierced with a knife, 3 to 5 minutes or longer, depending on the thickness of the fish. Spread about 1 tablespoon of the tarragon-fennel butter over the top of each fillet and cook only 1 minute more until butter starts to melt.

Remove to a serving platter and garnish each fillet, if desired, with a lemon slice, a tarragon sprig, and some Cucumber Watercress Relish.

GRILLED SALMON WITH GREEN MUSTARD SAUCE

This grilled salmon dish, garnished with a piquant mustard sauce flecked with bits of spinach and arugula, won enthusiastic approval several years ago from my spouse, who is not a salmon fan. I marinated fillets in white wine, orange juice, and soy sauce, then grilled and topped them with the green-hued mustard. The sauce looks striking against the coral flesh of the roasted salmon and complements the taste of the fish beautifully.

4 6- to 7-ounce salmon fillets

⅓ cup dry white wine

⅓ cup fresh orange juice

⅓ cup soy sauce

Vegetable oil for grill rack and oiling salmon

Kosher salt

Green Mustard Sauce (page 327)

Run your fingers over the salmon against the grain, and remove, with clean tweezers, any bones you feel. Place fillets, skin-side up, in a shallow nonreactive pan. In a small bowl, whisk together wine, orange juice, and soy sauce and pour over salmon. Cover fish with plastic wrap and refrigerate 2 hours, turning several times.

When ready to grill salmon, oil a grill rack and arrange 4 to 5 inches from heat source. Prepare grill for a hot fire (high temperature). Oil the skin sides of the salmon fillets. Place salmon, flesh-side up, on rack. If your grill has a lid, cover with the vents open or tent salmon loosely with aluminum foil. Cook until flesh is opaque and flakes easily when pierced with a knife, 6 to 10 minutes, depending on thickness of fish.

Salt fillets. Garnish each serving with a dollop of Green Mustard Sauce and pass any extra in a small bowl.

A mosquito, buzzing around in the backyard, can smell a potential target from 25 to 30 meters (about 21 to 38 yards) away!

HALIBUT FILLETS WITH TOMATO-ORANGE BUTTER

SERVES 4

4 tablespoons unsalted butter at room temperature

⅓ cup cherry or grape tomatoes, halved, seeded, and cut into ¼-inch dice

2 tablespoons chopped fresh basil, plus sprigs for garnish

1 tablespoon fresh orange juice

1 teaspoon grated orange zest

⅛ teaspoon red pepper flakes

Kosher salt

Vegetable oil for oiling grill rack and fish

4 7-ounce halibut fillets with skin left on, each ¾ to 1 inch thick

2 to 3 teaspoons balsamic vinegar

Halibut fillets are delicious when quickly grilled and topped with pats of butter seasoned with orange and tomato. I like to use firm, flavorful halibut for this recipe, but other mild fish fillets such as Chilean sea bass or salmon could be substituted. Depending on the fish you use, the cooking time might need to be adjusted. Thicker fish fillets will require a few extra minutes on the grill, while thinner ones will need less time.

Combine softened butter in a small bowl with tomatoes, chopped basil, orange juice and zest, red pepper flakes, and ⅛ teaspoon salt. Mix well to combine. (The butter can be prepared 1 day ahead. Cover and refrigerate; bring to room temperature before using.)

When ready to grill halibut, oil a grill rack and arrange 4 to 5 inches from heat source. Prepare grill for a hot fire (high temperature). Brush both skin and flesh sides of fillets with oil. Place fish, flesh-side down, on grill and cook 4 to 5 minutes. Turn and cook 4 to 5 minutes longer or until fish is cooked through and flakes easily. Drizzle each fillet lightly with a little balsamic vinegar. Salt lightly and spread each with some of the Tomato Orange Butter. Cook only a few minutes more until the butter just starts to melt. Remove and arrange fillets on a serving platter. Garnish each serving with a basil sprig and serve immediately.

SWORDFISH STEAKS with LIME CILANTRO BUTTER

This is a recipe to call upon when you want seafood with a delectable burst of flavor and have little time to spend cooking. Swordfish steaks are marinated in lime juice for half an hour, quickly grilled, then garnished with dollops of cool, piquant lime butter. Grilled or boiled corn on the cob and a plate of sliced tomatoes sprinkled with parsley would make simple accompaniments.

4 6-ounce swordfish steaks, ¾ to 1 inch thick

3 tablespoons fresh lime juice

Olive oil for oiling grill rack

Kosher salt

Lime Cilantro Butter (page 324)

4 thin lime wedges for garnish

4 fresh cilantro sprigs

SERVES **4**

Place swordfish steaks in a shallow nonreactive dish and pour the lime juice over them. Marinate at room temperature 30 minutes, turning fish several times to ensure even marinating.

When ready to grill fish, oil a grill rack and arrange 4 to 5 inches from heat source. Prepare grill for a hot fire (high temperature). Sprinkle fish with salt and grill 3 to 5 minutes per side, until flesh is opaque all the way through but still flaky. Do not overcook or fish will be dry.

To serve, place cooked fish on a serving plate and top each with 1½ to 2 tablespoons of the Lime Cilantro Butter, which will start to melt and flavor fish. Arrange lime wedges and cilantro sprigs as a garnish in center of each steak.

SWORDFISH STEAKS WITH MANGO LIME SALSA

4 6- to 7-ounce swordfish steaks, ¾ to 1 inch thick

2 tablespoons olive oil, plus extra for oiling grill rack

2 tablespoons fresh lime juice

¼ teaspoon salt

Freshly ground black pepper

Mango Lime Salsa (page 307)

These grilled swordfish steaks, mounded with a refreshing mango salsa, are perfect to serve when the temperature soars. There's another bonus that comes with this recipe–it doesn't demand a lot of your time. The marinade for the fish and the salsa takes about a quarter of an hour, and grilling the swordfish is a ten-minute job.

SERVES 4

Place the swordfish steaks in a shallow nonreactive dish or pan. In a small bowl, whisk together 2 tablespoons oil, lime juice, salt, and several grinds of pepper, and pour over the swordfish. Cover with plastic wrap and refrigerate 45 minutes or up to 2 hours.

When ready to grill fish, oil a grill rack and arrange 4 to 5 inches from heat source. Prepare grill for a hot fire (high temperature). Grill swordfish steaks about 3 to 5 minutes per side, or until fish is opaque all the way through, but still flaky. Watch carefully, as cooking time can vary depending on the thickness of the fish.

Arrange fish on a platter. Divide salsa evenly and mound on each of the fillets.

Typically, a person will endure three mosquito bites before deciding to put on a repellent.

SWORDFISH WITH TOMATO-ORANGE SALSA

¾ cup teriyaki sauce

⅔ cup dry sherry

4 teaspoons minced garlic

2 teaspoons minced peeled fresh ginger

1 teaspoon Asian sesame oil

6 5- to 6-ounce swordfish steaks, about 1 inch thick

Vegetable oil for oiling grill rack

Tomato-Orange Salsa (page 308)

This attractive main course, which is low in calories, is a perfect choice for those watching their weight. The accompanying salsa, which bursts with color and flavor, can be made several hours in advance and looks striking served atop the grilled swordfish.

SERVES 6

Combine the teriyaki sauce, sherry, garlic, ginger, and sesame oil in a small saucepan. Bring marinade to a boil. Set aside to cool.

Place the swordfish in a single layer in a shallow nonreactive dish. Pour marinade over the swordfish; turn to coat evenly. Cover and refrigerate fish 1½ hours, turning often.

Oil a grill rack and arrange 4 to 5 inches from heat source. Prepare grill for a hot fire (high temperature). Remove fish from marinade. Grill 3 to 5 minutes per side until fish is opaque all the way through, but still flaky. Do not overcook or fish will be dry. Transfer fish to a platter. Serve with Tomato Orange Salsa. (You may have some salsa left over; save for another use.)

Mosquitos are attracted to dark clothing so it's best to wear light clothes when outdoors.

PEPPER AND CORIANDER-COATED TUNA STEAKS

¼ cup coriander seeds, coarsely crushed

1 tablespoon dark brown sugar

2 teaspoons coarsely ground black pepper

3 tablespoons chopped fresh flat-leaf parsley

3 tablespoons grated orange zest (5 to 6 large thick-skinned oranges)

Vegetable oil for oiling grill rack and brushing tuna

6 6-ounce tuna fillets, about ¾ inch thick

Kosher salt

A sprinkling of orange zest and chopped parsley contrasts well with the spicy crushed coriander seed and cracked pepper crust on these tuna steaks. Tomato and Fennel Salad with Fennel Seed Dressing (page 191) and Sesame-Scented Sugar Snaps (page 161) are good side-dish possibilities.

SERVES 6

Mix coriander, sugar, and pepper in a small bowl and stir well to blend. (This spice mixture can be prepared 8 hours ahead. Cover and store at room temperature.)

When ready to grill tuna, prepare the garnish. Mix the chopped parsley and orange zest together in a small bowl and set aside.

Oil a grill rack and arrange 4 to 5 inches from heat source. Prepare grill for a hot fire (high temperature). While grill is heating, brush the tuna on all sides lightly with vegetable oil and sprinkle on both sides lightly with salt. Coat the tuna steaks on both sides with the spice mixture. Grill tuna until just a thin line of pink remains in center of each steak, 2 to 3 minutes per side. Watch carefully so that tuna is not overcooked and becomes dry.

Remove to a serving platter and spoon some of the parsley and orange zest mixture on top of each serving.

TUNA STEAKS TOPPED WITH WARM SHIITAKE MUSHROOMS

These grilled tuna steaks mounded with sautéed shiitakes are fairly low in fat, but definitely high in flavor. Orange, garlic, and ginger make complementary seasonings for the mushrooms, which can be cooked ahead and reheated. Grilled Asparagus (page 134) and Sesame and Ginger Coleslaw (page 178) are good partners for the tuna.

3   tablespoons vegetable oil, plus extra for oiling grill rack

2   small cloves garlic, peeled and crushed, plus 1 teaspoon minced garlic

8   ounces shiitake mushrooms, cleaned, stemmed, and caps cut into ¼-inch strips

1   cup reduced-sodium chicken stock

2   teaspoons minced peeled fresh ginger

1   teaspoon soy sauce

¼   cup chopped green onions including 2 inches of green stems

3   teaspoons grated orange zest, divided

Freshly ground black pepper

Kosher salt

4   6-ounce tuna steaks, about ¾ inch thick

2   teaspoons chopped fresh cilantro or flat-leaf parsley

SERVES 4

Combine 3 tablespoons oil and crushed garlic in a medium, heavy skillet over low heat. Heat slowly until garlic barely begins to color and is fragrant, 3 to 4 minutes. Be careful not to let garlic burn. Strain and discard garlic and pour half of the oil into a small bowl; set aside.

Return skillet with remaining garlic oil to medium-high heat, and when oil is hot, add mushrooms. Sauté, stirring, until mushrooms are softened, lightly browned, and begin to stick to pan. Add stock and bring to a boil. Cook, stirring occasionally, until stock has reduced by half, about 3 minutes. Add ginger, soy sauce, and the minced garlic. Continue to cook, stirring constantly, until almost all of the liquid has evaporated and mushrooms are very soft, 2 to 3 minutes more. Remove skillet from heat and stir in green onions and 2 teaspoons of the orange zest. Taste and season with several grinds of black pepper and salt, if needed. (The mushrooms can be prepared 3 hours ahead; reheat stirring over medium heat, then cover loosely with aluminum foil to keep warm.)

When ready to grill tuna, oil a grill rack and arrange 4 to 5 inches from heat source. Prepare grill for a hot fire (high temperature). Brush the steaks lightly on both sides with reserved garlic oil, then salt and pepper them generously. Have the warm mushroom relish nearby. Grill tuna until just a thin line of pink remains in center of each steak, 2 to 3 minutes per side. Do not overcook or tuna will be dry.

To serve, place steaks on a platter. Top each with some warm mushroom relish and sprinkle with remaining orange zest and the cilantro.

LANG'S GRILLED OYSTERS

While on vacation in North Carolina's Outer Banks, my friend Lang Bell went to a local fish market and was so smitten with a display of fresh oysters that he bought far more than his family could bear to shuck. When he returned to the store to ask what to do with the excess oysters, the fishmonger suggested grilling them, explaining that when placed over an open fire, oysters open on their own. My friend became an enthusiastic fan of cooking the shellfish with this method and shared his discovery with me. Tomato Fennel Confetti (page 316) is a festive garnish that pairs beautifully with the warm oysters.

3 dozen oysters in the shell
   Tomato Fennel Confetti (page 316)

SERVES 6 WITH 6 OYSTERS EACH

Arrange a grill rack 4 to 5 inches from heat source. Prepare a grill for a hot fire (high temperature), making certain if there are vents on the top and bottom chambers of the grill that they are open.

Scrub the oysters with a brush under cold running water. Discard any opened shells, which indicate the oyster is dead.

When grill is hot, place the oysters with their flat sides up on the rack. Cover the grill and cook 6 to 9 minutes, until the oysters begin to open about ¼ inch. Using tongs, remove the oysters onto a platter as they open, taking care not to spill the oysters' juices. Be careful, since the oysters will be very hot and give off steam.

Wearing kitchen mitts, pry the oysters the rest of the way open using an oyster knife or a paring knife. If you are worried about losing the juice, open oysters over a shallow bowl to catch the juices. Sever the muscles that connect the oysters to their shells, and leave the oysters in the cupped sides of the shells. You can pour any collected juice over the oysters.

Spoon 1½ to 2 teaspoons of the Tomato Fennel Confetti over each of the oysters. Serve immediately while oysters are still warm.

GRILLED LOBSTER TAILS
WITH CITRUS BUTTER

Lobster tails are delicious and attractive when cooked on the grill. Their shells turn a bright orange and are lightly charred after several minutes over a hot fire, while their flesh cooks to an opaque whiteness. A clean, refreshing citrus-flavored butter, which can be made a day ahead and reheated, is perfect for drizzling over the lobster meat.

Vegetable oil for oiling grill rack

4 ⅓- to ½-pound lobster tails

Salt

Freshly ground black pepper

Warm Citrus Butter (page 323)

1 bunch watercress for garnish (optional)

Orange wedges for garnish (optional)

SERVES 4

Oil a grill rack and arrange 4 to 5 inches from heat source. Prepare grill for a hot fire (high temperature).

Lay the lobster tails, shell-side down, on a work surface, and with a sharp pair of kitchen scissors or shears, cut off the transparent shells covering the tail meat. Start cutting along one side of the shell and continue around the tail fin section and up the other side. Salt and pepper the exposed lobster meat lightly and brush with some of the Warm Citrus Butter.

When grill is ready, place lobster tails, shell-side down, over the hot fire. Cook 10 minutes, or until the shells become bright orange. Turn and cook 5 to 10 minutes more or until flesh is opaque. Total cooking time will depend on the size of the lobster tails and the intensity of the heat. Watch carefully so you do not overcook lobsters and end up with dry, tough meat.

Remove to a platter and arrange tails flesh-side up. Garnish platter with several clusters of watercress and orange wedges, if desired. Pour Warm Citrus Butter into 4 small bowls. Serve each lobster tail with a bowl of butter for drizzling or for dipping.

BARBECUED SHRIMP IN THEIR SHELLS

This dish has been among my family's all-time favorites for years. I've lost track of where the original recipe came from, but over many summers I've fine-tuned the directions. I always use large unshelled shrimp and marinate them in a cooked mixture of butter, white wine, garlic, and green onions. Later, the marinade is reheated, strained, and reserved for use as a sauce. The shrimp, grilled until coral pink and curled, are served piled high on a platter. They are peeled at the table, then dipped into the warm butter sauce.

18 green onions (3 bunches), divided

12 tablespoons (1½ sticks) unsalted butter

12 medium cloves garlic, chopped

1⅓ cups dry white wine

2 tablespoons fresh lemon juice

1 teaspoon freshly ground black pepper

1½ pounds large shrimp in the shell, legs removed (see note)

1 cup chopped fresh flat-leaf parsley, divided

Vegetable oil for oiling grill rack

½ teaspoon Tabasco sauce, plus more if needed

Salt

1 lemon, cut into 6 wedges for garnish

Tabasco sauce is named after a state called Tabasco in southeastern Mexico.

SERVES **6**

Chop the green onions, including 2 inches of the green stems, and reserve 2 tablespoons for the garnish.

Melt the butter in a heavy nonreactive casserole over medium-low heat. Add the onions and garlic and cook, stirring, 3 minutes. Add the wine and simmer 15 minutes to blend flavors. Remove the pan from the heat and stir in the lemon juice and pepper. Set aside to cool to room temperature.

Using a paring knife, cut the shrimp down the back and devein, but do not peel. Toss the shrimp and ¾ cup of the parsley in the cooled butter mixture. Refrigerate, covered, 6 hours or overnight, turning occasionally.

When ready to grill shrimp, oil a grill rack and arrange 4 to 5 inches from heat source. Prepare grill for a hot fire (high temperature).

Meanwhile, remove the shrimp from the marinade. Heat the marinade in a medium, heavy saucepan to liquefy, then strain. Return the strained liquid to the pan, bring it to a boil, then cook over medium-high heat 5 minutes. Stir in the Tabasco sauce. Taste, and if desired, add more hot sauce for a spicier flavor. Salt mixture to taste. Cover the sauce to keep it warm.

When grill is ready, add the shrimp. (If you have a grill basket or a cooking grate, spread the shrimp on that and then place on the grill.) Grill until shrimp curl up and turn pink, 4 to 5 minutes total, turning once. Do not overcook, or the shrimp will become tough and the shells will be hard to remove.

Mound the shrimp on a warm serving platter. Garnish with the lemon wedges. Pour the sauce into 6 individual ramekins, then sprinkle remaining chopped parsley and reserved green onions over the sauce. Serve immediately.

VARIATION: For a smoked flavor, add to the prepared grill eight 2-inch hickory chunks, soaked in water for 15 minutes and then drained.

NOTE: Here's a guideline for unshelled shrimp sizes:
Medium—31 to 40 per pound
Large—21 to 30 per pound
Extra large—10 to 15 per pound

MIXED SEAFOOD GRILL WITH SESAME DIPPING SAUCE

Skewered shrimp and scallops, grilled quickly and served with a delectable Asian-accented dipping sauce, are a treat for seafood lovers. The sauce can be prepared a day ahead and the fresh herbs and sesame seeds stirred into it at serving time. The seafood needs only a few minutes on the grill.

SESAME DIPPING SAUCE

6 tablespoons honey

6 tablespoons unseasoned rice vinegar

1 tablespoon minced peeled fresh ginger

1 tablespoon soy sauce

1 tablespoon chili garlic sauce (see note)

1½ teaspoons dark roasted sesame oil

1½ teaspoons grated orange zest

2 tablespoons chopped fresh cilantro

2 tablespoons chopped fresh mint

2 tablespoons toasted sesame seeds (see page 15)

Salt

Vegetable oil for oiling grill rack

4 metal or wooden skewers (which have been soaked in water 30 minutes before using and patted dry)

12 sea scallops, side muscles trimmed

12 large shrimp, shelled and deveined but with tails intact

2 tablespoons chopped fresh cilantro

2 tablespoons chopped fresh mint

SERVES

TO MAKE THE SESAME DIPPING SAUCE: Whisk together the honey, rice vinegar, ginger, soy sauce, chili garlic sauce, sesame oil, and orange zest in a medium nonreactive bowl to blend well. (The sauce can be prepared 1 day ahead. Cover and refrigerate. Bring to room temperature before using.) When ready to use, remove 2 tablespoons of the sauce and reserve. Stir cilantro, mint, and sesame seeds into remaining sauce. Season with salt if needed.

Oil a grill rack and arrange 4 to 5 inches from heat source. Prepare grill for a hot fire (high temperature).

Thread each of 4 skewers alternately with 3 scallops and 3 shrimp. Brush the reserved 2 tablespoons of sauce over the fish.

Grill the skewers until scallops and shrimp are both cooked through, turning several times, about 4 to 5 minutes total. When done, the scallops will be opaque and the shrimp pink and curled.

To serve, **arrange skewers** on a serving plate and salt them lightly. Sprinkle with chopped cilantro and mint. Pour reserved dipping sauce into 4 small bowls. Serve each skewer with a bowl of the dipping sauce.

NOTE: Hot chili sauce with garlic can be found in the Asian section of many supermarkets and in Asian specialty food stores. Kame is a readily available brand that works well in this recipe.

CHAPTER 3

BACK
YARD
CLASSICS

FRIED CHICKEN, BOILED LOBSTERS, GREAT SANDWICHES, AND MORE

Many mouth-watering dishes that find their way to the backyard table are not cooked on the grill. Instead, they are prepared—often well in advance—in the kitchen, then transported outside. Such classics make up this chapter. Sesame Fried Chicken and Baked Ham with a Red Currant Mustard Glaze, each served cool rather than piping hot, are both great make-ahead entrées for outdoors. Steamed mussels accompanied by Saffron Mayonnaise and boiled lobsters set out with several dipping sauces are also temptations for a backyard crowd. Such dishes as Spicy Crab Cakes, Habanero Chicken Wings, and Golden Fried Clam Cakes can play dual roles, as appetizers or as a main course.

And, we can't forget about sandwiches—the ultimate picnic comfort food. Americans, the world's best sandwich makers, appreciate originality between their slices of bread, and have been the inventors of countless creations. On the following pages you'll find a dozen tempting combinations, from corned beef and coleslaw po' boys to egg salad clubs and New England lobster rolls.

SESAME FRIED CHICKEN WITH HONEY GLAZE

Growing up in the South, I remember that fried chicken was a staple at our table. My mother, who never thought of herself as a talented cook, was an expert at one thing—turning out golden morsels of chicken. She always followed two rules. First, she insisted that the floured pieces had to be placed into piping hot oil, preferably sizzling in a cast-iron skillet, so that the skin would brown immediately and form a crust. Second, she covered the browned chicken with a lid set slightly ajar, and cooked it for several minutes more to insure moist and tender meat. I used these same tried and true guidelines to produce crispy sesame-scented fried chicken. Drizzled with a delectable honey glaze, the chicken can be served warm or at room temperature.

1 3-pound frying chicken cut into 2 breasts, 2 wings, 2 thighs, and 2 legs (with backbone saved for another use)

Salt

Freshly ground black pepper

Canola oil for frying chicken

2 large eggs

½ cup milk

1 tablespoon toasted sesame oil

¼ teaspoon Tabasco sauce

½ cup all-purpose flour

⅔ cup unflavored dried bread crumbs

⅓ cup toasted sesame seeds (see page 15)

HONEY GLAZE

¼ cup honey

4 teaspoons rice vinegar

2 teaspoons toasted sesame oil

¼ teaspoon Tabasco sauce

1 bunch watercress for garnish (optional)

SERVES **4 to 6**

Season chicken pieces on all sides very generously with salt and pepper. Set aside.

Add enough canola oil to a large, heavy skillet, which will hold the chicken pieces in a single layer, to come 1 inch up the sides of the pan. Place skillet over high heat and watch carefully while you prepare the chicken.

In a shallow bowl, whisk together eggs to blend. Then whisk in milk, sesame oil, and Tabasco sauce. Spread flour on a dinner plate. Mix together bread crumbs and sesame seeds and spread on another dinner plate. Dredge each piece of chicken in flour, then dip in egg mixture, then coat with sesame–bread crumb mixture.

When oil is very hot, but not smoking, add all the chicken to the skillet and cook over moderately high heat until golden brown, 6 to 7 minutes. Turn and cook on the other side until golden, 6 to 7 minutes more. Reduce heat to low and place a lid slightly ajar on the skillet. Cook 12 minutes more, turning several times. This additional cooking will make chicken more tender. Remove and drain on paper towels.

TO MAKE THE GLAZE: Whisk together honey, vinegar, sesame oil, and Tabasco sauce in a small bowl.

Arrange chicken on a serving platter and drizzle with some honey glaze. Serve extra sauce in a small bowl. Garnish platter with two clusters of watercress, if desired. Serve warm or at room temperature.

Favorite backyard games include croquet, badminton, frisbee, touch football, and the increasingly popular Italian ball game of bocce.

HABANERO CHICKEN WINGS

Eastern European Jewish cooking meets the hot accents of Latin America in this dish. An assistant, Lesley Abrams-Schwartz, shared with me her Polish grandmother's recipe for oven-baked chicken wings coated with matzo meal. After devouring several batches of the crispy wings one day, we tried a variation, marinating the wings in hot habanero sauce before baking them. We loved the results. The pepper added an extra dimension of flavor (a decidedly hot, though not fiery, taste) to the chicken. You could offer these wings as a substantial appetizer or make them a main course. Either way, you might consider doubling the recipe, since they disappear quickly.

12 (2½ to 3 pounds) chicken wings

3 tablespoons habanero sauce (see note)

3 tablespoons vegetable oil, plus extra for coating baking pan

6 tablespoons unsalted matzo meal or flour

2 teaspoons kosher salt

1 teaspoon freshly ground black pepper

¾ to **1** teaspoon cayenne pepper

MAKES 12 WINGS

Place chicken wings in a large, shallow nonreactive pan. In a small bowl, whisk together habanero sauce and 3 tablespoons oil. Brush the habanero mixture over all surfaces of the wings. Cover wings with plastic wrap and refrigerate at least 45 minutes or up to 2 hours. Bring to room temperature 30 minutes before baking.

When ready to cook wings, arrange an oven rack at center position and preheat oven to 350 degrees F. Use a large, heavy roasting pan or 2 cast-iron skillets to cook the wings. Pour enough oil into the roasting pan or the skillets to coat the bottom(s) generously.

Place matzo meal, salt, and pepper in a plastic bag and shake to combine. Add wings, close bag, and shake until wings are coated with mixture. Arrange wings in a single layer in roasting pan or skillets, and sprinkle generously with cayenne. Bake wings 1 hour, then, using tongs or a fork, turn the wings and bake another 30 minutes. When done, wings should be crispy and a deep golden brown on both sides.

Remove from oven and arrange wings on a serving plate. Serve warm.

NOTE: You can find habanero sauce in the condiments section of the supermarket. McIlhenny's Tabasco Brand Habanero Sauce is my favorite to use in this recipe. Matzo meal can be found in most supermarkets.

CORNISH GAME HENS WITH MUSTARD AND ROSEMARY

These golden roasted Cornish hens accompanied by a delectable apricot and mustard–scented mayonnaise are served at room temperature. That means that all the preparation–both the roasting of the hens and the assembly of the sauce–can be done completely in advance. Serve the hens with the Orzo Salad with Vegetables and Herbs (page 206) and with some crusty French or Italian bread, and you won't need to bother with any last-minute cooking.

6 tablespoons unsalted butter at room temperature

⅓ cup finely chopped prosciutto, divided

2½ teaspoons Dijon mustard, divided

5 teaspoons chopped fresh rosemary, divided

Salt

Freshly ground black pepper

3 1½-pound Cornish game hens

1½ cups chicken broth

1 cup regular or reduced-fat (not nonfat) mayonnaise

3 tablespoons apricot preserves

1 bunch watercress

SERVES 6

Arrange an oven rack at center position and preheat oven to 400 degrees F.

Combine butter, half of the prosciutto, 1½ teaspoons of the mustard, and half of the rosemary in a bowl. Season with salt and pepper. Run your fingers under breast skin of each game hen to loosen skin from flesh. Rub 1 tablespoon of the seasoned butter under the breast skin of each hen. Sprinkle hens inside and out with salt and pepper, and place 1 teaspoon of seasoned butter in each cavity.

Place hens on a rack in a large roasting pan. Pour ⅓ cup stock over hens. Dot each hen with 1 teaspoon of seasoned butter. Roast 30 minutes, basting with remaining broth and butter every 10 minutes. Continue roasting without basting until juices run clear when thigh is pierced at thickest part, about 30 minutes more. (Internal temperature should be 180 degrees F when a thermometer is inserted in the inner part of the hens' thighs.) Remove hens and let rest. Prepare the mayonnaise. Reserve ¼ cup of the pan juices.

In a small bowl, mix together reserved pan juices, mayonnaise, apricot preserves, and remaining prosciutto, mustard, and rosemary. Let hens cool to room temperature and cut in half. (Hens and sauce can be made 1 day ahead. Cover and chill. Bring hens and sauce to room temperature 30 minutes before serving.)

Arrange hens on a large platter and garnish with several bouquets of watercress. Place sauce in a serving bowl.

BAKED HAM WITH A RED CURRANT MUSTARD GLAZE

Glazed baked ham, served at room temperature, is a fabulous make-ahead main course to serve a crowd. Sliced and arranged on a bed of watercress accompanied by a bowl of spicy Plum Chutney, this attractive ham does not require any last-minute attention. Scalloped Potatoes with Crème Fraîche and Gruyère (page 158) and a mixed greens salad tossed in a vinaigrette dressing could complete the menu.

1 6- to 7-pound fully cooked boneless ham, preferably from the shank half

¾ cup red currant jelly

6 tablespoons whole-grain Dijon mustard

1½ teaspoons ground ginger

1 bunch watercress for garnish
Plum Chutney (page 317)

SERVES **10**

Arrange an oven rack at lower third of oven and preheat oven to 325 degrees F. Place ham in a shallow roasting pan and bake for an hour.

While the ham is baking, whisk together jelly, mustard, and ginger in a saucepan over medium heat to make the glaze. Continue to whisk until the mixture has liquefied, 1 to 2 minutes. Remove from heat.

After the ham has been in the oven for an hour, remove it and score the top, making a grid pattern with a sharp knife and cutting through the skin. Then brush the top and sides of the ham generously with some of the glaze. Return to the oven and continue to cook, basting the ham with additional glaze every 10 minutes, until an instant-read thermometer inserted in the thickest part of the ham registers 140 degrees F. The total baking time should be about 10 to 12 minutes per pound. The temperature will rise another 5 degrees when the ham is removed from the oven.

Let rest for 15 minutes before carving.

To serve, slice ham and arrange overlapping slices on a platter. Brush slices with any remaining glaze. Garnish the platter with several bouquets of watercress and serve ham at room temperature with Plum Chutney.

ITALIAN COLD CUTS WITH ARTICHOKE, RED PEPPER, AND OLIVE CONFETTI

Your favorite Italian cold cuts, sliced and arranged on a platter, can be accompanied by a delicious artichoke relish and some crusty bread for a tempting first course. Or, offer this dish with a pasta salad as a simple, but delectable cold entree.

2 pounds thinly sliced assorted Italian cold cuts (Use a combination of your choice including such favorites as prosciutto, various salamis, and mortadella.)

2 loaves crusty Italian bread such as ciabatta, sliced

Artichoke, Red Pepper, and Olive Confetti (page 315)

SERVES 6 TO 8

Arrange cold cuts on a platter and place bread in a napkin-lined basket. Set out a bowl of Artichoke, Red Pepper, and Olive Confetti. Top each bread slice with some sliced cold cuts, then spoon a generous amount of Artichoke, Red Pepper, and Olive Confetti over the sliced meat.

Castroville, California, is the Artichoke Capital of the World. Marilyn Monroe was crowned the town's first Artichoke Queen in 1947.

RIBS, DEEP SOUTH STYLE

I grew up in Memphis, often called the Barbecue Capital of the United States, and have tasted myriad versions of barbecued ribs. This recipe, in which ribs are slow-baked in the oven rather than cooked over an open fire, is a personal favorite. The secret to their great taste is the homemade barbecue sauce, created years ago by my late father-in-law, a Southerner celebrated for his barbecued ribs. The ribs, brushed with the homemade sauce, are baked for a couple of hours until their outsides are crusty and brown and the meat beneath moist and succulent.

1 double recipe of Deep South Barbecue Sauce (page 322)

6 1½-pound slabs baby back pork ribs (9 pounds total)

½ cup plus 1 tablespoon cider vinegar

Kosher salt

Freshly ground black pepper

Cayenne pepper

SERVES **6** WITH 1 FULL SLAB PER PERSON, OR 12 WITH ½ SLAB PER PERSON

Arrange one rack in middle position of oven and another rack in lower third of oven. Preheat oven to 350 degrees F.

Reserve 1 cup of the barbecue sauce to serve with ribs.

Rinse ribs and pat dry with paper towels. Score white membrane on underside with a knife. Place a flat roasting rack in each of 2 large roasting pans. Brush ribs on both sides with vinegar. Season ribs generously on both sides with salt, black pepper, and cayenne and leave meaty-side up on roasting racks in pans. Brush both sides of ribs with some of the barbecue sauce and put in the oven. Baste top of ribs every 30 minutes with some of the barbecue sauce. After 45 minutes, reverse the pans, placing the pan on the middle rack on the lower rack, and vice versa. Cover ribs loosely with aluminum foil if they start to brown too quickly. Roast until ribs are a rich dark brown and tender when pierced with a knife, 1½ to 1¾ hours.

When done, place ribs on a large platter. Heat reserved barbecue sauce and any remaining basting sauce in a medium saucepan over medium heat, until bubbling. Pass warmed sauce to drizzle over each serving of ribs.

SHRIMP WITH CREOLE DIPPING SAUCE

SERVES **6**

Boiled shrimp dipped in a piquant remoulade sauce is a Louisiana favorite and a great dish to serve outdoors. The following recipe for Creole sauce was shared with me by a friend whose family lived in New Orleans for many years. A fail-proof version that takes only minutes to prepare in a blender or processor, it makes a perfect accompaniment to a platter of boiled shrimp.

CREOLE DIPPING SAUCE

1 cup vegetable or olive oil

½ cup tarragon vinegar

½ cup coarsely chopped green onions

½ cup coarsely chopped celery

¼ cup horseradish mustard or Dijon mustard

2 tablespoons ketchup

1 tablespoon paprika

1 teaspoon salt

½ teaspoon cayenne pepper

6 drops Tabasco sauce

2 small cloves garlic

2 teaspoons salt

3 pounds large shrimp, shelled and deveined but with tails left on (see note, page 99)

2 tablespoons chopped fresh flat-leaf parsley for garnish (optional)

TO MAKE THE CREOLE DIPPING SAUCE: Combine all the ingredients in a blender or food processor, and process until the mixture is smooth, about 1 minute. (The sauce can be made 2 to 3 days ahead. Cover and refrigerate. Bring to room temperature 30 minutes before using.) Makes about 3 cups sauce.

To prepare shrimp, bring 4 quarts water to a boil and add 2 teaspoons salt. Add the shrimp and cook until curled and pink, 3 to 4 minutes. Drain in a colander and rinse under cold water. Drain well and pat dry. The shrimp can be cooked up to 4 hours ahead. Cover and refrigerate.

To serve, fill 6 small bowls with Creole Dipping Sauce and place each on a dinner plate. Mound shrimp on a large platter and sprinkle with parsley, if desired.

ANN CLARK'S GOLDEN FRIED CLAM CAKES

1¼ cups all-purpose flour

2 teaspoons baking powder

¾ teaspoon salt

¼ teaspoon cayenne pepper

1 large egg

½ cup clam juice

¼ cup whole milk

1 cup (1 pound) chopped clams (see note)

Corn oil for deep-frying the clam cakes

1 to 1½ tablespoons chopped fresh chives or flat-leaf parsley for garnish (optional)

A New England friend, Ann Clark, shared this old family recipe for Golden Fried Clam Cakes. Chopped clams are encased in a milk and flour batter, which is added by spoonfuls to bubbling hot oil. The resulting cakes (which could easily be called clam fritters or puffs) are served piping hot mounded on a platter, and disappear within minutes at my friend's family reunions.

Sift together flour, baking powder, salt, and cayenne in a medium bowl. Set aside. In another medium bowl, whisk egg with clam juice and milk. Whisk in dry ingredients just until mixture is smooth. Stir in clams. Cover batter and refrigerate at least 3 hours, or even better, overnight.

When ready to fry clam cakes, fill a medium, heavy saucepan 3 inches deep with oil, and place over high heat. Use a deep-frying thermometer to determine when oil has reached 350 degrees F.

When ready, scoop 1 tablespoonful of batter for each clam cake into the hot oil. Fry 3 to 5 at a time, without crowding. Cook, turning once or twice with a slotted spoon, until the cakes are a rich golden brown on all sides, about 3 minutes. (Watch the temperature carefully and try to maintain 350 degrees; if temperature drops, raise heat, and if it gets too high, lower heat or take pot off the burner for a few minutes.) Remove cakes and drain on paper towels. Cover loosely with aluminum foil. Continue until all the batter is used. Mound clam cakes on a platter and garnish with chives or parsley, if desired. Serve hot.

NOTE: If you can't find chopped shucked clams, you can use clams in the shells. For 1 cup, you'll need about 4 pounds, depending on the variety of clams. Steam them in 3 cups simmering water until the shells open, about 5 minutes. Discard any unopened clams.

BOILED LOBSTERS WITH TWO DIFFERENT SAUCES

If you want to break with tradition and serve boiled lobsters with something more unusual than plain melted butter, quickly made Sesame Orange Mayonnaise served cold or Warm Citrus Butter are good choices. Both of these vibrantly flavored sauces can be prepared in advance to serve with lobsters.

Salt

6 1½-pound live lobsters

1 small bunch watercress (optional)

1 double recipe of Sesame Orange Mayonnaise (page 329) or 1 double recipe of Warm Citrus Butter (page 323)

SERVES 6

To cook lobsters, bring at least 9 quarts water to a boil in a large lobster pot or an extra-large stock pot set over high heat. (If you do not have a large pot, use 2 pots and fill each with 5 to 6 quarts of water and cook 3 lobsters in each one.) Add ½ tablespoon salt per quart of water to the pot(s). When the water returns to a boil, add the lobsters, and reduce heat to medium. Cover and simmer for about 12 minutes. Test for doneness by removing a lobster from the pot and twisting one of the thin legs on the body. If the leg pulls off easily and quickly, the lobsters should be done.

Remove lobsters to a platter and garnish with several clusters of watercress, if desired. Fill 6 small bowls with Sesame Orange Mayonnaise or with Warm Citrus Butter. Serve each lobster with a bowl for dipping.

Nearly 90 percent of the nation's lobster supply is caught off the coast of Maine.

SPICY CRAB CAKES

For many years, a former Northampton, Massachusetts, restaurant called Lady Bird served a version of these Asian-accented crab cakes to rave reviews. Chef Stefanie Shulman shared the original recipe, which I streamlined for home cooks. Hot chili sauce and cilantro are two unexpected ingredients that give big boosts of flavor to these little cakes.

3 slices good-quality white bread

½ pound fresh lump crab meat, picked over

½ cup finely diced red bell pepper

½ cup finely chopped red onion

⅓ cup chopped fresh cilantro

½ cup, plus 3 tablespoons hot chili sauce with garlic divided (see note)

1 large egg, lightly beaten

¼ teaspoon salt

Canola oil for sautéing

Early ketchups were prepared with mushrooms, onions, oysters, anchovies, lemons, or pickled walnuts. New Englanders added tomatoes to these blends in the late 1700s and became the originators of tomato ketchup.

MAKES **12** CRAB CAKES; SERVES 4 WITH 3 CRAB CAKES EACH

Arrange an oven rack at center position and preheat oven to 350 degrees F.

Pulse bread slices in a food processor until fine bread crumbs are formed. Remove bread crumbs and spread evenly on a baking sheet. Bake until just golden, about 5 minutes, stirring once. Remove from oven and place in a bowl.

Place crab meat in a clean kitchen towel and gently squeeze out any excess liquid. Combine crab meat in a large bowl with red bell pepper, onion, and cilantro. Stir well to blend. Add 3 tablespoons chili sauce, egg, and salt and mix well, then stir in the toasted bread crumbs. Chill mixture for 30 minutes or longer to firm.

Shape the crab mixture into 12 equal patties, each about 3 inches in diameter. Place on a baking sheet and cover with plastic wrap. (The crab cakes can be prepared 3 to 4 hours in advance. Keep covered and refrigerated.)

When ready to cook crab cakes, heat enough oil to coat the bottom of a medium (preferably nonstick) skillet over medium-high heat. When very hot, cook 3 to 4 crab cakes at a time until golden brown, about 1½ to 2 minutes per side. Turn them with a metal spatula. Remove to a serving platter and cover sautéed crab cakes loosely with aluminum foil to keep warm. Continue, adding more oil to coat the bottom of the pan if necessary, until all crab cakes have been cooked. (If you are doubling or tripling this recipe, it is easier to keep the crab cakes warm in a preheated 350-degree F oven. Transfer crab cakes as they are cooked onto a baking sheet, cover them loosely with foil, and place in oven.)

To serve, drizzle a little of the chili sauce over each crab cake. Place remaining chili sauce in a small bowl to pass. Serve crab cakes warm.

NOTE: Hot chili sauce with garlic can be found in the Asian section of many super-markets and in Asian specialty food stores. Kame is a readily available brand that works well in this recipe.

MOUNDS OF MUSSELS WITH SAFFRON MAYONNAISE

I don't think there is anything more spectacular than a platter piled high with steamed mussels, their sleek black shells spread wide open to reveal the tan tender morsels within. Certainly, nothing could be simpler to prepare. These mussels are steamed in white wine, butter, and shallots until their lids open. Then the mussels are removed and the cooking liquid is seasoned with saffron and reduced. It is whisked into mayonnaise to make a dipping sauce for the shellfish.

12 tablespoons (1 ½ sticks) unsalted butter

⅔ cup coarsely chopped shallots

6 medium cloves garlic, thinly sliced

3 cups dry white wine

1 cup fresh flat-leaf parsley sprigs

4 sprigs fresh thyme, or 2 teaspoons dried

2 large bay leaves

4 pounds (about 4 dozen) medium mussels in the shells, scrubbed (see note)

SAFFRON MAYONNAISE

1 teaspoon saffron threads, crushed

1½ cups regular or reduced-fat (not nonfat) mayonnaise

2 teaspoons chopped fresh flat-leaf parsley

SERVES

Melt 6 tablespoons of the butter in each of 2 large (6- to 8-quart) pots set over medium-high heat. When hot, put half of the shallots and garlic in each pot. Sauté, stirring, until softened, 2 to 3 minutes. Add half of the wine and half of the herbs to each pot. Bring mixture to a simmer. Add half of the mussels to each pot, trying to keep the hinged sides down. Cover and steam until the mussels are open, 5 to 7 minutes. Remove and discard any mussels that have not opened. Mound the mussels onto a large serving platter or in a large, shallow bowl. Cover loosely with foil to keep warm.

TO MAKE THE MAYONNAISE: Strain the cooking liquid from both pots and return 2 cups of the strained liquid to only 1 of the pots. Place over high heat. Add the saffron and cook until the mixture has reduced to about ½ cup and is slightly syrupy, 5 to 8 minutes or longer. Remove and cool 5 minutes, then whisk reduced mixture into the mayonnaise. Place in a small serving bowl and sprinkle with parsley.

Remove the foil from the mussels and serve with the Saffron Mayonnaise.

NOTE: Use the mussels as soon as possible after purchasing them. If you have to store them, refrigerate in a mesh bag or in a bowl, but not in a plastic bag (because they would suffocate). Cover with a damp towel. Live mussels should have tightly closed lids. If a mussel is open, place under cold running water. If the mussel does not close, discard it.

PO' BOYS WITH CORNED BEEF, CREAMY CARAWAY COLESLAW, AND SWISS

Po' boys, which originated in New Orleans as a cheap and quick sandwich for dock workers, are most often made with fried oysters, so this version is slightly different. The large soft-crusted Italian loaves typically used for such sandwiches are split and layered with sliced corned beef, Gruyère cheese, and a creamy slaw flavored with crushed caraway seeds. The oversize sandwiches are then cut into individual portions. Serve the sandwiches with crispy potato chips, kosher pickles, and olives.

2 1-pound soft-crusted Italian bread loaves, each about 12 to 14 inches long and 6 inches wide

1½ pounds thinly sliced corned beef

1 pound thinly sliced imported Swiss cheese such as Gruyère

Creamy Caraway Coleslaw (page 182)

SERVES 8

With a serrated knife, halve each loaf of bread horizontally. For each po' boy, arrange half of the corned beef on a bottom bread half, then cover with half of the sliced cheese. Using a slotted spoon, spread half of the coleslaw over the cheese layer and top with remaining bread half. Makes 2 large po' boys.

To serve, arrange po' boys on a wooden bread board or on a serving platter. With a serrated knife, cut each sandwich into 4 equal servings.

HAM, CHEDDAR, AND PLUM CHUTNEY ON WHOLE WHEAT

8 slices good-quality whole-wheat bread, lightly toasted

3 to **4** tablespoons Dijon mustard

8 ounces thinly sliced baked ham

8 ounces thinly sliced sharp white Cheddar cheese

About ½ to ¾ cup Plum Chutney (page 317)

1 to **1**½ cups loosely packed mixed lettuce greens

Toothpicks

Ham and cheese sandwiches are elevated to a new dimension when prepared with a sweet and tart plum chutney and topped with mixed greens. The chutney can be prepared several days in advance and refrigerated until needed.

SERVES 4

To assemble sandwiches, spread a bread slice generously with Dijon mustard. Top with 3 to 4 ham slices, 2 cheese slices, and 2 to 3 tablespoons Plum Chutney. Mound some greens on top and cover with another bread slice generously spread with mustard. Repeat to make 3 more sandwiches.

Cut sandwiches diagonally into quarters. Skewer quarters with toothpicks to secure. Arrange sandwiches on serving plates.

In the 18th century, John Montagu, the Earl of Sandwich, is said to have created the first sandwich when he refused to leave a card game and ate cold meat placed between slices of bread.

BLTs WITH BASIL MAYO ON TOASTED COUNTRY BREAD

8 thick slices (8 ounces) smoked bacon

8 ½-inch-thick slices country French bread (cut on the diagonal from a crusty loaf about 4 inches in diameter)

Basil Mayonnaise (page 328)

3 to 4 medium, ripe tomatoes, thinly sliced

1 small bunch of arugula, stemmed

Toothpicks

Here's a fabulous variation on classic bacon, lettuce, and tomato sandwiches. Quickly made basil mayonnaise adds extra flavor, and peppery arugula replaces traditional iceberg lettuce. A dense country loaf is a change from soft white bread.

SERVES 4

Fry bacon in a large, heavy skillet set over medium heat until crisp and golden brown. Remove and drain on paper towels.

Toast bread slices until golden. Brush 1 side of each slice with Basil Mayonnaise.

To assemble sandwiches, arrange a layer of tomato slices slightly overlapping on a bread slice. Top with 2 bacon slices, then with several arugula leaves. Cover with another bread slice. Cut the sandwich in half on the diagonal with a serrated knife. Repeat to make 3 more sandwiches. Skewer each half with a toothpick to secure, and arrange the sandwich halves on a serving plate. Serve immediately.

TURKEY, APPLE, AND CHEDDAR CLUBS

8 thin slices whole-wheat country or crusty sourdough bread

1 recipe Chutney Mayonnaise (page 330)

10 to **12** ounces thinly sliced smoked turkey

8 ounces thinly sliced medium-sharp white Cheddar cheese

1 large Granny Smith apple, halved and cored but not peeled

2 teaspoons fresh lemon juice

4 small romaine or red leaf lettuce leaves

Toothpicks or wooden skewers

These sandwiches, quickly made with easy-to-find ingredients, are perfect to serve for an outdoor lunch or light supper. The Chutney Mayonnaise, made with purchased dressing mixed with chopped mango chutney and curry powder, adds a distinctive flavor, while the crisp apple slices lend unexpected crunch. Offer the sandwiches with potato chips and glasses of Old-Fashioned Lemonade (page 214).

SERVES

Spread 1 side of each bread slice generously with 1 tablespoon or more of Chutney Mayonnaise. Top a slice with ¼ of the sliced turkey, then with ¼ of the sliced cheese. Slice each apple half thinly and toss slices with lemon juice in a small bowl. Arrange 4 to 5 slices over the cheese layer, then top with a lettuce leaf and another slice of bread. Repeat to make 3 more sandwiches.

Halve sandwiches on the diagonal and skewer halves with a toothpick to secure.

CHICKEN CLUBS À LA PROVENÇALE

I've never had a sandwich like this when in southern France, but the ingredients are redolent of Provence. Creamy goat cheese, fresh herbs, roasted red peppers, and mesclun greens are combined with roasted chicken and served on slices of country French bread. These sandwiches are filling enough for a substantial lunch or a light supper. If you don't have any leftover roasted or grilled chicken on hand, buy a roasted chicken from a local supermarket to save time.

GOAT CHEESE SPREAD

10 to **11** ounces soft creamy goat cheese

3 tablespoons chopped niçoise or kalamata olives

2½ tablespoons chopped fresh basil

1 tablespoon drained, chopped capers

2½ teaspoons chopped fresh thyme

2 teaspoons minced garlic

1 teaspoon freshly ground black pepper

SANDWICHES

8 ½-inch-thick slices crusty country French bread, lightly toasted

8 to **10** ounces roasted or grilled chicken, sliced (see note)

1 7-ounce jar roasted red peppers

1⅓ to **1½** cups loosely packed mesclun greens or mixed baby greens

2 teaspoons olive oil

1 teaspoon fresh lemon juice

Salt

Freshly ground black pepper

Toothpicks (optional)

SERVES

TO MAKE THE GOAT CHEESE SPREAD: Combine all ingredients in a nonreactive bowl and mix well to blend. (The spread can be made 1 day ahead; cover and refrigerate.)

TO MAKE THE SANDWICHES: Spread all the bread slices evenly on 1 side with the goat cheese mixture. (Depending on the size of your bread slices, you may not need to use all of the spread; save extra for another use. It is good on crackers or stuffed into cherry tomatoes.)

Arrange chicken on 4 of the slices. Drain, rinse, and pat the peppers dry, and use just enough to make an even layer over the chicken on each sandwich. (You may not need to use all of the peppers; save extras for another use.)

Toss the greens with the olive oil and lemon juice, and season generously with salt and pepper. Divide greens and mound on top of peppers. Cover sandwiches with remaining bread slices. Cut each sandwich in half and skewer halves with toothpicks, if desired. Serve immediately.

NOTE: These sandwiches are also good made with sliced, roasted turkey.

PAN-GRILLED WRAPS WITH CHICKEN, GINGER, AND PLUM SAUCE

4 8-inch flour tortillas

4 ounces cream cheese, plus more if needed

½ cup Asian plum sauce, plus more if needed (see notes)

½ cup chopped green onions including 2 inches of green stems

3 tablespoons minced peeled fresh ginger

1 small (2-pound) purchased roasted chicken (see notes)

1 bunch watercress, stemmed

Wooden skewers or toothpicks

Vegetable oil for oiling grill pan

These wraps fall into the category of "creative convenience" cooking and take no time at all to assemble. Flour tortillas are spread with a thin layer of cream cheese, then with Asian plum sauce. Chopped fresh ginger and green onions are added next, and finally slices of roasted chicken and watercress sprigs. Then the tortillas are rolled into cylinders and grilled in a stovetop pan. By buying plum sauce in the Asian condiment section of the grocery and purchasing a roasted chicken at the rotisserie counter, you'll save time but will not sacrifice flavor. Serve the wraps for a light lunch or supper along with a mixed greens salad.

SERVES 4

Place tortillas on a clean work surface. Spread each with a thin layer (about 2 tablespoons) of cream cheese, then with a thin layer (about 2 tablespoons) of plum sauce. Divide evenly and sprinkle green onions and ginger over tortillas.

Cut thin slices from breast of chicken. (Save dark meat for another use.) Place some sliced chicken on top of each tortilla. Lay enough watercress sprigs on top to form a 1-inch-wide band across the centers of tortillas. Then, roll tortillas up tightly into cylinders and fasten with skewers or toothpicks. (Wraps can be prepared 1 hour ahead; cover and refrigerate.)

When ready to grill wraps, oil a stovetop grill pan or coat the bottom of a large, heavy skillet with oil. Place grill pan or skillet over medium-high heat. Grill or sauté wraps, turning several times, until grill marks appear (if using a grill pan) or until lightly browned (if using a skillet) on all surfaces and sandwiches are hot inside, 2 to 3 minutes or longer.

Cut each tortilla diagonally into halves. Arrange a cluster of watercress sprigs on serving plate and surround with sliced wraps. Serve warm.

NOTES: Plum sauce is available in the Asian ingredient section of supermarkets or in Asian groceries.

: Try to buy a plain or lemon-roasted chicken; avoid barbecued and highly spiced birds for this recipe.

TUNA SALAD WITH OLIVES, TOMATOES, AND BASIL ON CRUSTY BAGUETTES

12 ounces white-meat tuna packed in water, drained and coarsely chopped

½ cup pitted chopped kalamata olives

6 tablespoons finely chopped celery

¼ cup chopped oil-packed sun-dried tomatoes

¼ cup chopped fresh basil

Scant ½ teaspoon red pepper flakes

Salt

6 tablespoons regular or reduced-fat (not nonfat) mayonnaise

2 tablespoons frozen orange juice concentrate, defrosted

2 teaspoons grated orange zest

2 best-quality crusty baguettes

About 1⅓ to 1½ cups lettuce greens such as baby spinach or Boston lettuce

Tuna salad made with sun-dried tomatoes, basil, and olives bound with an orange-scented mayonnaise is delicious served on crispy baguettes. Serve the sandwiches with potato chips and Old-Fashioned Lemonade (page 214).

SERVED 4

Combine tuna, olives, celery, sun-dried tomatoes plus 1 teaspoon of the oil in which they were packed, basil, red pepper flakes, and a generous pinch of salt in a bowl and mix well. Whisk together mayonnaise, orange juice concentrate, and orange zest in another bowl. Add to bowl with tuna and mix well. Taste and season with more salt if needed. (The salad can be prepared 3 hours ahead, cover and refrigerate.)

Cut four 6- to 8-inch-long pieces from the baguettes and slice in half horizontally. You may not need to use all of the baguettes. Spread a bread bottom with ¼ of the tuna salad, top with lettuce, and then with a bread top. Repeat to make 3 more sandwiches. Cut sandwiches in half or leave whole.

Potato chips were invented in 1853 in Saratoga Springs, New York, by George Crum.

CAPE COD FRIED SCALLOP ROLLS

Vegetable oil

⅔ cup all-purpose flour

½ teaspoon salt

¼ teaspoon black pepper

½ cup whole milk

16 large (about 1 pound) sea scallops, side muscles removed

4 sliced sandwich rolls (hot dog–style buns with crustless sides), lightly toasted

Quick Tartar Sauce (page 331)

Although my husband and I love the beautiful beaches and ocean views of Cape Cod, we confess that it's the area's incredible seafood dishes that keep us coming back year after year. The Fried Scallop Roll is one of my favorites. In fact, each summer I insist that we travel to Orleans' Rock Harbor, where a modest little spot on the water serves a fabulous version of these sandwiches. The freshest sea scallops imaginable are cut into bite-sized pieces, coated with flour, and deep fried. The crisp golden morsels are mounded on lightly toasted sandwich rolls and served with tartar sauce. From the first taste, I am in heaven. I love the slightly crunchy exterior of the scallops and the smooth texture beneath. Simple sides like sliced tomatoes, drizzled with oil and vinegar and sprinkled with herbs, plus corn on the cob, would make perfect accompaniments.

SERVES **4**

Fill a heavy, medium saucepan with enough oil to come 3 inches up the sides. Place over medium-high heat until hot, but not smoking (about 365 degrees F if you are using a deep-frying thermometer).

While the oil is heating, spread flour, salt, and pepper on a dinner plate and stir to mix well. Place milk in a bowl. Cut each scallop into 4 equal-sized pieces, and dip them in the milk. Remove and drain in a colander. Then, a handful at a time, coat in the flour until all scallops have been dredged.

When oil is ready, spread several thicknesses of paper towels on a work surface for draining cooked scallops. Use a slotted spoon to transfer a handful of the scallops to the saucepan. The oil will sizzle and bubble immediately. Cook the scallops until golden brown, stirring occasionally, only 1 to 2 minutes. Remove with the slotted spoon and drain on paper towels. Cover loosely with aluminum foil to keep warm. Continue until all scallops have been cooked.

Divide the scallops evenly and mound in the toasted buns. Serve scallop rolls with a bowl of tartar sauce. Serve immediately.

NEW ENGLAND LOBSTER ROLLS WITH SESAME ORANGE MAYONNAISE

½ recipe Sesame Orange Mayonnaise (page 329)

½ pound cooked lobster meat, diced (see note)

2 tablespoons finely chopped celery

1 green onion including 2 inches of green stems, finely chopped

3 to 4 sandwich rolls (hot dog–style buns with crustless sides), lightly toasted

1 tablespoon finely chopped fresh chives

1½ teaspoons sesame seeds, toasted (see page 15)

The New England coast boasts many seafood specialties, and lobster rolls are among the most celebrated. Traditionally, soft sandwich rolls are toasted and mounded with fresh lobster salad. In this version, mayonnaise scented with orange and sesame replaces the usual dressing in the salad and adds a refreshing flavor. The following recipe serves three to four but can be easily doubled.

SERVES  3 TO 4

Combine mayonnaise, lobster, celery, and green onion in a large nonreactive bowl. Mix well. (Mixture can be prepared 2 to 3 hours ahead; cover and refrigerate. Bring to room temperature 30 minutes before using.)

Mound each roll with some lobster salad and sprinkle lightly with chives and sesame seeds.

NOTE: One pound of lobster will yield ¼ pound cooked meat. Many fish markets will cook lobsters and remove the meat for you. The price is higher, but often worth it for the time it saves.

CRAB AND PISTACHIO SALAD SANDWICHES

1 pound fresh crab meat, picked over

½ cup finely diced celery

6 tablespoons regular or reduced-fat (not nonfat) mayonnaise

¼ cup coarsely chopped unsalted roasted pistachios (see note)

¼ cup chopped fresh flat-leaf parsley

4 teaspoons fresh lemon juice

4 teaspoons fresh orange juice

½ teaspoon grated lemon zest

½ teaspoon grated orange zest

Salt

Cayenne pepper

12 slices best-quality white bread (such as Pepperidge Farm), lightly toasted

6 Boston lettuce leaves (optional)

Tender, sweet fresh crab meat and crunchy chopped pistachios pair well in a mayonnaise-bound salad to use in sandwiches. The salad can be prepared several hours ahead and the sandwiches quickly assembled at serving time.

SERVES

Combine crab, celery, mayonnaise, pistachios, parsley, lemon and orange juices, lemon and orange zests, ½ teaspoon salt, and a small pinch of cayenne in a medium non-reactive bowl. Taste and season with more salt if needed. (The salad can be prepared 4 hours ahead; cover and refrigerate.)

Spread a slice of bread generously with crab salad and top with a lettuce leaf, if desired. Cover with a remaining bread slice. Repeat to make 5 more sandwiches.

NOTE: Shelled roasted pistachios are available in specialty groceries or food stores. If you can't find shelled pistachios, you can buy roasted nuts in their shells and shell them. It will not take long since you will need a small amount for this recipe.

EGG SALAD CLUB SANDWICHES

8 large hard-boiled eggs (see page 15)

15 or more Spanish olives (pimento-stuffed green olives)

¼ cup very finely chopped celery

Salt

Coarsely ground black pepper

¼ cup regular or reduced fat (not nonfat) mayonnaise plus extra for spreading on toasted bread

½ teaspoon Dijon mustard

8 slices good-quality white sandwich bread, lightly toasted

8 slices bacon, fried until crisp and golden

8 crisp red leaf lettuce leaves

6-inch wooden skewers

Pimento-stuffed olives and a hint of Dijon mustard take classic egg salad to a new level. The salad is mounded on toasted bread slices and topped with bacon and crisp red leaf lettuce. Served garnished with potato chips, cherry tomatoes, and sliced deli-style pickles, these sandwiches are good to serve for lunch or a light supper.

4 SERVES

Shell eggs, chop coarsely, and place in a large nonreactive bowl. Chop olives and add to bowl along with celery, ½ teaspoon salt, and ¼ teaspoon pepper. Mix gently to combine. Stir mayonnaise and mustard together and then add to egg mixture and mix well. Taste and season with more salt and pepper if desired. (The egg salad can be prepared 4 hours ahead. Cover with plastic wrap and refrigerate until needed.)

To assemble sandwiches, spread all bread slices on 1 side very lightly with some mayonnaise. Mound an equal amount of egg salad on each of 4 slices, break bacon slices in half, and arrange 4 halves on each sandwich. Top with lettuce leaves and remaining toasted bread slices. Slice sandwiches on the diagonal with a serrated knife and secure halves with wooden skewers.

To serve, arrange 2 skewered halves on each of 4 dinner plates.

BEEF IN THE ROUND SANDWICHES

1 6-ounce jar prepared horseradish, drained well

½ cup regular or reduced-fat (not nonfat) sour cream

6 tablespoons chopped dill pickle

¼ cup regular or reduced-fat (not nonfat) mayonnaise

2 teaspoons whole-grain Dijon mustard

¼ teaspoon salt

¼ teaspoon freshly ground black pepper

2 cups chopped red cabbage

2 6- to 8-inch round crusty sourdough breads

1 medium Granny Smith apple, halved and cored

2 teaspoons fresh lemon juice

¾ pound thinly sliced Gruyère cheese

1 pound thinly sliced rare roast beef

These sandwiches are a meal in themselves and ideal to serve at an outdoor buffet. They are made with rounds of sourdough, which are scooped out and layered with roast beef, Gruyère cheese, thin apple slices, and red cabbage slaw. These hearty sandwiches are cut into wedges for serving and would be good offered with A Mixed Bag of Beans (page 162) and a mixed greens salad tossed in a vinaigrette dressing.

SERVES 8

In a large bowl, stir together horseradish, sour cream, pickle, mayonnaise, mustard, salt, and pepper until well blended. Add cabbage and stir to combine. Set aside.

Slice each loaf of bread in half, horizontally through the center, into 2 rounds. Gently pull out most of the soft bread from the center of each half, leaving a ½-inch-thick edge.

Cut each apple half into very thin slices and toss in lemon juice.

On 1 of the bottom bread halves, layer half of the cheese, then half of the apples, and half of the roast beef. Use half of the cabbage mixture to cover the roast beef, then cover with a bread top. Repeat to make another sandwich. (Sandwiches can be prepared an hour ahead. Wrap in plastic wrap and refrigerate.)

To serve, place the sandwiches on a cutting board, and using a serrated knife, cut each into 4 wedges.

CHAPTER 4

VEGETABLE SIDEKICKS

Side dishes wield much more weight than their name implies. I think of them as supporting actors who help the lead shine in a play. And when it comes to backyard cooking, side possibilities are unlimited, as this chapter will reveal. Some of these vegetable recipes are fairly simple, others dressed up a bit, but all are delicious enough to make a lasting impression on your guests.

Grilled asparagus spears, slightly smoky from a short time on the fire, tender green beans tossed with olive oil and chives, and paper-thin sweet potato slices, deep fried until crisp, are simple but flavorful accompaniments. Corn on the cob is irresistible, boiled or grilled, then slathered with any of several seasoned butters found in this collection. As an alternative, consider a spicy Pepper Jack corn pudding made with scraped kernels of sweet summer corn.

Potatoes are the backyard cook's best friend, and you'll find more than one way to prepare them here. Skewered and grilled, wrapped in foil packages, then cooked atop hot coals, or baked in gratins, these spuds will enliven any barbecue menu. Tomatoes, zucchini, and eggplant—that beloved summer trinity—appear in many dishes, alone or in combination.

Any of these recipes will rescue your vegetarian guests from side-dish boredom. And what fabulous candidates these creations would make to take to a backyard barbecue when someone says to you: "Just bring a vegetable."

GRILLED ASPARAGUS SPEARS

This is one of the simplest, yet most delicious, ways I know to pre-pare asparagus. Thick spears are dipped in water seasoned with a little oil, then put atop a hot grill. Cooked until lightly charred and tender, they need only to be salted, peppered, and dusted with pars-ley when done.

2 teaspoons olive oil, plus extra for oiling grill rack

1½ pounds large asparagus spears

Kosher salt

Freshly ground black pepper

2 tablespoons chopped fresh flat-leaf parsley

SERVES 6

Oil a grill rack and arrange 4 to 5 inches from heat source. Prepare grill for a hot fire (high temperature). Combine 4 cups water and 2 tablespoons olive oil in a large bowl. Add asparagus and toss to coat well. Let stand 5 minutes. Drain and season with salt and pepper.

Grill asparagus until crisp-tender, turning frequently with tongs, about 6 minutes. Transfer to a platter. Taste and season with more salt and pepper if desired. Sprinkle with parsley.

ARTICHOKES WITH PECORINO, BLACK PEPPER, AND OLIVE OIL

Nothing could be easier than this dish, which calls for three ingredients plus salt and pepper. After artichokes are cooked and still warm, their inner leaves are removed and fuzzy chokes scraped out, and a sauce of virgin olive oil, grated Pecorino, and cracked pepper is poured into the center of each. For eating, the leaves are pulled off and dipped into the sauce, and the tender chokes are infused with flavor when you reach them. The artichokes make an attractive vegetable garnish to grilled steaks or lamb chops.

4 medium artichokes (about 8 ounces each)

½ cup fruity olive oil

6 tablespoons grated Pecorino Romano cheese (see note)

Cracked or coarsely ground black pepper

Kosher salt

SERVES 6

Bring a large pot of water to boil over medium-high heat. While water is coming to a boil, prepare artichokes. Cut off and discard stem from each artichoke so they will sit upright without wobbling. Place each artichoke on its side, and using a sharp knife, cut off and discard about ¾ inch of the top. Using scissors, trim and discard sharp tips from artichoke leaves.

Place artichokes in boiling water. Cover with lid slightly ajar, and cook artichokes until bases are tender when pierced with a knife and when leaves around base can be pulled off easily, 25 to 30 minutes. Remove and drain artichokes upside down on a plate for 5 minutes.

While artichokes are resting, prepare sauce. In a small bowl, mix together olive oil, cheese, 1 teaspoon pepper, and ¼ teaspoon salt. Taste and add more salt and pepper if needed.

To serve, arrange 1 artichoke upright on each of 4 salad plates. Spread the leaves open and using a spoon, scoop out the fuzzy center chokes. Salt and pepper the cavities, then ladle 1 tablespoon of the sauce into each artichoke. Divide remaining sauce among 4 small ramekins or bowls and place beside artichokes on salad plates. To eat, pull off leaves and dip in sauce. The hearts will be nicely seasoned with sauce when you have pulled off the outer leaves.

NOTE: Pecorino Romano, a pale yellow, hard Italian cheese made from sheep's milk, is available in most groceries. You can substitute Parmigiano-Reggiano if desired, but the Pecorino Romano has a sharper flavor.

GRILLED CORN ON THE COB WITH SEASONED BUTTERS

Corn on the cob grilled in the husks is delicious served slathered with any of the three seasoned butters suggested here. The Curry Butter has a very distinctive flavor but does not overpower the corn, the Lime Cilantro Butter is more delicate but very refreshing, while the Red Bell Pepper Basil Butter complements the corn beautifully with its big, assertive tastes.

8 ears of corn in the husks

Curry Butter (page 323), Lime Cliantro Butter (page 324), or Red Bell Pepper Basil Butter (page 324)

SERVES **8**

Pull back, but do not remove, husks from each ear of corn. Remove and discard all the corn silk. Pull husks back over corn. Place corn in a large bowl or pot of cold water, and soak 10 minutes. Remove corn from water and pat dry.

Prepare a charcoal grill for a hot fire (high temperature), and when the coals are hot and gray, nestle the ears of corn in the coals. Cook 20 to 30 minutes, until kernels are hot. Remove with tongs. Serve ears with charred husks pulled back or removed, as desired, on a warm serving platter with any of the seasoned butters.

NOTE: If you have a gas grill, you can remove the husks and silk from the corn ears and wrap each individually in aluminum foil and grill on high about 25 to 30 minutes, turning them several times. You can also boil corn for 5 minutes and serve it with the seasoned butters.

An average ear of corn contains 800 kernels.

SPICY FRIED CORN, VIDALIAS, AND RED PEPPERS

1 tablespoon unsalted butter

1 tablespoon olive oil

1 cup chopped Vidalia onion

5 cups fresh corn kernels (8 to 10 ears of corn)

1 large red bell pepper, cut into ¼-inch dice

Salt

Sugar

⅔ cup light cream

1 teaspoon whole-grain Dijon mustard

Scant ⅛ teaspoon cayenne pepper

2 tablespoons chopped fresh chives

This bright combination of sautéed corn, sweet onions, and red bell peppers, simmered in light cream along with dashes of cayenne and Dijon mustard, can be prepared several hours in advance and left at cool room temperature. At serving time it will need only to be quickly reheated. Pair this spicy side dish with grilled salmon fillets, with barbecue ribs, or with hamburgers or turkey burgers.

SERVES **4 TO 5**

Heat butter and olive oil in a large, heavy skillet (cast iron works particularly well) over medium-high until very hot. Add onion and cook, stirring 2 minutes. Add corn, red bell pepper, 1 teaspoon salt, and 1 pinch of sugar. Sauté until vegetables have browned lightly, 5 to 6 minutes. Stir the mixture only occasionally so vegetables will stick to bottom of pan and brown.

In a bowl, whisk together cream, mustard, and cayenne, and add to vegetables in pan. Cook, stirring constantly, until cream has been almost entirely absorbed, about 3 minutes. Taste and add more salt and sugar if needed. (Corn mixture can be prepared 3 hours ahead; cover loosely with lid or with foil and leave at cool room temperature. Reheat, stirring.)

To serve, mound corn mixture in a serving bowl and sprinkle with chives.

GOLDEN CORN CAKES TOPPED
WITH GOAT CHEESE AND BACON

Pan fried until golden crisp, these little cakes are made with a corn-meal batter to which creamy goat cheese and sautéed corn and onions have been added. I serve them topped with a swirl of extra goat cheese, bits of crumbled bacon, and a sprinkling of minced green onions. Throughout the corn season, try them as a garnish to grilled or barbecued meats and poultry.

5 thick slices (4 to 5 ounces) bacon

2 cups fresh corn kernels (about 4 ears of corn)

1 cup chopped yellow onion

¾ cup buttermilk

1 large egg

About 5 ounces creamy goat cheese, divided

1 cup yellow cornmeal

2 teaspoons baking powder

1 teaspoon salt

½ teaspoon baking soda

⅛ teaspoon cayenne pepper

Vegetable oil for sautéing

1 bunch of green onions including 2 inches of green stems, chopped

Sauté bacon in a large, heavy skillet (preferably cast iron) over medium heat until crisp, and drain on paper towels. Chop coarsely and reserve for garnish. Reserve 2 tablespoons of the bacon drippings in skillet and discard the rest.

With skillet over medium heat, sauté corn and onions, stirring, until onions are golden brown, about 5 minutes. Remove from heat.

In a large bowl, combine buttermilk, egg, and ¼ cup of the goat cheese and whisk to blend. Add cornmeal, baking powder, salt, baking soda, and cayenne. Mix well. Stir in sautéed corn and onions; mixture will be thick.

Generously coat the skillet in which corn and onions were sautéed with a thin film of oil, and place over medium heat. When oil is quite hot, drop ⅛ cup batter for each corn cake into pan, leaving space around each to allow for spreading. Flatten each cake slightly with a spatula. Cook until golden brown on bottoms, about 1 minute, then turn and flatten again and cook 1 to 2 minutes more or until golden brown on bottoms and cooked through.

Drain on paper towels. When one batch of cakes is done, remove to a baking sheet and cover loosely with foil. Continue until all the batter has been used. (Corn cakes can be prepared 4 hours ahead; cool to room temperature and cover loosely with plastic wrap. Reheat, uncovered, on an ungreased baking sheet in preheated 400-degree F oven until crisp and heated through, 5 to 8 minutes.)

To serve, arrange corn cakes on a serving platter, top each cake with a generous teaspoon of the remaining goat cheese, and sprinkle with green onions and bacon.

PEPPER JACK CORN PUDDING

Butter for greasing pan

3 tablespoons vegetable oil

1 cup chopped leeks (white and light green parts only)

4 cups fresh corn kernels (7 to 8 ears of corn)

½ teaspoon salt

¼ teaspoon ground nutmeg

Generous ⅛ teaspoon cayenne pepper

4 large eggs

2 cups half-and-half

8 ounces pepper Jack cheese, grated

A generous amount of grated pepper Jack cheese gives this corn pudding its heat and distinguishes it from others. It can be made ahead and reheated, and complements such dishes as Ribs, Deep South Style (page 110) and Old-Fashioned Barbecued Chicken (page 82).

SERVES **6**

Arrange an oven rack at center position and preheat oven to 350 degrees F. Butter a shallow 2-quart ovenproof baking dish.

Heat oil in a large, heavy skillet over medium heat until hot. Add leeks and sauté, stirring, until softened, about 2 minutes. Add corn and cook, stirring, 5 minutes more. Remove from heat and stir in salt, nutmeg, and cayenne. Set aside.

In a large bowl, whisk eggs and half-and-half together until blended. Stir in corn mixture and cheese, and mix well. Transfer to the baking dish.

Bake until a knife or tester inserted into the middle comes out clean, and top is slightly brown, 35 to 45 minutes. Remove and cool 5 minutes. (The pudding can be prepared 1 day ahead. Cool, cover, and refrigerate. Reheat in a preheated 350-degree F oven for 25 minutes or longer.) Serve warm.

CORN AND TOMATO PUDDING WITH BASIL

2 tablespoons olive oil, plus extra for oiling baking dish

1½ cups chopped yellow onion

5 cups fresh corn kernels (8 to 10 ears of corn)

⅛ teaspoon ground nutmeg

Salt

Freshly ground black pepper

2½ cups half-and-half

3 large eggs

2 large egg whites

¼ teaspoon Tabasco sauce

2 cups diced seeded tomatoes, drained

½ cup chopped fresh basil

This mouth-watering corn pudding can be baked ahead, then reheated with its tomato topping. A garnish of chopped fresh basil adds flavor and color. The baked corn would be good served with grilled burgers or fish. Try it with Goat Cheese–Stuffed Turkey Burgers (page 45) or with Barbecued Salmon with a Mahogany Glaze (page 86).

Arrange an oven rack at center position and preheat oven to 350 degrees F. Oil a 2-quart baking dish and set aside.

Heat 2 tablespoons oil in a heavy, large skillet over medium-high heat, then add onions. Sauté until onions are translucent, about 4 minutes. Add corn kernels and sauté until cooked through, about 6 minutes. Stir in ground nutmeg. Season to taste with salt and pepper. Let mixture cool to room temperature.

Combine half-and-half, eggs, egg whites, and Tabasco sauce in a large bowl and whisk to blend. Stir corn mixture into custard. Pour into prepared dish. Bake until custard is set, about 30 minutes. (Pudding can be prepared 5 hours ahead to this point. Remove and leave at room temperature. Reheat until warm in a preheated 350-degree F oven until hot, and continue.)

Remove pudding from oven and season tomatoes with salt and pepper. Sprinkle evenly over pudding and return to oven. Bake until tomatoes are heated through, about 8 minutes. Sprinkle with basil and serve.

POLENTA TRIANGLES WITH CORN, RED PEPPERS, AND GREEN ONIONS

These golden polenta triangles studded with bits of corn, sweet bell peppers, and green onions make an exceptionally good side to serve with grilled steaks, lamb, or chicken. The triangles can be completely assembled a day ahead and need only to be heated in the oven at serving time.

1½ tablespoons unsalted butter, plus extra for greasing pan

1 tablespoon vegetable oil

2 cups fresh corn kernels (4 ears of corn)

½ cup finely diced red bell pepper

3 green onions including 2 inches of green stems, chopped

Kosher salt

2 pinches (scant ⅛ teaspoon) cayenne pepper

3¾ cups reduced-sodium chicken stock

1 cup yellow cornmeal

6 ounces grated Monterey Jack cheese, divided

Monterey Jack cheese is named after David Jacks, a 19th-century cheese maker who lived near Monterey, California.

MAKES 16 POLENTA TRIANGLES; SERVES 8

Butter an 8-inch square baking pan and set aside.

Heat oil in a medium, heavy skillet (preferably cast iron), set over medium-high heat. When hot, add corn, and cook until corn starts to brown, 6 to 8 minutes. Stir only occasionally so that corn can caramelize and develop a roasted flavor. Add bell pepper and onions, and stir and cook 2 minutes more. Add 1 teaspoon salt and cayenne. Taste and, if needed, season with additional salt. Set aside while you prepare polenta.

Pour chicken stock into a medium, heavy saucepan over medium-high heat and bring to a boil. Gradually add cornmeal in a fine stream, whisking constantly until mixture is quite thick, 5 to 8 minutes.

As soon as mixture is thick, whisk in 1½ tablespoons butter and 1 cup of the cheese, and continue whisking until both have melted. Stir in corn mixture. Taste and season with more salt if needed.

Immediately pour polenta into buttered pan, and using a rubber spatula, smooth the top so it is even and level. Cool to room temperature. Cover with plastic wrap and refrigerate until chilled and firm, 1 hour or longer. (Polenta can be prepared 1 day ahead; keep refrigerated.)

To bake polenta, arrange an oven rack at center position and preheat oven to 350 degrees F. Line a baking sheet with generously buttered foil.

Cut polenta into 16 triangles. (Cut polenta into 2 triangles and continue to cut each triangle in half until you have 16.) Arrange triangles on baking sheet and sprinkle each with some of the remaining cheese. Bake until heated through and cheese has melted, about 10 minutes.

NOTE: If you prefer, you can omit cutting the polenta into triangles, and serve it from the baking pan. Sprinkle the polenta with the remaining cheese and reheat in a preheated 350-degree F oven until hot, 15 minutes or longer.

GRATIN OF EGGPLANT AND TOMATOES

Victorine Fernandes, who lives in the same Parisian building where my husband and I often rent an apartment, arrived at our door one summer evening with a beautiful eggplant and tomato gratin. From the first bite, I swooned over the delicious combination of flavors. The talented cook had assembled a multilayered dish of sliced tomatoes and eggplant seasoned with herbes de Provence. When I asked for the recipe, my neighbor explained that she had no written directions, but offered instead to come and prepare the dish with me. I've made this gratin many times since then on both sides of the Atlantic. It can be baked several hours in advance and served either at room temperature or reheated.

½ cup olive oil, plus extra for oiling baking pan

⅓ cup, plus 1 ½ tablespoons unflavored dried bread crumbs, divided

3 pounds ripe, but not mushy, tomatoes, peeled (see page 16)

1 1-pound eggplant

⅓ cup chopped fresh flat-leaf parsley

3 large cloves garlic, minced

Kosher salt

Freshly ground black pepper

3 tablespoons herbes de Provence (page 20)

Arrange an oven rack at center position and preheat oven to 400 degrees F.

Lightly coat the bottom of a medium (2-quart) ovenproof baking dish with olive oil. Sprinkle with 1½ tablespoons of the bread crumbs.

Slice tomatoes into ¼-inch-thick rounds and set aside. Cut the eggplant into thin ⅛-inch-thick rounds and set aside. Combine parsley and garlic, and set aside.

Make a layer of tomato slices in the baking pan; salt and pepper generously and sprinkle with a generous teaspoon of herbes de Provence. Top with a layer of eggplant slices and repeat seasonings. Spread the parsley and garlic mixture over the eggplant. Make another layer of tomatoes and seasonings, followed by another layer of eggplant and seasonings. Finally, make 1 last layer of tomatoes and seasonings. Drizzle remaining olive oil over the tomatoes and coat with remaining bread crumbs.

Bake until vegetables are tender when pierced with a knife and crust is golden and crisp, 50 to 60 minutes. Remove and cool 15 minutes. Serve warm or at room temperature. There are often juices in the bottom of the pan after this gratin has been baked. This is normal, as the vegetables give off some of their water during the cooking process. The juices are delicious when mopped up with a piece of good bread. (The gratin can be baked 5 hours ahead and left at room temperature. Reheat in a preheated 400-degree F oven until warm, 20 minutes or longer.)

GOLDEN EGGPLANT SLICES WITH BASIL

I have used this recipe time and again when I needed an easy, make-ahead vegetable dish for an outdoor menu. Breaded eggplant slices are quickly pan-fried until golden, then seasoned with cider vinegar, and left to marinate for several hours. The eggplant, served at room temperature with a garnish of julienned fresh basil, is especially good with grilled lamb or chicken.

1 1-pound eggplant
   Salt
   Freshly ground black pepper
2 large eggs, beaten
1 cup unflavored dried bread crumbs
   Vegetable oil for pan frying
3 tablespoons cider vinegar
2 teaspoons minced garlic
1½ tablespoons finely julienned fresh basil

SERVES 4 TO 5

Peel the eggplant and cut into ⅛-inch-thick round slices. Discard 2 or 3 of the smaller slices from either end. (Add them to a compost heap if you have one.) Salt and pepper the slices on both sides.

Put the eggs in a shallow bowl and spread the bread crumbs on a dinner plate. Dip each eggplant slice in the eggs and then in bread crumbs, coating thoroughly. Place on a baking sheet or a large platter. Continue until all slices are coated with bread crumbs.

Generously cover the bottom of a large, heavy skillet with oil and place over medium-high heat. When hot, add enough eggplant slices to fit comfortably in a single layer in pan. Cook until a rich golden color, 2 to 3 minutes per side. Drain slices on paper towels.

Pour half of the vinegar into a shallow nonreactive dish or onto a platter that will accommodate the slices in a single layer. Top with eggplant slices and sprinkle with remaining vinegar and the garlic. Let stand at room temperature for 2 to 4 hours.

To serve, remove and discard garlic from eggplant. Arrange eggplant slightly overlapping on a platter and sprinkle with julienned basil.

GREEN BEANS TOSSED WITH OLIVE OIL AND CHIVES

Keep this dish simple: Use the tenderest and youngest beans you can find, blanch them quickly, and toss them with olive oil and snipped fresh chives. Then season them with fleur de sel, a very flavorful sea salt from France. The beans make a perfect partner to all manner of grilled meats, chicken, and fish.

2 pounds thin young green beans, trimmed

¼ cup extra-virgin olive oil

2 tablespoons chopped fresh chives

Sea salt such as fleur de sel

SERVES 6

Blanch green beans in a large pot of boiling salted water until crisp-tender, about 4 to 5 minutes. Drain.

Transfer beans to a large bowl. Toss with oil and chives. Season with salt (no more than about ½ teaspoon if using fleur de sel, which is strong in taste).

NOTE: If you can't find small, thin green beans, use regular size beans, and cook about 8 minutes.

GREEN BEANS WITH BALSAMIC BUTTER

Chopped shallots, cooked in balsamic vinegar until tender and the vinegar has reduced to a syrup, make a distinctive seasoning to stir into softened butter. This balsamic butter can be used to season many green vegetables, but it is especially good tossed with tender green beans.

½ cup balsamic vinegar

6 tablespoons minced shallots (2 large shallots)

4 tablespoons (½ stick) unsalted butter at room temperature

2 pounds green beans, trimmed

Kosher salt

SERVES 8

Combine balsamic vinegar and shallots in a small, heavy saucepan over medium heat. Stir mixture constantly, and reduce until only a little syrup remains and balsamic vinegar is mostly absorbed into the shallots. Watch carefully to make certain mixture doesn't burn. This should take 4 to 5 minutes. Transfer mixture to a small bowl and cool completely.

Using a fork or rubber spatula, add softened butter to shallots in bowl, and mix until shallots are evenly distributed throughout butter. (The butter can be prepared 1 day ahead; cover and refrigerate. Bring to room temperature 30 minutes before using.)

Bring a large pot of water to full boil, and add green beans and 1 tablespoon salt. Cook beans until tender, about 8 minutes. Drain beans well and pat dry with a clean kitchen towel. Toss beans in a large bowl with Balsamic Butter; mix well to coat all beans with butter. Salt beans to taste.

GREEN BEANS AND LIMAS WITH PECORINO

SERVES **6 TO 8**

This dish is best cooked and served immediately, but all the ingredients can be prepared in advance. When ready to serve, you will need only to quickly blanch the green beans and limas, then toss them with the other seasonings.

1 6- to 8-ounce piece of Pecorino Romano cheese

Kosher salt

1 pound (about 3 cups) frozen baby lima beans, defrosted (see note)

1 pound tender young green beans, trimmed and cut diagonally into 2-inch pieces

3 tablespoons extra-virgin olive oil

½ to ¾ teaspoon freshly ground black pepper

Cut the cheese into ¼-inch-thick slices and cut each slice into ¼-inch dice to yield ¾ cup. (You may not need to use all of the cheese.)

Bring a large pot of salted water to a boil over high heat. Add limas and cook 4 minutes, then add green beans and cook until both beans are just tender, 6 to 8 minutes more. Remove and drain beans in a colander. Pat beans dry with a clean kitchen towel, then put in a serving bowl.

Add olive oil, pepper, and diced cheese and mix well. Season with salt to taste. Serve warm.

NOTE: If you want, you can omit the limas and use 2 pounds of green beans. In that case, the total cooking time for the beans will be 6 to 8 minutes.

Lima beans originated in South America and were named for Peru's capital.

FRIED VIDALIA ONION RINGS SCENTED WITH ROSEMARY

1 large (10- to 12-ounce) Vidalia onion

⅔ cup all-purpose flour

⅓ cup yellow cornmeal

Kosher salt

½ teaspoon baking powder

¼ teaspoon cayenne pepper

1 cup buttermilk

1 large egg, lightly beaten

2 tablespoons chopped fresh rosemary, plus several sprigs for garnish

Vegetable oil for frying onions

During a visit to Florida, I was invited by my aunt to lunch at her local golf club. Along with chicken salad sandwiches, we ordered fried onion rings, which arrived piping hot mounded on a large platter. I knew these golden rings, fried to a perfect crispness and subtly seasoned, were special from my first bite. The crust had a slightly crunchy texture due to cornmeal in the batter, and cayenne pepper provided a hint of spiciness. At home I successfully substituted sweet Vidalias for yellow onions, and discovered that though best when cooked and eaten immediately, the rings can be fried an hour or two ahead and reheated in a hot oven. Amazingly, the heat restores the crispy texture to the onions. Pair these onion rings with grilled steaks, chops, or hamburgers for a winning combination.

Vidalia onions, considered the sweetest onions in the world, are grown only in Georgia in a 20-county area defined by the state legislature.

SERVES **4 TO 6**

Preheat oven to 350 degrees F, and line a large baking sheet with aluminum foil. Arrange a double thickness of paper towels on a work surface for draining onions.

Slice onion into ¼-inch-thick slices. Divide slices into rings and set aside. Sift flour, cornmeal, ½ teaspoon salt, baking powder, and cayenne into a small bowl. Mix buttermilk and egg in a medium bowl. Add flour mixture and whisk well to combine. Stir in chopped rosemary.

Add enough oil to come about 4 inches up the sides of a medium, heavy saucepan. Heat over medium heat until hot (a thermometer should register 375 degrees F). Dip a small onion ring in the batter, then drop into oil. If onion sizzles immediately, oil is ready for frying.

Dip several onion rings in batter and, using a fork or a slotted spoon, place carefully in hot oil. Cook until rings are deep golden brown and crisp, about 2 minutes. As rings are cooked, remove with a slotted spoon to drain on paper towels, then transfer to baking sheet, and place in preheated oven. Cook remaining rings in batches, draining them and keeping them warm, until all are fried. (To prepare onion rings ahead, fry onions, drain on paper towels, then transfer to baking sheet and leave uncovered at cool room temperature for up to 2 hours. Reheat in preheated 350-degree F oven until hot and crisp, 5 to 8 minutes. Watch carefully.)

To serve, sprinkle cooked onion rings generously with kosher salt. Place on a serving platter and garnish with rosemary sprigs.

The first Vidalia onions were sold in 1931 and cost $3.50 for a 50-pound bag.

BALSAMIC ROASTED ONIONS

4 medium red onions

¼ cup olive oil

Salt

Freshly ground black pepper

6 tablespoons (¾ stick) unsalted butter

3 tablespoons sugar

6 tablespoons balsamic vinegar

1 tablespoon chopped fresh flat-leaf parsley

These onions make a great side dish to grilled steaks or chops. Since a recipe will easily serve 10, these oven-roasted onions are an excellent, make-ahead side dish to serve a crowd.

Position 1 rack in center and 1 rack in bottom third of oven. Preheat oven to 500 degrees F. Line 2 large baking sheets with foil.

Cut onions through root ends into ¾-inch-thick wedges. Toss in a medium bowl with oil. Arrange onions, cut-side down, on baking sheets. Sprinkle with salt and pepper. Roast until onions are brown and tender, rotating pans in oven and turning onions over once, about 45 minutes.

Meanwhile, melt butter in a small, heavy saucepan over medium-high heat. Add sugar and stir until sugar dissolves. Remove from heat. Add vinegar, return to heat, and simmer until mixture thickens slightly, about 2 minutes. (Onions and balsamic glaze can be made 1 day ahead. Cool; cover separately and chill. Reheat onions in 375-degree F oven about 15 minutes. Stir glaze over low heat to reheat.)

Arrange onions on a platter and drizzle with the glaze. Sprinkle with parsley.

Ancient Egyptians saw the onion as a symbol of eternity and buried them with their Pharaohs.

GRILLED POTATO **AND ONION PACKAGES**

⅔ cup olive oil

2 tablespoons chopped fresh thyme or 2 teaspoons dried, plus thyme sprigs for garnish (optional)

1 tablespoon Dijon mustard

Salt

Freshly ground black pepper

2 pounds (about 4 large) white potatoes, peeled, sliced ¼ inch thick

2 large red onions, halved, sliced ½ inch thick

Nonstick vegetable oil spray

Seasoned potatoes and onions encased in neat aluminum foil packages can be placed on the grill alongside grilled steaks, chops, or burgers. When done, the foil of each package is split to reveal the tender seasoned vegetables inside.

SERVES **6**

Combine oil, chopped thyme, mustard, 1 teaspoon salt, and 1 teaspoon pepper in a large bowl. Whisk to blend well. (This mustard oil can be prepared 6 hours ahead. Cover and let stand at room temperature.)

Arrange a grill rack 4 to 5 inches from heat source. Prepare grill for a hot fire (high temperature).

Add potatoes and onions to mustard oil. Toss to coat. Set six 18-by-9-inch sheets of heavy-duty aluminum foil on a work surface. Spray foil with nonstick vegetable oil spray. Divide vegetables evenly among foil sheets, placing them in the center of the left half of each. Sprinkle vegetables with salt and pepper. Fold right half of foil over vegetables. Then fold edges of packages together to seal tightly.

Grill packages until potatoes are tender and golden brown, turning occasionally, about 25 minutes. To check for doneness, carefully remove 1 package from the grill, unfold the foil, and test a potato with the tip of a knife to see if it is tender. When done, remove packages from grill. Slit top of foil and fold back. Garnish potatoes with thyme sprigs, if desired. Serve vegetables in foil packages.

SKEWERED ROSEMARY RED SKINS

Salt

1½ pounds small (1 to 1½ inches in diameter) red-skin potatoes

2½ tablespoons olive oil plus extra for oiling grill rack

2½ tablespoons Dijon mustard

3 medium cloves garlic, minced

2½ tablespoons finely chopped fresh rosemary

Coarsely ground black pepper

6 to 8 long metal or wooden skewers (which have been soaked in water 30 minutes before using and patted dry)

These grilled potatoes are always a crowd pleaser and can be almost completely prepared in advance. I toss parboiled baby red skins in a mixture of olive oil, mustard, minced garlic, and chopped fresh rosemary before skewering them. The skewered potatoes, which can rest at room temperature several hours, are then grilled for several minutes until lightly charred. The potatoes would make a distinctive garnish to grilled steaks, lamb, or chicken. And, in the unlikely event that there are any leftover potatoes, they could be tossed in a vinaigrette dressing and served as a salad.

SERVES 6 TO 8

Bring a large pot of salted water to a boil. Scrub potatoes, but do not peel. Halve potatoes and add to boiling water. Cook until tender but not mushy, 10 to 12 minutes. Test potatoes with a sharp knife to see if they are done. Remove and drain in a colander. Cool potatoes 10 minutes.

Whisk together oil, mustard, garlic, rosemary, ½ teaspoon salt, and ½ teaspoon pepper in a large bowl. Add cooked potatoes and toss well to coat. Taste a potato and season with more salt and pepper if desired. Remove and skewer the potatoes with cut sides up. Cover with plastic wrap and leave at room temperature for up to 4 hours.

When ready to grill potatoes, oil a grill rack and arrange 4 to 5 inches from heat source. Prepare grill for a hot fire (high temperature). Grill skewers, turning several times until potatoes are browned well, about 10 minutes. Remove and arrange skewers on a serving platter.

HORSERADISH AND MUSTARD-SCENTED POTATO GRATIN

Butter for greasing baking dish

1 cup half-and-half

1 cup chicken stock

2 teaspoons Dijon mustard

3 pounds Yukon Gold, russet, or red-skin potatoes

Salt

Freshly ground black pepper

6 ounces Gruyère cheese, grated

⅓ cup drained, prepared horseradish

1½ tablespoons chopped fresh flat-leaf parsley

I love to serve this crusty potato gratin, accented by the hearty taste of horseradish, with grilled steaks or chops and a tossed green salad. Chicken stock and half-and-half are used in place of heavy cream in this dish to shave a few calories.

SERVES **6 TO 8**

Preheat oven to 400 degrees F. Butter a 9-by-13-inch baking pan generously.

In a mixing bowl, whisk together half-and-half, chicken stock, and mustard. Set aside while you prepare the potatoes.

Peel potatoes and cut into ⅛-inch-thick slices. Overlap ⅓ of the potatoes in the prepared pan. Season generously with salt and pepper and sprinkle with ½ cup cheese. Using a slotted spoon, scatter ⅓ of the horseradish evenly over potatoes. Repeat to make 2 more layers. Then whisk half-and-half mixture again and pour over potatoes.

Bake potatoes until tender, top is crusty and golden brown, and almost all of the liquid has evaporated, about 1 hour. Remove and cool 10 minutes. (The dish can be covered loosely with aluminum foil and left to rest up to 30 minutes at room temperature before serving.) Sprinkle with parsley just before serving.

POTATO GRATIN WITH MUSTARD AND WHITE CHEDDAR CHEESE

SERVES 6

1½ teaspoons unsalted butter, plus extra for greasing baking dish

½ cup fresh white bread crumbs

1½ teaspoons dried thyme

½ teaspoon salt

½ teaspoon freshly ground black pepper

8 ounces sharp white Cheddar cheese, grated

2 tablespoons all-purpose flour

2½ pounds russet potatoes, peeled, thinly sliced

2 cups reduced-sodium chicken broth

½ cup heavy cream

3 tablespoons Dijon mustard

This rich and creamy potato gratin is best when served soon after baking. However, since it needs to rest 15 minutes once out of the oven, you could use this quarter hour to complete a menu by quickly grilling steaks or chops and assembling a green salad.

Melt butter in a large, heavy skillet over medium heat. Add bread crumbs and stir until crumbs are golden brown, 5 to 6 minutes. Remove and cool crumbs. (The bread crumbs can be prepared 1 day ahead. Cover and leave at room temperature.)

Arrange an oven rack at center position and preheat oven to 400 degrees F. Butter a 2-quart ovenproof baking dish.

Mix thyme, salt, and pepper in a small bowl. Toss grated Cheddar and flour in a large bowl. Arrange ⅓ of the potatoes over bottom of prepared dish. Sprinkle ⅓ of thyme mixture over them, then ⅓ of cheese mixture. Repeat to make 2 more layers.

Whisk chicken broth, cream, and mustard in a medium bowl to blend. Pour broth mixture over potatoes, lifting layers gently with a fork or knife as you pour so that this liquid is evenly distributed.

Bake 45 minutes. Sprinkle buttered crumbs over top. Bake until potatoes are tender and top is golden brown, about 45 minutes longer. Let stand 15 minutes before serving.

YUKON GOLDS BAKED WITH ARUGULA AND BACON

Butter for greasing baking dish

12 ounces sliced bacon, chopped

2½ cups heavy cream

1½ cups whole milk

3½ pounds Yukon Gold potatoes, peeled, thinly sliced

1½ teaspoons salt

1½ teaspoons freshly ground black pepper

8 ounces arugula, stemmed, coarsely chopped

8 ounces Gruyère cheese, grated

I love the assertive tastes of bacon and arugula in this gratin of golden, crusty potatoes. This dish serves ten easily, so it is perfect for a big gathering. Another bonus is that the gratin can be baked a day ahead and reheated when needed. It is good offered as a side dish to grilled steaks or lamb chops.

SERVES 10

Arrange an oven rack at center position and preheat oven to 375 degrees F. Butter a 9-by-13-inch baking dish.

Cook bacon in a large, heavy skillet over medium-high heat until crisp. Using a slotted spoon, transfer bacon to paper towels and drain.

Mix cream and milk in a 4 cup measure.

Layer ⅓ of the potatoes in prepared dish, overlapping them slightly. Season with ½ teaspoon *each* salt and pepper. Top potatoes with ½ of the arugula, then sprinkle ⅓ of the cheese and ⅓ of the bacon over this layer. Pour ⅓ of the cream mixture over potatoes. Repeat to make another layer. Make a final layer of potatoes. Sprinkle with salt and pepper, and with remaining cheese and bacon. Pour remaining cream mixture over this layer.

Bake gratin, uncovered, until potatoes are tender and cream mixture thickens, about 1 hour and 15 minutes. Let stand 15 minutes before serving. (Can be made 1 day ahead. Cool slightly; chill uncovered, until cold, then cover and keep refrigerated. Reheat, covered with foil, in 375-degree F oven about 30 minutes.)

SCALLOPED POTATOES WITH CRÈME FRAÎCHE AND GRUYÈRE

Nothing could be easier than this delicious side dish made with only three primary ingredients: potatoes, crème fraîche, and cheese. Layers of thinly sliced potatoes are spread with a thin coating of crème fraîche, sprinkled with cheese, then put in the oven. Baked until a rich golden crust forms and covers the tender slices beneath, this gratin makes a good partner for grilled steaks or chops.

Butter for greasing baking dish

2 pounds baking potatoes such as russet

Salt

Freshly ground black pepper

1 cup crème fraîche (page 20)

4 ounces Gruyère or sharp white Cheddar cheese, shredded

SERVES **6**

Arrange an oven rack at center position and preheat oven to 375 degrees F. Butter a 2-quart shallow baking dish.

Peel potatoes and cut into ⅛-inch-thick slices. Spread half the slices over the bottom of prepared dish. Salt and pepper slices generously. Using a rubber spatula, spread half the crème fraîche over the potatoes, then sprinkle half the cheese over the crème fraîche. Make a second layer in the same way using the remaining ingredients.

Bake gratin for 10 minutes. Lower heat to 350 degrees F. Continue to cook until potatoes are tender when pierced with a knife and a golden brown crust has formed on top, 30 to 35 minutes more. Remove from oven and serve hot.

Idaho is the "Land of Famous Potatoes."

BOURSIN POTATOES

Butter for greasing baking dish

1 cup heavy cream

1 cup half-and-half

1 5-ounce package Boursin cheese with herbs, broken into small chunks

3 pounds new red potatoes, unpeeled

Salt

Freshly ground black pepper

1½ tablespoons chopped fresh flat-leaf parsley or chives

The creamy garlic-and-herb-scented cheese known as Boursin is the secret to these scalloped potatoes. It is stirred into a warm mixture of cream and half-and-half to form a quick, but delicious, sauce for sliced potatoes. This golden gratin would make a good side dish to offer with grilled steaks, lamb, or chicken.

SERVES 8

Arrange an oven rack at center position and preheat oven to 400 degrees F. Butter a 9-by-13-inch ovenproof baking dish.

Combine cream, half-and-half, and Boursin in a medium saucepan over medium heat. Whisk constantly until cheese has melted and mixture is smooth. Remove and set aside.

Slice the potatoes thinly (about ⅛ to ¼ inch thick) and arrange half of them in the prepared dish in slightly overlapping rows. Generously season potatoes with salt and pepper. Pour half of the cream and cheese mixture over them. Repeat to make a second layer.

Bake until top is golden brown and potatoes are tender when pierced with a knife, 55 to 60 minutes. Remove and sprinkle with parsley.

SWEET POTATO CHIPS

The secret to producing crispy sweet potato chips lies in slicing the tubers very thinly. The slices must be quickly fried in hot oil for a few minutes, and drained on paper towels. The chips, served piping hot or at room temperature, are a delicious garnish to grilled burgers. They would also make a colorful accompaniment to the Chili-Rubbed Sirloins with Guacamole Salsa (page 24).

2 pounds red-skinned sweet potatoes (see note)

Canola oil for frying chips

Kosher salt

SERVES 6 TO 8

Peel sweet potatoes. Using a large, sharp knife, carefully slice potatoes crosswise into paper-thin rounds.

Pour oil into a medium, heavy saucepan to a depth of 3 inches and heat to 325 degrees F. Working in batches, fry sweet potato slices until they begin to curl and brown in spots, stirring occasionally, about 3 minutes. Using a slotted spoon, transfer chips to paper towels to drain. Season with salt. Transfer to a serving bowl.

Serve warm or at room temperature. (The chips can be made 3 hours ahead.)

NOTE: Sweet potatoes, a member of the morning glory family, come in many varieties, but two varieties are commonly available in our markets. One has tan skin and pale yellow, almost golden flesh that is somewhat dry. The other, often erroneously called "yams," has copper-colored skin and bright orange, moist flesh beneath. It is the latter that is best used in this recipe.

SESAME-SCENTED SUGAR SNAPS

This is such a simple recipe, but it boasts great flavor and visual appeal. Fresh, tender sugar snap peas are steamed, then tossed with aromatic, toasted sesame oil and crunchy toasted sesame seeds. I like to serve these with Salmon Fillets with Fresh Tarragon and Crushed Fennel (page 87) or with Tuna Steaks Topped with Warm Shiitake Mushrooms (page 94).

Kosher salt

1 pound sugar snap or snow peas, ends snipped off and strings removed

1½ teaspoons toasted sesame oil, plus more if needed

1 teaspoon toasted sesame seeds (see page 15)

SERVES **6**

Bring 1½ inches of water and a generous pinch of salt to a boil in a large saucepan. Insert steamer basket and add prepared peas. Steam for 2 to 3 minutes or until peas are bright green and just tender. (If you do not have a steamer, simply blanch peas in boiling lightly salted water to cover until bright green and just tender, 1 to 2 minutes.) Drain peas, pat dry, and place in a serving bowl.

Toss peas with sesame oil and toasted sesame seeds, then season to taste with salt. If desired, drizzle a little extra sesame oil over the peas and toss to mix. Serve warm.

A MIXED BAG OF BEANS

1 15½-ounce can cannellini beans

1 15½-ounce can navy beans

1 15½-ounce can baby butter beans (see notes)

1 15½-ounce can pinto beans

2 14½-ounce cans stewed tomatoes

⅓ cup unsulfered molasses (see notes)

2 tablespoons light brown sugar

2 tablespoons prepared mustard

1 teaspoon salt

½ teaspoon freshly ground, coarse black pepper

5 thick slices (about 5 ounces) bacon

1 medium onion, thinly sliced

Emily Bell, my longtime assistant, helped create this dish, and refers to this recipe as "quick as a wink" baked beans. The "quick" refers to the speedy assembly achieved by using a mixture of different canned beans, which are rinsed and drained, then embellished in a matter of minutes with such robust ingredients as stewed tomatoes, molasses, mustard, brown sugar, sautéed onions, and bacon. After a little more than an hour in the oven, they are good enough to rival even the best "from scratch" beans.

SERVES 6

Arrange an oven rack at center position and preheat oven to 350 degrees F.

Pour all the beans into a large colander and rinse under cold running water, then drain well. Combine in a large bowl. Drain tomatoes in the same colander and then put in a food processor and lightly pulse just to chop tomatoes coarsely. Add to bowl of beans along with molasses, brown sugar, mustard, salt, and pepper. Mix well and set aside.

Cut 3 bacon slices crosswise into 1½-inch pieces and sauté in a medium skillet over medium heat until browned. Drain on paper towels. In the same pan, sauté the onion in the bacon drippings until softened and lightly browned, about 3 minutes. Add onion and cooked bacon to the beans and stir to mix.

Pour beans into a shallow 2-quart baking dish and spread evenly. Cut the remaining 2 bacon slices into 1½-inch pieces and scatter on top of beans.

Bake uncovered 1¼ to 1½ hours, until bacon on top of casserole is crisp and browned. Serve hot.

NOTES: If you cannot find baby butter beans, regular butter beans can be substituted.

: Both sulfered and unsulfered molasses are available. The latter is lighter and has a cleaner flavor.

ROASTED TOMATO SLICES WITH OLIVES AND HERBS

SERVES 6

Although sliced tomatoes, sprinkled with slivered olives, chopped green onions, and fresh herbs, could easily be served uncooked at room temperature, you might be surprised to learn that this dish is far more enticing when quickly baked in the oven and offered warm. The heat seems to intensify the flavors of the tomatoes, which make a fine accompaniment to grilled lamb or steaks.

3 to 4 tablespoons olive oil

3 large just-ripe tomatoes (about 1½ pounds)

Kosher salt

Freshly ground black pepper

⅓ to ½ cup slivered, pitted kalamata olives

⅓ cup chopped green onions including 2 inches of green stems

1 tablespoon chopped fresh flat-leaf parsley

1 tablespoon chopped fresh basil

2 teaspoons red wine vinegar

1 teaspoon minced garlic

Arrange an oven rack at center position and preheat oven to 350 degrees F. Lightly coat the bottom of a 9-by-13-inch ovenproof baking dish with 2 to 3 tablespoons oil.

Cut tomatoes into ½-inch-thick slices. Arrange slightly overlapping in prepared pan. Salt and pepper slices generously.

In a small bowl, combine olives, onions, parsley, basil, vinegar, garlic, and 1 tablespoon olive oil. Mix well and sprinkle over the tomatoes. (Tomatoes can be prepared 3 hours ahead; cover with plastic wrap and leave at cool room temperature.)

Bake until tomatoes are hot, about 10 minutes. Remove and serve while warm. Do not overcook, or tomatoes will become mushy.

CARAMELIZED ZUCCHINI AND ONIONS

"Less is more" is a cooking concept I embrace, and nowhere is this philosophy more evident than in Provence, where dishes are simple and unadorned. Redolent of the cooking of this part of France is the following recipe, which calls for only two ingredients plus olive oil and salt. Onions and zucchini are slowly sautéed in olive oil until caramelized and fork tender. They would make a fine accompaniment to Lamb Chops with Crushed Garlic, Rosemary, and Red Pepper Flakes (page 64) or to Fennel and Rosemary–Coated Chicken (page 74).

1 pound (about 3 medium) yellow onions

2 to **2¼** pounds small zucchini

6 tablespoons olive oil, divided

1 to **1¼** teaspoons fleur de sel or kosher salt

SERVES 4

Halve onions lengthwise and slice thinly. Cut zucchini in half lengthwise and cut each half into ½-inch-thick half-moon slices.

Heat 2 tablespoons of the oil in a large, heavy skillet set over medium heat until hot. Add onions and cook, stirring often, until onions are wilted and browned, 8 to 10 minutes. While cooking, the onion slices should stick slightly to the bottom of the pan so that they brown and caramelize. Remove onions with a slotted spoon and set aside while you cook the zucchini.

Add remaining oil to same skillet and place over medium heat. When hot, add zucchini and cook, stirring occasionally, for 10 to 12 minutes or until vegetables are tender and well browned, but not mushy. While cooking, the zucchini slices should stick slightly to the bottom of the pan so that they brown and caramelize. Stir the onions back into the pan and heat and stir 1 minute more.

Season vegetables with salt. (Vegetables can be cooked 2 hours ahead. Remove from heat and leave in pan. Reheat, stirring, over medium heat.) To serve, mound in a bowl and serve warm.

ZUCCHINI, POTATOES, AND TOMATOES GREEK STYLE

1½ pounds medium zucchini

1½ pounds medium Yukon Gold potatoes

1 to 1½ pounds ripe tomatoes

1 medium-large onion, chopped

3 medium cloves garlic, chopped

1½ to 2 teaspoons tomato paste

1 tablespoon chopped fresh mint

1 tablespoon chopped fresh flat-leaf parsley

Kosher salt

Freshly ground black pepper

6 to 8 tablespoons extra-virgin olive oil

½ cup crumbled feta cheese (optional)

⅓ cup slivered kalamata olives (optional)

A few years ago, I watched and took notes as a Greek friend, Georgos Andrikidis, assembled this glorious vegetable dish. He sliced zucchini and potatoes; chopped garlic, onions, and tomatoes; then layered the vegetables in a large baking pan, adding fresh mint and parsley as seasonings. After pouring a generous amount of olive oil over the mixture, he baked the gratin slowly so that the flavors of the vegetables melded and their texture became soft and delicate. Crumbled feta and sliced kalamata olives are typical garnishes for this preparation, but if the vegetables are fresh from the market, the gratin can stand on its own without embellishments.

SERVES 6

Arrange an oven rack at center position and preheat oven to 350 degrees F.

Cut zucchini into ½-inch-thick rounds and place in a large bowl. Peel potatoes and cut into ½-inch-thick rounds and add to bowl. Quarter tomatoes, and chop coarsely (without seeding); add to bowl. Mix in chopped onion, garlic, tomato paste, and herbs. Season with 1½ teaspoons salt and several grinds black pepper.

Spread vegetables evenly in a 9-by-13-inch (or similar size) ovenproof baking dish and pour olive oil over them. Toss to distribute oil. Bake, uncovered, until potatoes are fork tender and zucchini extremely soft, about 1½ hours. Remove, and when cool enough, taste and season with additional salt and pepper if needed. If desired, sprinkle dish with feta and olives. Serve warm.

CRISPY ZUCCHINI AND CORN CAKES

These crisp golden cakes, made with grated zucchini and fresh corn kernels, can be served the moment they come out of the frying pan or several hours later, after a quick reheating in a hot oven. They would make a fine side dish to serve with Barbecued Salmon with a Mahogany Glaze (page 86) or with Garlic-Scented Sirloins with Red and Yellow Pepper Relish (page 25).

2   small (about ½ pound) zucchini
    Kosher salt
1   cup fresh corn kernels (2 to 3 ears corn)
1   cup buttermilk
1   large egg
2   teaspoons baking powder
½   teaspoon freshly ground nutmeg
½   teaspoon baking soda
⅛   teaspoon cayenne pepper
1   cup yellow cornmeal
    Vegetable oil for sautéing corn cakes

6

SERVES : MAKES 12 TO 14 CAKES

Arrange an oven rack at center position and preheat oven to 200 degrees F.

Grate zucchini coarsely and place in a large sieve or colander. Sprinkle with 1 teaspoon salt. Let stand for 3 to 4 minutes. Without rinsing, place zucchini in a clean kitchen towel and squeeze to extract as much liquid as possible.

Mix squeezed zucchini in a medium bowl with corn. In a separate large bowl, mix together buttermilk, egg, baking powder, 1 teaspoon salt, nutmeg, baking soda, and cayenne. Stir in cornmeal, then add zucchini and corn.

Add enough oil to coat the bottom of a large, heavy skillet (cast iron works well) or griddle, and place over medium heat. When hot, ladle a scant ¼ cup batter for each cake into pan, leaving space around each for it to spread. Cook until golden on bottom, about 2 to 3 minutes, then turn and cook until other side is golden, 1 to 2 minutes more.

Place cooked cakes on a baking sheet in preheated oven and continue, adding more oil to pan as needed, until all the batter is used. When done, taste a cake and sprinkle with additional salt if desired. (The corn and zucchini cakes can be made 3 hours ahead. Leave on baking sheets at room temperature. At serving time reheat cakes, uncovered, in a preheated 350-degree F oven until hot and crispy, about 10 minutes. Watch carefully.)

Serve cakes slightly overlapping on a serving platter.

NOTE: The corn cakes can be served garnished with dollops of sour cream and a sprinkling of chives or parsley.

PROVENÇAL SUMMER VEGETABLE TART

This special tart—a three-layer creation composed of a butter-rich pastry crust, a savory goat cheese filling, and a garnish of sautéed Provençal vegetables—is a true showstopper. It can be made completely in advance and tastes good served either warm or at room temperature. Make it the star attraction of a lunch or a light supper, accompanied by a mixed green salad in a vinaigrette dressing, or offer it as a side dish to grilled lamb or chicken.

TART

Butter-Rich Savory Pie Dough (page 18)

5 ounces creamy goat cheese

½ cup heavy cream

3 large eggs, lightly beaten

¼ cup sour cream

⅛ teaspoon salt

Generous pinch of cayenne pepper

TOPPING

2 tablespoons olive oil

1 small red bell pepper, cut into ½-inch-thick julienne strips

½ medium fennel bulb, cored and cut lengthwise into ½-inch-thick slices

1 small (5 to 6 ounces) zucchini, halved lengthwise and cut into ½-inch-thick slices

1 small (5 to 6 ounces) yellow squash, halved lengthwise and cut into ½-inch-thick slices

5 grape or small cherry tomatoes, quartered lengthwise

½ teaspoon salt

1 tablespoon chopped fresh basil

8

SERVES 8 AS A FIRST COURSE OR SIDE DISH; 4 TO 6 AS AN ENTRÉE

TO MAKE THE TART: Roll dough out on a lightly floured surface into a 12-inch round. Carefully transfer to a 9-inch tart pan with removable bottom. Trim overhanging dough to 1 inch. Fold overhanging dough in and press to form double-thick sides. Pierce bottom of dough with a fork. Wrap tart in plastic wrap and freeze for 30 minutes.

Arrange an oven rack at center position and preheat oven to 400 degrees F. Bake crust until golden brown, piercing with fork if crust bubbles, about 20 minutes. Remove and cool 5 minutes.

Lower oven temperature to 375 degrees F.

In a medium bowl, whisk together cheese, heavy cream, eggs, sour cream, salt, and cayenne. Pour into shell and bake until filling is set, about 25 minutes. Remove and cool 10 minutes.

TO MAKE THE TOPPING: While tart is baking, heat oil until hot in a large, heavy skillet over medium heat. Add red bell pepper and fennel and sauté, stirring, until softened, about 4 minutes. Add zucchini and squash and sauté, stirring, 4 minutes more or until all vegetables are tender. Remove from heat and stir in tomatoes. Season generously with salt. Mound vegetables on top of tart and sprinkle with basil. If serving warm, serve within 30 minutes. If serving at room temperature, tart can be prepared 4 hours ahead; leave, uncovered, at cool room temperature.

CHAPTER 5

SALADS

WITH SPECIAL TOUCHES

For those who think all salads come from a cellophane package and a bottle, this chapter should prove that there are far more interesting alternatives. Potato salad and coleslaw, two backyard menu staples, are featured in several different versions. These potato salads are made with red skins, Yukon Golds, and sweet potatoes, and tossed with mayonnaise, yogurt, or warm bacon dressings. Coleslaw gets updated with accents of Parmesan cheese, sesame seeds, fresh ginger, or olives.

And, what tastes better with a juicy grilled steak or chop than a mixed greens salad? From the unique Grilled Caesar to the Mesclun Salad with Fennel, Oranges, and Figs, the following pages provide plenty of inspiration for the backyard cook. For those times when you want salad to stand on its own, as a light main course for lunch or supper, you'll find scrumptious chicken and turkey salads and a distinctive wild rice and smoked salmon combination that will fit the bill.

I love to prepare salads made with beans or pasta when entertaining outdoors, because they're so easy to assemble in advance. The ones featured here are tried and true crowd-pleasers. I've watched guests take seconds, even thirds, of the BLT Pasta Salad, and witnessed with amazement as a huge bowl of Black Bean, Tomato, and Avocado Salad disappeared in minutes.

Ever versatile, these salads can embellish alfresco menus in more than one way. Use them as a first course to start a meal, as an entrée to anchor it, or as a side dish in a supporting role.

OLD-FASHIONED POTATO SALAD

2 pounds Yukon Gold potatoes

4 large hard-boiled eggs, divided
(see page 15)

1½ cup chopped celery

½ cup chopped yellow onion

½ cup regular (not reduced-fat or nonfat)
mayonnaise

2½ teaspoons fresh lemon juice, plus
more if needed

1½ teaspoons cider vinegar

1½ teaspoons ball-park mustard
(not Dijon)

Kosher salt

⅛ teaspoon cayenne pepper

¼ cup chopped fresh flat-leaf parsley

This is classic potato salad at its best, made with plain, honest ingredients. Yukon Golds, peeled and diced, hold up well after cooking, and are combined with chopped hard-boiled eggs, celery, and onions. The dressing, made with purchased mayonnaise, ball-park mustard, plus splashes of cider vinegar and lemon, is enhanced by the addition of mashed hard-boiled eggs, which adds body as well as rich satisfying flavor. People always take seconds of this potato salad, and a friend once confided to me that her teenage son had consumed an entire bowl at one sitting!

SERVES **6**

Bring a large pot with 3 quarts of water to a boil. While water is coming to a boil, peel and cut potatoes into 1-inch dice. Add diced potatoes to boiling water and cook about 10 minutes, or until tender (not mushy) when pierced with a knife. Remove and drain well in a colander.

Place potatoes in a large nonreactive bowl and cool to room temperature. Chop 3 of the eggs and add to the bowl along with the celery and onion. Mix well to blend.

Mash the remaining egg in a small bowl, then add the mayonnaise, 2½ teaspoons lemon juice, vinegar, mustard, 1 teaspoon salt, and cayenne. Whisk well to blend. Add to bowl with potatoes and mix well to combine. Taste and season with more salt and a little lemon juice if needed. Cover with plastic wrap and refrigerate until needed. (Salad can be made 6 hours ahead; bring to room temperature 30 minutes before serving.) When ready to serve, sprinkle salad with parsley.

GERMAN POTATO SALAD WITH **FRESH DILL**

2	pounds (about 12) small red-skin potatoes
4	ounces (6 to 8 slices) bacon, cut into ½-inch dice
½	cup finely chopped red onion
½	cup white wine vinegar
2	teaspoons whole grain Dijon mustard
2	teaspoons sugar
	Kosher salt
	Freshly ground black pepper
¼	cup chopped fresh dill, plus 2 or 3 sprigs for garnish

German potato salad distinguishes itself from other tuber salads because it is served warm, rather than cold. Both the potatoes and the delicious bacon dressing are still hot when tossed together. This version, which has a lively accent of chopped fresh dill, would make a fine accompaniment to grilled pork chops or bratwursts.

SERVES 6

Bring a large pot of water to a boil over high heat and add potatoes. Bring to a boil again and cook potatoes until just tender when pierced with a knife, 12 to 15 minutes. (Don't overcook or potatoes will be mushy.) Drain potatoes in a colander and cool just long enough so that you can handle them comfortably. Peel potatoes, if desired, or leave skins on. Slice into ¼-inch-thick slices. Place in a bowl, and cover with a clean kitchen towel to keep warm.

In a large, heavy skillet, sauté the bacon pieces until brown and crisp, 2 to 3 minutes. Remove with a slotted spoon and drain on paper towels. Pour off and discard all but about 3 tablespoons of the drippings in the pan. Place pan over medium-low heat until hot. Add onion and sauté, stirring, until soft, about 2 minutes. Whisk in vinegar, ½ cup water, mustard, sugar, 2 teaspoons salt, and ¼ teaspoon pepper. Simmer 1 minute or more, until mixture has reduced by about ⅓.

Add potatoes to skillet. Toss gently, coating potatoes with dressing. Let potatoes sit for 2 to 3 minutes to absorb dressing. Sprinkle with bacon pieces and chopped dill, and toss gently. Season with more salt and pepper if needed.

Arrange potato salad in an attractive shallow serving bowl and garnish the center with a bouquet of dill sprigs. Serve warm.

ROASTED POTATO SALAD WITH DILL AND MINT DRESSING

Roasted, rather than boiled, potatoes tossed in a dressing made with sour cream, yogurt, and chopped fresh herbs make this potato salad different from the usual offerings. It is delicious served with grilled lamb or chicken or as an accompaniment to baked ham or ribs.

¼ cup olive oil, plus extra for oiling baking sheet

3 pounds red-skin potatoes, unpeeled

6 cloves garlic, peeled

1 teaspoon dried dill (see note)

Salt

Freshly ground black pepper

⅓ cup plain regular or reduced-fat (not nonfat) yogurt

⅓ cup regular or reduced-fat (not nonfat) sour cream

⅔ cup chopped red onion

⅓ cup chopped fresh dill, plus an extra sprig for garnish

2 tablespoons chopped fresh mint leaves, plus an extra sprig for garnish

1 pint cherry or grape tomatoes for garnish

The most popular side dish prepared on the grill is the roasted potato, followed by steamed vegetables, then marinated vegetables.

SERVES

Arrange an oven rack at center position and preheat oven to 375 degrees F. Generously oil a large, heavy, rimmed baking sheet.

Halve potatoes, then cut each half into ¾-inch-thick wedges and spread them on the oiled baking sheet. Process ¼ cup oil, garlic, dried dill, ¾ teaspoon salt, and ½ teaspoon pepper in a food processor or blender, until the garlic is very finely minced. Remove and pour the garlic-scented oil over the potatoes in the pan. Toss the potatoes until they are all coated, then spread them in a single layer in the pan.

Roast potatoes, stirring them every 10 minutes to prevent sticking, until they are golden brown and tender, 45 to 55 minutes. Transfer contents of pan, scraping everything, including oil and roasted garlic bits, into a large bowl. Cool potatoes to room temperature.

To prepare dressing, whisk together yogurt and sour cream in a small bowl and then stir in red onion, fresh dill, mint, ½ teaspoon salt, and ¼ teaspoon pepper. Add to bowl with cooled potatoes and toss well to mix. (If not using immediately, cover and refrigerate up to 4 hours. Bring to room temperature 30 minutes before serving.)

To serve, mound salad in center of a shallow serving bowl or on a platter. Garnish with a border of cherry or grape tomatoes and a sprig of fresh dill and mint in center.

NOTE: Dried dill works best as a seasoning when roasting potatoes. Fresh dill is used in the dressing and as a garnish in this salad.

ROASTED SWEET POTATO SALAD
WITH **LIME** AND **HONEY**

"Lime and honey are a heavenly partnership," remarked one of my students after tasting this salad, in which tart and sweet flavors are beautifully balanced. Cubes of roasted sweet potatoes are tossed with a lime and honey dressing, then dusted with a sprinkling of cilantro. The salad makes a colorful dish that is especially good as an accompaniment to grilled pork or chicken.

3 pounds red-skinned sweet potatoes (see note, page 160)

¼ cup olive oil

Kosher salt

2 tablespoons lime juice, plus more if needed

2 teaspoons grated lime zest

2 tablespoons honey

¼ cup chopped fresh cilantro for garnish

SERVES 6

Arrange an oven rack at lower position and preheat oven to 450 degrees F. Line a large baking sheet (or use 2 standard sheets) with aluminum foil. Peel sweet potatoes and cut into 1-inch cubes to yield 8 cups. Spread cubes on baking sheet, and drizzle with olive oil. Toss well so that all cubes are lightly coated. Sprinkle 2 teaspoons salt over potatoes. (If using 2 sheets, divide ingredients equally between them.)

Roast potatoes, stirring every 10 minutes, until cubes are brown around the edges and tender when pierced with a knife, about 20 to 25 minutes. Watch carefully, as they can start to burn quickly. (If using 2 baking sheets, place 1 sheet on lower level and the other on center level. Reverse sheets after 15 minutes.) Transfer potatoes to a serving bowl and let cool to room temperature.

Whisk together lime juice, zest, and honey in a small bowl. Pour over potatoes and toss gently to mix. Taste and season with more salt and 1 to 2 teaspoons additional lime juice if needed. (Salad can be assembled 30 minutes ahead; leave at room temperature.)

When ready to serve, sprinkle salad with cilantro.

COLESLAW WITH SPANISH OLIVES

When a friend arrived at our house with this out-of-the-ordinary coleslaw, I loved the unique flavor but couldn't figure out what made this version so distinctive. When I quizzed my pal, Betty Couvares, she explained that her mother, while making coleslaw one day, discovered too late that she was out of vinegar and tossed in chopped Spanish olives instead. This serendipitous creation has remained a favorite in my friend's family for years. The olives (the taste I couldn't detect) impart a salty, slightly tart note and keep the slaw from being cloyingly sweet. This slaw goes well with Ribs, Deep South Style (page 110) and with Barbecued Salmon with a Mahogany Glaze (page 86).

1 medium (2-pound) green cabbage with attractive outer leaves

2 medium carrots, finely chopped

1 ¼ cups (about 7 ¼ ounces) whole Spanish olives stuffed with pimentos (see note)

3 tablespoons regular (not reduced-fat or nonfat) mayonnaise

3 tablespoons chopped fresh chives

SERVES 6

Remove 4 to 5 of the attractive outer leaves from cabbage, rinse, and pat dry. Store in a plastic bag in the refrigerator until you are ready to garnish slaw.

Cut cabbage into ¼-inch-wide slices until you get to the core. Discard the core and chop the cabbage slices coarsely. Measure 8 cups chopped cabbage and put into a medium nonreactive bowl. (Save extra cabbage for another use.)

Add carrots to cabbage. Chop olives and add to bowl. Stir in mayonnaise and mix well. Cover with plastic wrap and refrigerate for at least 3 hours. (The slaw can be prepared up to 6 hours ahead. Keep refrigerated.)

To serve, line a shallow serving bowl with the reserved cabbage leaves. Stir chives into slaw and mound in bowl.

NOTE: Spanish olives stuffed with pimentos, usually sold in glass jars, are available in the condiment section of the grocery. I've tried other olives, including French, Italian, and Greek types, but this recipe always works best with the ordinary Spanish olives.

SESAME AND GINGER COLESLAW

1 small (1- to 1½-pound) green cabbage

3 cups peeled, shredded carrots

2 cups fresh spinach leaves, stemmed and thinly sliced, plus additional spinach leaves for garnish

½ cup plus 1 tablespoon rice wine vinegar

¼ cup dark roasted sesame oil

¼ cup sugar

3 tablespoons minced peeled fresh ginger

2 teaspoons soy sauce

Salt

3 tablespoons sesame seeds, toasted (see page 15)

Cabbage, spinach, and carrots provide a trio of complementary colors and textures in this slaw. Tossed with a distinctive dressing made with toasted sesame oil and fresh chopped ginger, it is particularly good with Pork Tenderloins with Peach Ginger Sauce (page 66) and with Grilled Lobster Tails with Citrus Butter (page 97).

SERVES **6**

Quarter the cabbage lengthwise and remove the tough core. Slice quarters thinly to yield 6 cups. (Save extra cabbage for another use.) Combine sliced cabbage, carrots, and spinach in a large nonreactive bowl.

In a medium bowl, combine vinegar, sesame oil, sugar, ginger, and soy sauce. Whisk well to blend sugar with liquids. Pour dressing over cabbage mixture and toss well to combine. Cover and refrigerate for at least 2 hours. (Slaw can be prepared 4 hours ahead; bring to room temperature before serving.) Taste and season with salt if needed.

To serve, line a shallow serving bowl or a platter with spinach leaves. Mound slaw on top and sprinkle with sesame seeds.

> *Coleslaw is derived from the Dutch* koolsla, *which means cabbage* (kool) *and salad* (sla).

RED AND YELLOW PEPPER COLESLAW IN LIME DRESSING

3 tablespoons plus 1 teaspoon fresh lime juice, plus extra if needed

1½ teaspoons grated lime zest

3 tablespoons chopped fresh cilantro

2 tablespoons honey

1 tablespoon ground cumin

Salt

6 tablespoons olive oil

1 medium (2-pound) green cabbage with attractive outer leaves

1 small red bell pepper

1 small yellow bell pepper

A variation on a classic, this slaw is made with thin julienned cabbage and thin strips of red and yellow bell peppers tossed in a lime and honey dressing. The slaw, which is best when made a few hours in advance, makes a fine accompaniment to barbecued chicken and is a delicious garnish to grilled salmon.

SERVES **4 TO 5**

Combine lime juice, lime zest, cilantro, honey, cumin, and ¾ teaspoon salt in a large nonreactive bowl, and whisk well to blend. Whisk in olive oil.

Remove 4 to 5 of the attractive outer leaves from cabbage, rinse, and pat dry. Store in a plastic bag in the refrigerator until you are ready to garnish slaw.

Quarter the cabbage lengthwise and remove the tough core. Slice quarters thinly to yield 7 cups. (Save extra cabbage for another use.) Place in a large nonreactive bowl.

Slice bell peppers into strips ¼ inch wide and 2 inches long. Add bell peppers to cabbage.

To assemble slaw, toss cabbage and bell peppers with the dressing. Taste and, if desired, add extra lime juice and salt. Cover and refrigerate at least 2 hours. (Slaw can be made 4 hours ahead; bring to room temperature 30 minutes before serving.)

To serve, line a shallow serving bowl with reserved cabbage leaves. Using a slotted spoon, mound slaw on top.

PARMESAN BLACK PEPPER COLESLAW

During a visit to Cape Cod, I ordered Parmesan Black Pepper Coleslaw at a seaside restaurant, but much to my disappointment, the dish arrived without the faintest hint of cheese and with no visible specks of pepper. Still, I liked the idea. The mellow taste of Parmesan and spicy black pepper seemed like such a winning combination that I tried a version myself, adding significant amounts of Parmigiano-Reggiano and coarsely ground pepper to a creamy mixture of sliced cabbage and red bell peppers. The slaw turned out to be especially good with barbecued chicken and with grilled sausages.

1 large (2½-pound) green cabbage with attractive outer leaves

1 large red bell pepper

½ cup white wine vinegar

¼ cup olive oil

3 tablespoons sugar

Coarsely ground black pepper

Salt

1 6- to 8-ounce piece of Parmesan cheese, preferably Parmigiano-Reggiano, at room temperature (so that it will be easy to grate)

3 tablespoons regular or reduced-fat (not nonfat) mayonnaise

3 tablespoons regular or reduced-fat (not nonfat) sour cream

SERVES **6 TO 8**

Remove 4 to 5 of the attractive outer leaves from cabbage, rinse, and pat dry. Store in a plastic bag in the refrigerator until you are ready to garnish slaw.

Quarter the cabbage lengthwise and remove the tough core. Slice quarters thinly to yield 12 cups. (Save extra cabbage for another use.) Place in a large nonreactive bowl.

Slice bell pepper lengthwise into thin strips; cut strips in half and add to bowl with cabbage.

In a small bowl, whisk together vinegar, oil, sugar, 2¼ teaspoons pepper, and ¾ teaspoon salt. Pour over cabbage mixture and toss to coat well. Marinate, uncovered at cool room temperature, 30 minutes.

Grate cheese using the coarse side of a hand grater or a food processor to yield 1½ cups. (You will probably have some cheese left over.) Be sure to grate cheese coarsely, not finely, for this recipe. Add to the slaw mixture.

Whisk together the mayonnaise and sour cream; add to the cabbage mixture, and toss well. Cover bowl with plastic wrap and refrigerate 2 hours. (Slaw can be made 6 hours ahead; bring to room temperature 30 minutes before serving.)

Taste and season with more salt and pepper if needed. Line a shallow serving bowl with the reserved cabbage leaves and mound slaw on top.

CREAMY CARAWAY COLESLAW

SERVES **6 TO 8**

1 medium (2-pound) green cabbage with attractive outer leaves

½ cup regular or reduced-fat (not nonfat) sour cream

½ cup regular or reduced-fat (not nonfat) mayonnaise

¼ cup white wine vinegar

2 tablespoons sugar

1 teaspoon salt

1 teaspoon caraway seeds, crushed, plus more if needed (see page 15)

¼ teaspoon celery seeds, crushed, plus more if needed (see page 15)

Freshly ground black pepper

6 green onions including 2 inches of green stems, finely chopped

All the traditional slaw ingredients–cabbage, vinegar, sugar, mayonnaise, and sour cream–can be found in this recipe, but it is the hint of crushed caraway seeds that gives the dish its distinctive taste. Mounded on a bed of cabbage leaves, this slaw makes an attractive side dish to serve with barbecued ribs or chicken, or with grilled sausages.

Remove 4 to 5 of the attractive outer leaves from cabbage, rinse, and pat dry. Store in a plastic bag in the refrigerator until you are ready to garnish slaw.

Quarter the cabbage lengthwise and remove the tough core. Slice quarters thinly to yield about 8 cups. (Save extra cabbage for another use.) Place in a large nonreactive bowl.

In a small nonreactive bowl, stir together sour cream, mayonnaise, vinegar, sugar, salt, caraway seeds, celery seeds, and several grinds of pepper. Pour over cabbage and add chopped green onions; mix well. Cover and refrigerate until well chilled, at least 2 hours. (Slaw can be made 6 hours ahead; bring to room temperature 30 minutes before serving.)

Taste slaw, and if you prefer a stronger caraway and celery seed flavor, crush another ½ teaspoon caraway seeds and ⅛ teaspoon celery seeds and stir into the slaw.

To serve, line a shallow serving bowl with reserved cabbage leaves. Mound slaw on top.

CABBAGE, HAM, AND GRUYÈRE SALAD

The Auvergne, a region in the interior of France, is known for hearty dishes, one of which is **Salade Auvergnate.** *A combination of sliced cabbage, ham, and Gruyère cheese, tossed in a vinaigrette dressing along with chopped walnuts and golden raisins, this delicious salad is a study in contrasts. The cheese and ham lend salty notes and are well paired with the sweetness provided by the raisins. I purchased this salad (which I think of as French coleslaw) so often during long stays in France that one day I finally decided to assemble a homemade version in my tiny French kitchen. This "French slaw" is good offered as a first course or as a garnish to grilled chicken or lamb chops.*

3 tablespoons red wine vinegar

1 tablespoon Dijon mustard

½ cup plus 1 tablespoon olive oil

1 small (1- to 1½-pound) green cabbage with attractive outer leaves

¾ pound thinly sliced (about ⅛ inch thick) cooked ham

¾ pound thinly sliced (about ⅛ inch thick) Gruyère or Emmenthaler cheese

¾ cup coarsely chopped walnuts

¾ cup golden raisins

Salt

½ cup chopped fresh flat-leaf parsley

Whisk together vinegar and mustard in a large nonreactive bowl. Gradually whisk in oil. Set aside.

Remove 4 to 5 of the attractive outer leaves from cabbage, rinse, and pat dry. Store in a plastic bag in the refrigerator until you are ready to garnish slaw.

Quarter the cabbage lengthwise and remove the tough core. Slice quarters thinly to yield 4 cups. (Save extra cabbage for another use.) Place in a large nonreactive bowl.

Cut ham into strips about ¼ inch wide and 2 inches long. Cut cheese into strips the same size.

Add ham, cheese, walnuts, and raisins to bowl with cabbage. Pour dressing over cabbage mixture and toss to coat well. Taste and season generously with salt. Refrigerate at least 2 hours to let flavors meld. (Salad can be made 4 hours ahead; bring to room temperature 30 minutes before serving.)

To serve, line a shallow serving bowl or platter with reserved cabbage leaves. Taste salad again and season with more salt if needed. Stir in parsley. Mound salad on cabbage leaves.

SERVES 6

GRILLED CAESAR SALAD

For years I overlooked Caesar salad both for family meals and when entertaining. That changed, however, when I discovered a grilled Caesar salad made with lightly grilled wedges of romaine lettuce brushed with an anchovy-scented mayonnaise. Cooking teachers Vicki and Steve Caparulo created this recipe and willingly shared it along with some make-ahead tips.

DRESSING

3 large cloves garlic

¾ cup regular or reduced-fat (not nonfat) mayonnaise

6 tablespoons grated Parmesan cheese, preferably Parmigiano-Reggiano, divided

4 canned anchovy fillets rolled with capers

2 tablespoons extra-virgin olive oil

1 tablespoon fresh lemon juice

1 teaspoon Worcestershire sauce

1 teaspoon Dijon mustard

SALAD

¼ cup extra-virgin olive oil, plus extra for oiling grill rack

2 medium cloves garlic, minced

¼ teaspoon kosher salt

1 medium (1- to 1¼-pound) head romaine lettuce, about 8 to 9 inches long

Freshly ground black pepper

SERVES

TO MAKE THE DRESSING: Pulse garlic in the bowl of a food processor or in a blender until minced. Add mayonnaise, 2 tablespoons of the Parmesan cheese, anchovy fillets, olive oil, lemon juice, Worcestershire sauce, and mustard, and process until smooth. (Dressing can be made 2 hours ahead; cover and refrigerate. Bring to room temperature 15 minutes before using.)

TO MAKE THE SALAD: In a small bowl, whisk together ¼ cup olive oil, garlic, and salt. Set aside for 15 minutes for flavors to develop. Remove and discard any outer bruised leaves from romaine. Quarter the lettuce lengthwise and set aside.

Oil a grill rack and arrange 4 to 5 inches from heat source. Prepare grill for a hot fire (high temperature). Lightly brush the cut sides (including stalk and leaves) of each lettuce quarter with the garlic-scented oil. Grill lettuce quarters, cut-side down, until lightly browned, about 2 minutes. The leaves should be very slightly charred but still hold their shape.

Arrange lettuce quarters, cut-side up, on 4 dinner plates. Brush some of the dressing over and under the leaves of each quarter, then drizzle each serving decoratively with a little more dressing. Sprinkle each serving with 1 tablespoon of the remaining Parmesan cheese and season with a generous grating of pepper. Place any extra dressing in a small bowl to pass.

The Caesar Salad was invented in the 1920s by Caesar Cardini, a restaurant owner and chef in Tijuana, Mexico.

WATERCRESS, CARROT, AND ORANGE SALAD IN A HONEY DRESSING

3 large navel oranges

4 small (8 to 10 ounces total) carrots

Salt

2 tablespoons honey

2 tablespoons white wine vinegar

2 tablespoons canola oil

¾ teaspoon ground cumin

2 large bunches attractive watercress, stemmed

Peppery watercress makes a fine partner to sweet carrots and oranges in this salad, all of which are tossed in a refreshing orange and honey dressing scented with cumin. The salad makes an excellent accompaniment to grilled lamb or fish.

SERVES 6

Grate enough peel from 1 orange to make 2 teaspoons zest and place in a nonreactive salad bowl. Juice orange to yield 2 tablespoons of juice and add to salad bowl. Using a sharp paring knife, cut away skin and all white pith from remaining 2 oranges. Cut between membranes to remove orange segments, and add to salad bowl.

Bring a large saucepan of water to a boil. Cut carrots on the diagonal into thin, ¼-inch-thick slices. Add 1 teaspoon salt and carrots to pot and cook until just tender, about 3 minutes. Drain in a colander and pat dry. Add carrots to salad bowl.

Add honey, vinegar, oil, cumin, and ½ teaspoon salt to bowl and stir gently to combine. (The salad can be prepared 2 hours ahead to this point. Cover with plastic wrap and leave at cool room temperature. Stir salad again when ready to serve.)

To finish salad, add sprigs of watercress to salad and toss well to coat. Taste and add more salt if needed. Mound salad on 6 individual salad plates. Serve immediately.

Ancient Romans ate salads with dressings, much like ours today, and called them herba salata (Latin for "salted herb"), from which the word "salad" is derived.

MESCLUN SALAD WITH FENNEL, ORANGES, AND FIGS

This Provençal-inspired salad is made with peeled orange segments, julienned fennel, and sliced dried figs, which are tossed with a generous amount of mesclun greens. With its bracing orange dressing, this would make a refreshing side dish to offer with the Provençal Summer Vegetable Tart (page 168) for a light backyard supper. It also makes a fine accompaniment to grilled lamb or chicken.

DRESSING

1½ tablespoons fresh orange juice

1½ teaspoons grated orange zest

1½ tablespoons white wine vinegar

Salt

Freshly ground black pepper

1½ tablespoons olive oil

SALAD

2 large navel oranges

1 medium bulb fennel

6 dried Black Mission figs

5 to 6 cups mesclun greens

SERVES 4

TO MAKE THE DRESSING: Combine orange juice, orange zest, vinegar, ¼ teaspoon salt, and several grinds of pepper in a small nonreactive bowl, and whisk well to combine. Whisk in olive oil. (The dressing can be prepared 3 to 4 hours ahead; cover and refrigerate. Bring to room temperature 30 minutes before needed and whisk well before using.)

TO ASSEMBLE THE SALAD: Peel oranges, removing all skin and white pith underneath, then cut between the membranes to remove the segments from the orange. Place in a salad bowl.

Trim and discard lacy stalks from fennel. Halve bulbs lengthwise and remove and discard tough triangular cores. Cut fennel lengthwise into very thin julienne strips and add to salad bowl.

Stem figs and slice thinly lengthwise. Add to bowl along with mixed greens. Pour ⅔ of the dressing over the salad and toss well. Taste and add more salt and pepper if needed.

Divide salad among 4 dinner plates and drizzle with remaining dressing.

PEAR, CHEDDAR, AND GREENS WITH HONEY DRESSING

SERVES **6**

HONEY DRESSING

6 tablespoons canola oil

¼ cup honey

3 tablespoons white wine vinegar

2 to **3** teaspoons finely chopped fresh rosemary or 1 teaspoon dried rosemary, crushed

Kosher salt

SALAD

7 to **8** cups torn greens (oakleaf lettuce, Boston, or red or green leaf lettuce all work well)

2 small ripe pears (Bartletts work well)

4 ounces extra-sharp white Cheddar cheese cut into julienned strips about 2 inches long by ¼ inch wide

¼ cup coarsely chopped pecans

This salad bursts with fresh, clean flavors. Mixed greens are tossed in a honey and rosemary vinaigrette, then topped with sliced pears, strips of Cheddar cheese, and chopped pecans. The honey provides a slightly sweet taste, which complements the juicy pears and salty cheese, while the rosemary is an unexpected but inviting accent. This salad would make a tempting garnish for grilled sausages, pork chops, or chicken.

TO MAKE THE DRESSING: Whisk together oil, honey, vinegar, rosemary, and ¼ teaspoon salt in a small nonreactive bowl. (The dressing can be prepared 1 day ahead; cover and refrigerate. Bring to room temperature before using.)

TO ASSEMBLE THE SALAD: Toss greens in a large bowl with half the dressing. Season to taste with salt. Divide and arrange the salad on 6 salad plates.

Halve pears lengthwise and core. Then cut lengthwise into thin slices and place in the same bowl the greens were in. Add the cheese strips and toss with remaining dressing. Garnish each serving with some pears and cheese. Sprinkle each portion with some chopped pecans.

MUSHROOM AND ARUGULA SALAD WITH SHAVED PARMESAN

Robust, peppery arugula leaves; thin, snowy white mushroom slices; and shaved Parmigiano-Reggiano cheese form a winning salad combination when tossed simply in balsamic vinegar and olive oil. For the best results, be sure to use Italian Parmigiano-Reggiano cheese, which is aged longer than domestic varieties and has a more complex taste. This salad complements grilled beef steaks or lamb chops.

3   tablespoons balsamic vinegar

    Kosher salt

    Coarsely ground black pepper

¼   cup extra-virgin olive oil

1   pound button or cremini mushrooms, cleaned, dried, and sliced thinly through the stems (see note)

⅔   cup coarsely chopped arugula leaves plus an extra bunch for garnish

1   4- to 6-ounce piece of Parmigiano-Reggiano cheese, at room temperature

SERVES 4 TO 6

Combine vinegar, ½ teaspoon salt, and a generous ¼ teaspoon pepper in a salad bowl and whisk well. Whisk in olive oil. Add mushrooms and chopped arugula, and toss to coat well.

Using a vegetable peeler, shave enough thin strips from the piece of Parmigiano-Reggiano to make ⅔ cup, and stir gently into the salad just to combine. Taste, and, if needed, add more salt and pepper, then toss again.

To serve, arrange reserved, undressed arugula leaves, overlapping, as a border on a serving platter, and mound the salad on top. Serve at room temperature.

NOTE: As a time saver, buy packages of sliced mushrooms at the grocery. Be sure the mushrooms are very fresh—firm, bright white, and without any dark spots.

RED, YELLOW, ORANGE, AND GREEN HEIRLOOM TOMATO SALAD

The summer farmers' market in my small New England town was the inspiration for this recipe. It's there that I discovered glorious, multihued heirloom tomatoes with their interesting names. Reds often include Cherokee Purple, yellows have names like Nebraska Wedding and Indian Mist, orange strains are labeled Jaune Flame and Marisol, while greens are called Green Zebras and Pineapple. There are many more varieties, and any will do in this recipe. Choose an assortment of varying colors, sizes, and tastes (using some tomatoes that are high acid and some that are low). Heirloom tomatoes are so full of flavor that they need little embellishing. They make a stunning salad when cut into wedges and arranged around a mound of greens dressed with vinaigrette.

3 pounds heirloom tomatoes (red, yellow, orange, and green varieties of your choice)

2 tablespoons red wine vinegar

1 teaspoon Dijon mustard

Salt

Freshly ground black pepper

⅓ cup extra-virgin olive oil

1 to 2 large bunches arugula, stemmed, or mixed greens such as mesclun (enough to make 8 cups)

SERVES 6

Cut tomatoes lengthwise into ½-inch-thick wedges. Place in a large nonreactive bowl and set aside.

Whisk vinegar, mustard, ¾ teaspoon salt, and several grinds of pepper together in a small bowl. Gradually whisk in olive oil. Pour half of this mixture over the tomatoes, and marinate for 10 to 15 minutes.

When ready to serve, toss arugula in a mixing bowl with enough of the remaining dressing to just coat lightly. Taste and season with more salt and pepper if needed.

Use a large ceramic or glass platter, and mound the greens in the center. Taste the tomatoes and season with more salt and pepper if needed. Then using a slotted spoon, arrange a border of tomatoes around the greens. Serve immediately.

TOMATO AND FENNEL SALAD WITH FENNEL SEED DRESSING

SERVES **6**

FENNEL SEED DRESSING

2 tablespoons white wine vinegar

4 teaspoons chopped fresh tarragon

1 teaspoon Dijon mustard

1 teaspoon fennel seeds, crushed (see page 15)

   Salt

   Freshly ground black pepper

6 tablespoons extra-virgin olive oil

SALAD

1½ pounds fennel bulbs

3 large (about 1½ pounds total) tomatoes cut lengthwise into ¾-inch-thick wedges

3 cups watercress sprigs, stemmed

This delicious salad is perfect for showcasing glorious summer tomatoes. Cut into wedges and combined with thinly sliced fennel and watercress sprigs, they are then tossed in a vinaigrette dressing scented with crushed fennel seeds and fresh tarragon. This colorful salad could accompany Pepper and Coriander–Coated Tuna Steaks (page 93), Hickory Smoked Turkey Breast with Herb Stuffing (page 80), or Bacon-Wrapped Filet Steaks Topped with Roasted Garlic Butter (page 28).

TO MAKE THE DRESSING: Combine vinegar, tarragon, mustard, fennel seeds, ½ teaspoon salt, and several grinds of pepper in a small nonreactive bowl, and whisk well to blend. Gradually whisk in olive oil. (Dressing can be made 3 hours ahead; cover and leave at cool room temperature. Whisk well before using.)

TO MAKE THE SALAD: Trim and discard lacy stalks from fennel bulbs. Halve bulbs lengthwise and remove and discard tough triangular cores. Slice fennel lengthwise very thinly into ⅛-inch-thick slices, to make 3 cups.

Toss fennel slices, tomato wedges, and watercress sprigs in a large salad bowl. Add the dressing and toss well.

EMILY BELL'S FORKLIFT SALAD

2 cups (2 medium) peeled, seeded, and diced cucumbers

2 cups (4 to 5 large) seeded and diced plum tomatoes

2 cups (about 2 medium) chopped red bell peppers

1 15½-ounce can garbanzo beans, drained, rinsed, patted dry, and coarsely chopped

1 cup (3 to 4 stalks) coarsely chopped celery

½ cup chopped red onion

3 tablespoons plus 1 teaspoon white wine vinegar

2 generous teaspoons minced garlic

Kosher salt

Freshly ground black pepper

1 teaspoon whole-grain Dijon mustard

¼ cup olive oil

3 tablespoons chopped fresh mint

3 tablespoons chopped fresh basil

3 tablespoons chopped fresh flat-leaf parsley

This colorful chopped salad, cleverly named "Forklift Salad" by its creator, is made with a bounty of vegetables dressed in vinaigrette. It can be prepared several hours in advance so there is no last-minute work other than adding a sprinkle of chopped herbs. Serve it in an attractive salad bowl, or for a delicious variation, try it mounded atop grilled flatbread slices.

8

SERVES

Combine cucumbers, tomatoes, red bell peppers, beans, celery, and onion in an attractive nonreactive serving bowl. In another bowl, whisk together vinegar, garlic, 1½ teaspoons salt, 1 teaspoon pepper, and mustard. Gradually whisk in oil. Pour over vegetables and toss well. Let marinate 45 minutes or up to 2 hours at room temperature.

At serving time, sprinkle the vegetables with the herbs and mix well. Taste and season with more salt and pepper if needed. Serve the salad with a slotted spoon.

AVOCADO, MANGO, AND **ARUGULA SALAD**

SERVES 6

The soft, tender texture of avocados and mangoes balances the crisp red onions and the crunchy garnish of toasted pumpkin seeds in this salad. The refreshing taste of orange in the dressing is a nice counterpoint to peppery arugula. This is a good salad to offer with grilled fish, chicken, or pork.

DRESSING

4 teaspoons red wine vinegar

2 teaspoons fresh orange juice

2 teaspoons grated orange zest

Salt

5 tablespoons olive oil

SALAD

1 ripe avocado

1 ripe mango

½ cup very thinly sliced red onion

6 cups (6 ounces) packed stemmed arugula leaves or baby spinach

2 generous tablespoons roasted and salted pumpkin seeds (see note)

TO MAKE THE DRESSING: Combine vinegar, orange juice, and 1 teaspoon orange zest, and ⅛ teaspoon salt in a small nonreactive bowl. Whisk mixture to combine well. Gradually add olive oil. (The dressing can be made 1 day ahead; cover and refrigerate. Bring to room temperature, and whisk well before using.)

TO MAKE THE SALAD: Peel avocado and remove pit. Cut avocado into ¼ inch cubes and set aside. Peel mango and cut flesh from pit. Cut flesh into ½-inch cubes and set aside.

Pour half the salad dressing into a large bowl and add avocado, mango, and onion. Toss gently, being careful not to crush the diced avocado. Add arugula and remaining dressing and toss gently again. Taste and season lightly with more salt if needed.

To serve, divide salad among 6 salad plates. Garnish each serving with 1 teaspoon of pumpkin seeds and a sprinkle of orange zest. Serve immediately.

NOTE: Roasted and salted pumpkin seeds are available in some supermarkets and in health food stores.

WATERCRESS, CUCUMBER, AND BELGIAN ENDIVE SALAD WITH MUSTARD SEED DRESSING

MUSTARD SEED DRESSING

1½ teaspoons mustard seeds

1½ tablespoons cider vinegar

3½ teaspoons fresh lemon juice

Kosher salt

¾ teaspoon Dijon mustard

Freshly ground black pepper

⅓ cup canola oil

SALAD

1 large cucumber

2 small (about 10 ounces each) Belgian endives

2 bunches (about 12 ounces) watercress, stemmed

Crisp, refreshing cucumbers, slightly bitter Belgian endive, and peppery watercress make a refreshing salad combination that is especially good with grilled fish or chicken. Try it with Grilled Salmon with Green Mustard Sauce (page 88) or with Fennel and Rosemary–Coated Chicken (page 74).

SERVES

TO MAKE THE DRESSING: Heat a small, medium skillet over medium heat until hot, reduce the heat to low, and add mustard seeds. Toast the seeds, shaking the skillet occasionally. The seeds will start to darken to a gray color and pop in 4 to 5 minutes. When they are popping and fragrant, remove skillet from heat and cool seeds completely. Place cooled seeds in a small self-sealing bag and crush them with a rolling pin or a meat pounder until coarsely ground. Set aside.

In a small bowl, whisk together vinegar, lemon juice, 1¼ teaspoons salt, mustard, and several grinds of black pepper. Slowly whisk in oil, then add crushed mustard seeds. (The dressing can be prepared 1 day ahead; cover and refrigerate. Bring to room temperature and whisk well before using.)

TO MAKE THE SALAD: Peel cucumber, halve it lengthwise, seed it, and slice it thinly; put in a salad bowl. Halve Belgian endives lengthwise, remove the cores, then cut into ¼-inch-julienne strips, and add to the bowl with the cucumbers. Add 3 tablespoons of the dressing and toss to mix. Add watercress and mix well, adding just enough additional dressing to coat the salad lightly. (You may not need to use all of the dressing.) Taste and add more salt and pepper if needed. Mound salad in a serving bowl. Serve immediately.

KATHIE ALEX'S BROCHETTES OF MELON, PROSCIUTTO, AND FRESH MOZZARELLA

One hot summer day in Provence, my good friend Kathie Alex, a talented teacher who lives and teaches in the south of France, served me these exquisite brochettes. Wedges of perfectly ripened melon, ribbons of paper-thin prosciutto, and little balls of fresh mozzarella were skewered and drizzled lightly with a basil-scented olive oil. The sweetness of the melon, the saltiness of the ham, and the silky smooth texture of the mozzarella all worked beautifully together. I wasted no time asking for the recipe, and have served these brochettes many times since. Use them as a salad to open a meal or offer them as a side dish to grilled fish or chicken.

1 bunch fresh basil

½ cup extra-virgin olive oil

1 medium clove garlic, peeled

1 small (about 2 pounds) ripe cantaloupe

16 paper-thin slices best-quality prosciutto

8 small balls of fresh mozzarella di buffala or one large (6- to 7-ounce) ball

8 metal or wooden skewers, preferably short rather than long skewers

AS A FIRST COURSE OR AS A LIGHT SIDE DISH.

8

SERVES

Pull off 16 large basil leaves; rinse them and pat dry. Rinse and dry remaining basil and reserve for garnish.

Combine olive oil, garlic, and basil leaves in a food processor or blender, and process, pulsing machine several times, until the basil and garlic are finely chopped and blended into the oil. Set aside. (The oil can be prepared 4 hours ahead; cover and leave at room temperature.)

Halve cantaloupe through the stem and scoop out and discard seeds. Cut each half into 4 wedges. Cut off skin and discard. Cut each wedge in half, crosswise.

Trim and discard any excess fat from prosciutto slices, then cut each slice in half lengthwise.

Drain mozzarella balls or, if you are using a large piece of mozzarella, drain and cut it into eight 1-inch cubes.

To assemble the brochettes, skewer 1 piece of melon. Next, take a strip of prosciutto and gather it together as if you were making a ruffle and skewer it. Next add a mozzarella ball or cube, and follow with another strip of ruffled prosciutto, and another melon wedge. Repeat to make 7 more skewers.

Arrange skewers on a serving platter and drizzle with the basil oil. Garnish the plate with several small bouquets of reserved basil leaves.

CHICKEN SALAD WITH FIGS AND GREEN BEANS IN BLUE CHEESE DRESSING

Using a purchased roasted chicken from your local grocery makes this an easy dish to prepare. Cut into chunks, the chicken is tossed in a creamy blue cheese dressing along with blanched green beans, slivered dried figs, and toasted walnuts. The assertive flavors—the salty cheese paired with the sweet figs—and the interesting textures—the crunchy nuts, the crisp beans, and tender chicken— all contribute to make this an out-of-the-ordinary chicken salad. The recipe can be doubled or tripled easily for large crowds.

BLUE CHEESE DRESSING

3 ounces Roquefort cheese, crumbled

½ cup regular or reduced-fat (not nonfat) mayonnaise

¼ cup regular or reduced-fat (not nonfat) sour cream

2 tablespoons red wine vinegar

2 teaspoons fresh lemon juice

½ clove garlic, minced

SALAD

Salt

¾ pound green beans, trimmed

12 dried Black Mission figs

1 2½-pound plain roasted chicken (see note)

1 cup toasted walnuts chopped, divided, (see page 15)

3 green onions including 2 inches of green stems, thinly sliced

Several Boston or red leaf lettuce leaves

*Picnic originates from two French words—*piquer *(to pick) and* nique *(a triffle).*

TO MAKE THE DRESSING: Combine cheese and mayonnaise in a mixing bowl, and mash cheese into mayonnaise with a rubber spatula or wooden spoon. Add remaining ingredients and whisk well to combine. Don't worry if a few lumps of blue cheese remain. (Dressing can be prepared 1 day ahead; cover and refrigerate. Bring to room temperature before using.)

SERVES 8

TO MAKE THE SALAD: Bring a pot of salted water to boil, and cook green beans until tender, 6 to 8 minutes. Drain in a colander under cold running water, then pat dry. Cut beans into 1-inch pieces and place in a large bowl.

Place figs in a bowl, cover with hot water, and soak to soften, 8 to 10 minutes. Pat figs dry, remove and discard stems, and cut into slivers. Add to bowl with beans.

Remove and discard skin from chicken. Cut chicken into bite-sized pieces to yield approximately 3 cups. Add to bowl with beans and figs along with ¾ cup of the walnuts and the green onions. (If not serving immediately, cover and refrigerate for up to 2 hours. Bring to room temperature before using.)

To serve, pour blue cheese dressing over chicken and other ingredients and toss to coat well. Taste and add salt if needed. Arrange a border of lettuce leaves on a serving platter and mound salad in center. Garnish salad with remaining ¼ cup walnuts.

NOTE: Purchase plain unseasoned chicken; avoid barbecued, Italian, or other strongly flavored birds for this recipe.

EASY CHICKEN SALAD WITH CHUTNEY AND LIME

1   cup regular or reduced-fat (not nonfat)
    mayonnaise

½   cup mango chutney

1   3-pound plain roasted chicken
    (see note, page 197)

¾   cup coarsely chopped walnuts

½   cup chopped celery

⅓   cup chopped red bell pepper

¼   cup chopped fresh cilantro

3   limes, divided

    Kosher salt

    Freshly ground black pepper

1   small head Boston or garden lettuce

As time savers, I use a purchased roasted chicken and opt for the convenience of store-bought mayonnaise and chutney for this chicken salad. The chicken is cubed and combined with chopped red bell peppers, celery, chutney, and cilantro and bound with the mayonnaise. Fresh lime zest and juice add a refreshing note. This quickly made salad is attractive mounded in a shallow bowl lined with lettuce leaves and garnished with lime wedges. It's also delicious served as a sandwich spread on lightly toasted white bread or as a filling for pita pockets.

SERVES 6

Place mayonnaise in a medium nonreactive bowl. Cut any large pieces of mango in the chutney into small dice, add the chutney to the mayonnaise, and stir to mix.

Remove and discard skin from chicken. Cut chicken into ¾-inch cubes to yield 4 cups and add to the mayonnaise mixture. Add walnuts, celery, bell pepper, and cilantro and mix well.

Juice 2 of the limes and add 3 tablespoons of the juice to the chicken salad; stir to mix. Season with salt and pepper to taste. (The chicken salad can be prepared 4 hours ahead; cover and refrigerate. Bring to room temperature 15 minutes before serving.)

To serve, arrange a bed of lettuce leaves in a shallow serving bowl or on a platter. Mound with chicken salad. Slice remaining lime into ½-inch wedges and garnish platter with wedges. Serve each portion on a bed of lettuce with a lime wedge.

TURKEY SALAD with PEACHES and SESAME

SALAD

1½ pounds roasted turkey breast

2 cups seedless red or green grapes or a combination, halved

1¼ cups finely chopped celery

½ cup chopped green onions including 2 inches of green stems

DRESSING

1 cup plus 2 tablespoons regular or reduced-fat (not nonfat) mayonnaise

4 tablespoons peach preserves

2 tablespoons minced peeled fresh ginger

1 tablespoon Asian sesame oil

1½ teaspoons grated lemon zest

1½ teaspoons, plus 2 tablespoons fresh lemon juice, divided

GARNISH

4 ripe peaches

1 small head Boston or red leaf lettuce

2 to 3 tablespoons toasted sesame seeds (see page 15)

Chunks of tender roasted turkey breast tossed with juicy grapes, crunchy celery, and green onions make a tempting combination when tossed in a mayonnaise dressing flavored with peaches and sesame oil. To save time, I buy turkey breast already roasted at my local grocery store. This salad is attractive served on a bed of lettuce as a light main course.

SERVES 6

TO MAKE THE SALAD: Remove and discard skin from turkey. Cut turkey into ¾-inch cubes. Combine turkey, grapes, celery, and green onions in a large bowl.

TO MAKE THE DRESSING: Whisk together mayonnaise, peach preserves, ginger, sesame oil, lemon zest, and 1½ teaspoons of the lemon juice. Add to the turkey mixture and mix well. (The salad can be prepared 4 hours ahead; cover and refrigerate.)

When ready to serve, peel peaches and cut into ½-inch wedges. Sprinkle the remaining lemon juice over the peach wedges. Arrange 2 to 3 lettuce leaves on each of 6 dinner plates and mound with salad, arranging the peach wedges on the side. Sprinkle with toasted sesame seeds.

In 17th-century France, a picnic meant a potluck style of meal—almost two hundred years later the word "picnic" came to signify an outdoor meal.

WILD AND WHITE RICE SALAD WITH ASPARAGUS AND SMOKED SALMON

Wild and white rice provide a dark and light background for this cooling summer salad laced with sliced asparagus, chopped fennel, and bits of smoked salmon. A lemon vinaigrette adds a cool, refreshing note. The salad makes an attractive main course to serve when the weather is unbearably hot. I like to place it on an outdoor buffet table along with a platter of cheeses, a plate of sliced tomatoes and cucumbers, and a basket of crusty French bread.

SALAD

4⅓ cups chicken stock, divided, plus extra if needed (see note)

1 cup wild rice

½ cup converted white rice

Salt

¾ pound slim asparagus, tough stems cut off and spears sliced into ½-inch pieces

2 cups chopped fennel (lacy stems discarded and bulbs cored before being chopped)

4 ounces thinly sliced smoked salmon, cut into ½-inch dice

½ cup chopped pecans, toasted (see page 15)

⅓ cup finely chopped green onions including 2 inches of green stems

3 tablespoons chopped fresh tarragon, plus several sprigs for garnish

DRESSING

¼ cup fresh lemon juice

2 teaspoons grated lemon zest

½ teaspoon Dijon mustard

Salt

Freshly ground black pepper

½ cup olive oil

TO MAKE THE SALAD: Bring 3 cups of the chicken stock to a boil in a medium saucepan over high heat and add wild rice. Cover pan, lower heat, and simmer until almost all stock is absorbed and rice kernels have cracked, 45 to 55 minutes. Watch carefully, and if stock is absorbed before rice is done, add extra stock. When done, remove from heat and let stand, covered, 10 minutes. Drain rice well.

While wild rice is cooking, prepare white rice and vegetables. Bring remaining 1⅓ cups chicken stock to a boil in another medium saucepan and add white rice; cook until tender, about 15 minutes. Drain well and set aside.

Bring 2 quarts lightly salted water to a boil and add asparagus. Cook for 1 minute, then add fennel and continue to cook, about 3 minutes. Remove to a large colander and place under cold running water until vegetables are cool, then drain completely.

In a large nonreactive bowl, gently stir together both rices, asparagus, fennel, salmon, pecans, onions, and chopped tarragon.

TO MAKE THE DRESSING: Whisk together lemon juice and zest, mustard, ½ teaspoon salt, and ½ teaspoon pepper in a small bowl. Gradually whisk in olive oil. Pour dressing over salad ingredients and toss well. Taste salad and add more salt and pepper if needed. (The salad can be made 2 hours ahead; cover and refrigerate. However, when asparagus sit in the lemon dressing longer than 30 minutes, they start to lose their bright green color, so toss all ingredients together except asparagus and stir them in just before serving.)

To serve, mound salad in a shallow serving bowl and garnish with a bouquet of fresh tarragon sprigs.

NOTE: Cooking the two rices in chicken stock adds extra flavor to these grains. Regular chicken stock works well; if you use reduced-sodium stock, you will probably need to season the salad with additional salt.

BLACK BEAN, TOMATO, AND AVOCADO SALAD FOR A CROWD

When you are cooking for a crowd, this salad, which can be made several hours in advance and serves twelve, is an ideal choice. Vibrantly colored ingredients including black beans, yellow bell peppers, jalapeños, avocados, tomatoes, and red onions are tossed in a cumin lime dressing and seasoned with cilantro. Using canned beans saves time and does not sacrifice flavor in this dish. The salad could be served with grilled chicken, steaks, or shrimp, or offered as a side dish to hamburgers. If you have any salad left over, combine it with cooked rice, grated Monterey Jack cheese, and shredded greens, as a filling for burritos.

CUMIN LIME DRESSING

¾ cup olive oil

6 tablespoons fresh lime juice

1 tablespoon grated lime zest

4 teaspoons ground cumin

   Salt

   Freshly ground black pepper

SALAD

4 15-ounce cans black beans, drained, rinsed, and patted dry

1 cup chopped yellow bell pepper

1 cup chopped red onion

1 cup diced celery

½ cup chopped fresh cilantro

3 jalapeño peppers, minced

3 avocados, cut into ½-inch dice

2 cups (about 8) chopped plum tomatoes

SERVES 12

TO MAKE THE DRESSING: Whisk together olive oil, lime juice, lime zest, cumin, and 1½ teaspoons salt, and several grinds of pepper in a medium nonreactive bowl. (Dressing can be made 1 day ahead; cover and refrigerate. Bring to room temperature before using.)

TO MAKE THE SALAD: Combine beans, bell pepper, onion, celery, cilantro, and jalapeños in a large nonreactive bowl, and mix well. Pour in dressing, and stir to coat all ingredients well. Gently stir in avocados and tomatoes. Taste, and add more salt and pepper if needed. Cover with plastic wrap, and refrigerate at least 2 hours to marinate. (Salad can be prepared 5 hours ahead. Bring to room temperature before serving.)

To serve, mound salad in a large shallow bowl or on a platter.

Pinto beans get their name from the Spanish word pinto, *which means "painted."*

RICH TERAPAK'S THREE BEANS PLUS SALAD

SERVES 8 TO 10

This salad, created by Rich Terapak, a talented cook and attorney from Columbus, Ohio, is an updated version of the classic bean salads that were so popular in the '60s and '70s. I marvel at how quickly and easily this salad can be assembled. Using canned black, pinto, and garbanzo beans, which are rinsed thoroughly then dried, saves a huge amount of time. The bean trio is combined with red onions, bell peppers, jalapeños, grape tomatoes, and herbs, then tossed in a cumin vinaigrette dressing. Bits of creamy goat cheese are added as a garnish at serving time.

SALAD

- **3** 15-ounce cans black beans, drained, rinsed, and patted dry
- **1** 15-ounce can garbanzo beans, drained, rinsed, and patted dry
- **1** 15-ounce can pinto beans, drained, rinsed, and patted dry
- **1** pint grape or cherry tomatoes, halved lengthwise
- **1** cup chopped yellow or red bell pepper
- **1** cup chopped red onion
- **1** tablespoon minced jalapeño pepper (see page 17)

DRESSING

- ½ cup olive oil
- ¼ cup red wine vinegar
- **2** teaspoons ground cumin
- ¼ cup chopped fresh cilantro
- ¼ cup chopped fresh flat-leaf parsley
- Kosher salt
- Freshly ground black pepper
- **4** to **5** ounces creamy goat cheese, crumbled or broken into small pieces

TO MAKE THE SALAD: Place all the beans in a large nonreactive bowl. Add tomatoes, bell pepper, onion, and jalapeño, and mix well.

TO MAKE THE DRESSING: Whisk together oil, vinegar, and cumin in a small bowl. Pour over the bean mixture. Add cilantro, parsley, 1 teaspoon salt, and several grinds of black pepper. Taste and season with additional salt and pepper if needed. (The salad can be prepared 5 hours ahead; cover and refrigerate. Bring to room temperature 30 minutes before serving.)

To serve, mound salad in a large shallow bowl and sprinkle with crumbled goat cheese.

EXTRA-SPECIAL TABBOULEH WITH AVOCADO AND FETA

SERVES **4 TO 6**

½ cup bulgur (see note)

12 ounces plum tomatoes, seeded, chopped

1 cup chopped fresh flat-leaf parsley

4 green onions including 2 inches of green stems, chopped

½ cucumber, peeled, seeded, finely chopped

4 radishes, chopped

½ cup crumbled feta cheese

¼ cup chopped fresh mint

1 tablespoon grated lemon zest

6 tablespoons olive oil

3 tablespoons fresh lemon juice

Salt

Freshly ground black pepper

2 avocados, pitted, peeled, sliced

Tabbouleh became popular in the United States in the 1970s, when it began to appear on the menus of many health food restaurants. This version includes some extra additions. Chopped radishes and crumbled feta are stirred into the salad along with the traditional tomatoes, cucumbers, and mint. Then the tabbouleh is mounded on a platter and surrounded with a colorful garnish of sliced avocados.

Combine 1½ cups hot water and bulgur in a large bowl. Cover tightly and let stand until bulgur is tender, about 45 minutes. Strain bulgur, and place in a clean dry towel; squeeze out any excess liquid. Return bulgur to bowl.

Add tomatoes, parsley, onions, cucumber, radishes, cheese, mint, and lemon zest to bulgur. Stir to combine.

Whisk oil and lemon juice in a medium bowl to blend. Season dressing to taste with salt and pepper. Add all but 2 tablespoons dressing to bulgur mixture. Toss to combine. Season tabbouleh to taste with salt and pepper.

Add avocado slices to remaining dressing; toss to coat. Mound tabbouleh on a serving platter. Garnish with avocado slices.

NOTE: Bulgur, also called cracked wheat, can be found in supermarkets and in natural food stores.

BLT PASTA SALAD

Salt

1 pound farfalle (bow-tie) pasta

2 tablespoons olive oil

8 ounces bacon slices, cut into 1-inch pieces

4 cups grape tomatoes, halved length wise

1½ cups (3 to 4 ounces) stemmed, coarsely chopped arugula (see note)

1 cup chopped red onion

DRESSING

½ cup regular or reduced-fat (not nonfat) mayonnaise

1 cup grated Parmesan cheese, preferably Parmigiano-Reggiano, divided

1 tablespoon white wine vinegar

Coarsely ground black pepper

America's favorite sandwich fixings–bacon, tomatoes, and lettuce–are equally good in a pasta salad. Crispy bits of fried bacon, sweet grape tomatoes, chopped arugula, and minced red onions are tossed with bow-tie pasta, then coated with a Parmesan mayonnaise dressing. This side dish, which can be made an hour in advance, would be excellent served with Fennel and Rosemary–Coated Chicken Breasts (page 74) or with Grilled Lemon Parsley Veal Chops (page 36).

Bring a large pot of salted water to a boil and add pasta. Cook according to package instructions, until al dente (just tender to the bite), then drain and transfer to a large, shallow nonreactive serving bowl. Toss pasta with olive oil and set aside.

In a large, heavy skillet set over medium heat, fry the bacon until crisp and golden, then drain on paper towels. Add the bacon, tomatoes, arugula, and onion to bowl with pasta and mix well.

TO MAKE THE DRESSING: In a small bowl, whisk together mayonnaise, half of the Parmesan cheese, vinegar, and 1 teaspoon pepper. Add to bowl with pasta and toss well to coat pasta with dressing. Add the remaining Parmesan cheese, and toss well to mix. Taste and season salad with more salt and pepper if needed. (Salad can be prepared 1 hour ahead. Cover with plastic wrap and leave at cool room temperature.)

SERVES 8

NOTE: I love the assertive taste of arugula in this salad, but if you can't find it, you could substitute watercress sprigs.

ORZO SALAD WITH VEGETABLES AND HERBS

A quartet of vegetables–sugar snap peas, tomatoes, cucumbers, and green onions–adds distinctive notes of color and texture to this summer salad, which is seasoned with a lemon dressing and garnished with specks of mint and parsley. Try it with Fennel and Rosemary–Coated Chicken (page 74), with Pork Loin in a Rosemary Jacket (page 68), or with Cornish Game Hens with Mustard and Rosemary (page 107).

SALAD

Salt

6 to **8** ounces sugar snap peas, trimmed, cut into ¾-inch pieces

2⅔ cups (about 21 ounces) orzo (rice-shaped pasta)

1¼ cups diced tomatoes

¾ cup diced peeled cucumber

½ cup chopped green onions including 2 inches of green stem

¼ cup chopped fresh flat-leaf parsley

¼ chopped fresh mint

2 teaspoons finely grated lemon zest

DRESSING

3 tablespoons fresh lemon juice

1½ teaspoons grated lemon zest

1 teaspoon minced garlic

½ cup olive oil

Salt

Freshly ground black pepper

1 head Boston lettuce

SERVES

TO MAKE THE SALAD: Bring a large pot of salted water to a boil. Add sugar snap peas; cook 1 minute, then use a slotted spoon to transfer peas to a strainer. Rinse with cold water and drain. Add orzo to same pot. Boil until tender but still firm to bite, about 8 minutes. Drain and cool.

In a large nonreactive bowl, mix together orzo, sugar snap peas, tomatoes, cucumber, green onions, parsley, mint, and lemon zest.

TO MAKE THE DRESSING: Combine lemon juice, lemon zest, and garlic in a medium bowl. Gradually whisk in olive oil. Add 1½ teaspoons salt and ¼ teaspoon pepper.

Pour enough dressing over the salad to coat well. You may have a little dressing left over. Season salad with salt and pepper, if needed. (The salad can be made 1 hour ahead. Do not let it sit longer, or the peas and onions will start to lose their bright color. Cover salad and refrigerate. Bring to room temperature before serving.)

To serve, line a shallow serving bowl with lettuce leaves. Mound salad in bowl.

CHAPTER 6

COO
LDR
IN
KS

When you're hosting a backyard event—a lunch, supper, small cocktail party, or maybe a late afternoon get-together with neighbors—planning the food often takes priority over all else. More often than not, we give little thought to the drinks. Wine, beer, and sodas are common and acceptable choices, but why not be more creative? With just a little extra effort you can prepare a signature drink that your guests will long remember.

You'll find a host of tantalizing drinks in this chapter. There's more than one recipe for lemonade—so popular that it could be declared America's national drink. Iced teas and coffees with new twists, and bracing creations made with freshly squeezed lime or orange juice, are other thirst-quenchers. Peaches, raspberries, and coconut are featured in thick, icy-cold smoothies. And, drinks with spirits include classic backyard sangria, piña coladas, mojitos from Cuba, and *caipirinhas* from Brazil.

JULEP ICED TEA

Like mint juleps, this thirst-quenching drink is made by combining crushed mint leaves with sugar. Strong brewed tea and freshly squeezed lemon juice, however, replace the bourbon. The creation of a talented Mississippi cook, Lynn Wilkins, this tea is a perfect refreshment to serve with any backyard meal.

4 to **5** lemons

2 cups loosely packed fresh mint leaves

6 standard-size black tea bags, preferably English Breakfast tea

4 cups boiling water

1 cup sugar

Ice cubes

SERVES **6 TO 8**; MAKES 2 QUARTS

Carefully, with a sharp paring knife or with a vegetable peeler, remove the rind from 1½ lemons. Be careful to cut away just the colored portion of the rind, and not the white bitter pith beneath. Cut the strips into thin julienne and set aside. Juice enough of the lemons to yield ⅔ cup and set aside.

Put mint leaves in a large, heat-proof glass bowl or measuring cup, and use your fingers to rub the leaves against the bottom of the bowl to bruise and break them to help release their flavor. Add lemon rind and tea bags, and cover with boiling water. Steep for 10 minutes, then remove tea bags. Mix in sugar and lemon juice and steep another 10 minutes. Strain the mixture into a nonreactive pitcher and add 4 cups cold water. Cover and refrigerate until chilled. Serve tea over ice in tall glasses.

INDIAN ICED TEA

Tea brewed with spices came to America from India, where it is known as chai *(sounds like "shy") or* Masala chai. *Typically, these hot teas are sweetened and served with milk. Chilled variations like the following, however, make tempting drinks for warm-weather months. This version, which does not call for sugar or milk, is delicious served in tall glasses over ice.*

4 standard-size orange pekoe tea bags

16 bay leaves, broken in half

16 green cardamom pods (crushed)

2 cinnamon sticks, broken in half

Ice cubes

4 : MAKES 1 QUART : SERVES

Bring 4 cups water to a boil in a medium saucepan. Remove from heat and transfer to a heat-proof bowl. Add tea bags and all the spices. Let the tea steep only 2 minutes, then remove and discard the tea bags. Let the spices steep for an additional 5 minutes. Strain tea and cool. Chill until cold.

Serve in 4 tall glasses over ice.

The tea bag was invented accidentally in the early 20th century by New Yorker Thomas Sullivan, a tea merchant who placed samples in small hand-sewn silk bags, rather than in costly tins; his clientele brewed the tea in the bags and begged for more.

SPICED ICED COFFEE

SPICED COFFEE

½ cup freshly ground coffee, preferably a mild roast such as Colombian

2½ teaspoons ground cardamom

1½ teaspoons sugar, plus more if needed

1 teaspoon ground cinnamon

½ teaspoon freshly grated nutmeg

WHIPPED CREAM GARNISH

¾ cup heavy cream

1½ tablespoons confectioners' sugar, plus more if needed

1 tablespoon brandy

Ice cubes

This delectable ice-cold coffee is so rich and satisfying that it could replace dessert. However, I think it is best served with such home-made cookies as Pecan Shortbread Cookies (page 275) or Chocolate Heaven Cookies (page 276) for an afternoon or late-evening treat. A mild coffee, rather than a dark strong roast, works best so that the flavors of the spices are not overpowered.

SERVES

TO BREW COFFEE: Use a drip-style coffeemaker (preferably an automatic). Combine ground coffee, cardamom, sugar, cinnamon, and nutmeg in filter cup. Mix gently with a spoon to combine spices with coffee. Add 5½ cups water to water chamber and brew according to manufacturer's directions. When coffee is brewed, cool to room temperature, then cover and refrigerate until well chilled.

TO MAKE WHIPPED CREAM GARNISH: Whip cream with an electric mixer on medium speed until it starts to mound softly, then beat in the 1½ tablespoons confectioners' sugar and brandy. Continue beating just until stiff peaks start to form. If not using right away, cover bowl of whipped cream with plastic wrap and refrigerate. (Whipped cream garnish can be prepared 1 day ahead.)

To serve, divide coffee evenly among six 8-ounce glasses. Stir 1 tablespoon of the whipped cream into each glass and mix until blended. If you want the coffee to have a sweeter taste, season with a little additional sugar. Fill each glass with ice and garnish each serving with a generous dollop of the whipped cream. Serve immediately.

Hawaii is the only state in the United States that grows coffee.

CARAMEL ICED COFFEE

1 cup freshly ground coffee, preferably a mild roast such as Colombian

½ cup Best Ever Caramel Sauce (page 332) or purchased caramel sauce (see note)

1 cup whole milk

4 teaspoons dark rum

Ice cubes

Rich caramel sauce and dark rum turn simple, iced coffee into something extra special for backyard sipping on a lazy day or night. A mild roasted coffee such as Colombian works best in this recipe.

SERVES 4

TO BREW COFFEE: Use a drip-style coffeemaker. Add 7 cups water to water chamber and brew according to manufacturer's directions. Then transfer to a heat-proof bowl or pitcher and refrigerate until chilled.

When ready to serve, place 2 tablespoons caramel in each of 4 medium glasses. Add ¼ of the coffee (about 1 cup), ¼ cup milk, and 1 teaspoon rum to each glass. Fill each glass with ice cubes and serve immediately.

NOTE: Mrs. Richardson's Butterscotch Caramel Sauce, which is available in most supermarkets, works well in this recipe.

OLD-FASHIONED LEMONADE

The base for this delectable lemonade—a sugar syrup, blended with lemon and lime juices, then infused with mint leaves—can be made several days in advance and kept on hand in the refrigerator. A thirsty soul needs only to fill a glass with syrup and water, add some ice, then sip in contentment.

2 cups sugar

1 cup fresh lemon juice (about 6 lemons)

¼ cup fresh lime juice (2 to 3 limes)

¾ cup loosely packed fresh mint leaves, plus mint sprigs for garnish

Ice cubes

Thin lemon slices for garnish

SERVES 12

Combine 2½ cups water and the sugar in a medium saucepan over medium heat. Stir until sugar has dissolved, then simmer 5 minutes. Remove from heat and cool about 20 minutes. Add lemon and lime juices to the sugar syrup. Place mint leaves in a medium nonreactive bowl, and pour the lemon-lime mixture over them. Let the mixture stand for 1 hour. Strain the lemonade into a jar, and keep it covered in the refrigerator. (The base can be stored in the refrigerator for 4 days.)

To serve, pour ⅓ cup lemonade base in a glass. Stir in ⅔ cup water. Fill the glass with ice cubes, and garnish it with a sprig of mint and a lemon slice.

Lemonade first appeared in the 17th century in France.

RASPBERRY LEMONADE

One hot summer day, my husband and I lunched in Boston's Museum of Fine Arts. I ordered a Raspberry Lemonade, expecting that the drink would be made from commercial concentrates. What a surprise to discover from my first inviting sip that the icy cold beverage had been prepared with fresh ingredients. A courteous waitress was kind enough to tell me how the lemonade was made.

1½ cups sugar

1½ cups fresh raspberries, plus
    6 raspberries for garnish (optional)

1 cup plus 2 tablespoons fresh lemon
    juice, strained (6 to 7 lemons)

Ice cubes

Thin lemon slices for garnish

SERVES 6

Combine 2½ cups water and the sugar in a medium saucepan over medium heat. Stir until the sugar has dissolved, then simmer 5 minutes. Remove from heat and stir in 1½ cups raspberries. Pour into a food processor or blender and process until raspberries are completely puréed into the liquid. Remove and stir in lemon juice. (You don't need to strain this mixture to remove the raspberry seeds.) Taste, and if you want a tarter flavor, add up to 1 tablespoon of additional lemon juice. Transfer to a nonreactive pitcher, cover, and refrigerate until chilled. (Lemonade can be made 1 day ahead; keep refrigerated.)

To serve, fill six 8-ounce glasses with ice and pour in lemonade. Slit each lemon round halfway through and slip onto the rim of a glass. If desired, float a raspberry in each glass.

LIME SPRITZERS

8 large mint leaves

½ cup sugar

¾ cup fresh lime juice

3 cups club soda, chilled

   Ice cubes

A cooking student gave me the recipe for this drink and explained that she had created it after enjoying a similar version during a visit to Bangkok. The spritzers take only minutes to assemble and make a refreshing pick-me-up to sip on a warm day.

SERVES 4

Chop mint leaves finely, then put them in a medium bowl and crush with a pestle or the back of a spoon. Add sugar, and crush sugar and mint together. Add lime juice, and stir to dissolve sugar.

Pour into a nonreactive pitcher and stir in soda. Fill four 8-ounce glasses with ice cubes, and add some of the lime spritzer mixture to each.

SERVES 1

FRENCH LEMONADE

The French have a "make it yourself" type of lemonade. At any café in France, if you order a citron pressé *(pronounced see-trone pres-say), a waiter will appear with a tall glass partially filled with freshly squeezed lemon juice, a shaker of sugar, a pitcher of water, and a spoon. You then make your own lemonade, adjusting the sweetness and tartness to your own individual taste. The following recipe for a single* citron pressé *calls for sparkling water, but you could use plain water if you like.*

1 large lemon

2 teaspoons sugar, plus more if needed

   Ice cubes

   Sparkling water

Juice the lemon and strain juice into a tall glass. Stir the sugar into the lemon juice. Fill the glass with ice cubes, then with sparkling water. Taste and add more sugar if desired.

ORANGE SPARKLERS

4 oranges, plus thin orange slices for garnish (optional)

1 lemon

¼ cup sugar

2⅔ cups sparkling water (such as Perrier), chilled

Ice cubes

Citrus flavors are the stars of these drinks. Made with freshly squeezed orange and lemon juices, sugar syrup, and sparkling water, they are good served any time of the day. If you want a spirited version, you can replace the sparkling water with champagne.

SERVES 4 ; MAKES 1 QUART

Carefully, with a vegetable peeler or sharp paring knife, remove the rind from the oranges and lemon. Be careful to cut away just the colored portion of the rind, and not the white bitter pith beneath. Combine the peels, ⅔ cup water, and sugar in a large nonreactive saucepan set over high heat. Stir to dissolve sugar and bring mixture to a boil. Remove and let mixture cool to room temperature.

Halve oranges and lemons and juice them. Add the juices to the cooled sugar syrup and mix well. Refrigerate until well chilled, 1 hour or longer. (The orange and lemon mixture can be made 1 day ahead; cover and refrigerate.)

To serve, strain the chilled mixture, discarding the orange and lemon rinds. Add the Perrier or sparkling water to the juice mixture and transfer to a large pitcher. Serve over ice in tall glasses. If desired, garnish each serving with a half orange slice.

Oranges were not named for their color; the origin of their name comes from the Sanskrit word naranga, *the roots of which mean "fragrant."*

RASPBERRY BANANA SMOOTHIES

These thick, icy cold smoothies, colored hot pink by the raspberries, are perfect for a mid-afternoon or late-night refresher. Serve them with straws so you can slowly sip the delicious puréed fruits.

2 medium ripe bananas

12 ounces frozen unsweetened raspberries

½ cup piña colada fruit juice or mix (see note)

4 mint sprigs for garnish

SERVES 4

Place unpeeled bananas in freezer for 30 to 40 minutes to chill. Then peel them and cut into chunks. Combine in a food processor or in a blender with frozen raspberries and process several seconds to purée. Add piña colada juice and process a few seconds more to mix well.

Fill four 8-ounce glasses with fruit mixture. Garnish each serving with a mint sprig and a straw. Serve immediately while icy cold.

NOTE: A nonalcoholic piña colada mix such as Coco Lopez works well in this recipe.

PEACH SMOOTHIES

2 cups (4 medium) peeled and diced ripe yellow peaches

1 cup vanilla ice cream

3 tablespoons sugar, plus more if needed

2 teaspoons fresh lemon juice, plus more if needed

½ teaspoon vanilla extract

4 ice cubes

Peaches and cream, always a winning duo, are the primary ingredients in these thick, rich smoothies. Sweet, ripe peaches, vanilla ice cream, and a hint of lemon and vanilla are all that is needed to produce these satisfying drinks.

SERVES **2**

Combine all ingredients in a blender or food processor and process until smooth. Taste and add extra lemon or sugar if needed. Pour into 2 tall glasses. Serve immediately, with straws, while they are icy cold.

NOTE: If you want to double this recipe, it is best to make the smoothies in two batches so that all the ingredients will fit comfortably into a processor or blender.

COCONUT BANANA SMOOTHIES

SERVES 4

- **1** 14-ounce can coconut milk (not reduced fat)
- **2** cups (4 small) peeled and diced bananas
- **1** cup vanilla ice cream
- **¼** cup sugar
- **4** teaspoons fresh lime juice
- **2** teaspoons vanilla extract
- **12** ice cubes

These tropically inspired smoothies, made with puréed bananas, coconut milk, and vanilla ice cream, are best served icy cold with a straw. You could serve them in place of dessert for a light backyard supper or enjoy them as a late-afternoon treat on a hot day.

Combine all ingredients in a blender or food processor and process until smooth. Pour into 4 tall glasses. Serve immediately, with straws, while icy cold.

CAIPIRINHAS

Caipirinha, *a celebrated Brazilian drink, is made with lime juice, sugar, and a strong sugarcane brandy known as* **cachaça.** *The popularity of this South American libation has spread far beyond the country's borders so that today its primary ingredient,* **cachaça,** *is widely available. The following recipe serves four and takes only minutes to assemble.*

- **2** cups ice cubes
- **½** to ¾ cup *cachaça*
- **¼** cup fresh lime juice
- **¼** cup sugar

SERVES 4

Coarsely crush ice cubes in a food processor or blender. Divide evenly among 4 wine glasses. In a medium bowl, stir together ½ cup *cachaça,* lime juice, and sugar until sugar is dissolved. Divide evenly and pour over ice in each glass. Taste and, if desired, add 1 tablespoon more of *cachaça* to each glass. Serve cold.

GRAPEFRUIT RED WINE SPRITZERS

These spritzers call for just four ingredients. Grapefruit juice and sugar are heated until the latter has dissolved, then red wine and sparkling water are added. These refreshing drinks, which can be made several hours in advance, are attractive served in ice-filled wine glasses garnished with twists of grapefruit peel.

1⅓ cups fresh or bottled pink grapefruit juice (not from concentrate)

⅓ cup sugar

1 cup sparkling water (such as Perrier)

½ cup dry red wine

Ice cubes

6 strips grapefruit peel (about 3 inches by ½ inch) for garnish (optional)

SERVES

Combine grapefruit juice and sugar in a medium nonreactive saucepan over medium heat, and stir until sugar has dissolved, 1 to 2 minutes. Remove from heat and stir in sparkling water and wine. Cover and refrigerate to chill. (Spritzers can be prepared 5 hours ahead; keep refrigerated until needed.)

Fill 6 medium wine glasses with ice and add some of the grapefruit spritzer mixture to each. If desired, garnish each serving with a twist of grapefruit peel.

The late 19th century was when many soda pops first appeared—Dr. Pepper was invented in 1885 in Waco, Texas; Coca-Cola in 1886 in Atlanta, Georgia; and Pepsi in 1898 in New Bern, North Carolina .

CAPE COD COOLERS

Cranberries and oranges, a refreshing twosome, are combined with white wine to make these tempting coolers. They take only minutes to assemble and are an attractive beverage to offer as a mid-afternoon thirst quencher or as a cooling drink to accompany an outdoor meal.

3½ cups cranberry juice cocktail

1½ cups fresh or bottled orange juice (not from concentrate)

1 cup dry white wine

Ice cubes

1 navel orange, cut into very thin round slices

SERVES **6 TO 8**; MAKES ABOUT 1¾ QUARTS

Combine cranberry juice cocktail, orange juice, and white wine in a nonreactive pitcher, and stir to blend. Refrigerate an hour or longer until well chilled.

To serve, fill tall glasses with ice and pour cranberry cooler mixture into each. Make a slit with a sharp knife halfway through each orange slice and place on the rim of each glass.

MOJITOS

½ cup fresh lime juice (6 limes)

2 tablespoons plus 2 teaspoons sugar

2 teaspoons chopped fresh mint leaves

½ to **1** cup white rum

½ cup club soda

Ice cubes

4 thin round lime slices for garnish

The mojito, a popular drink in Cuba, has found its way from this nearby island to our shores. This version, prepared with lime juice, sugar, mint, white rum, and club soda, is close to the original. However, in Cuba a milder form of mint called **yerba buena** *is used.*

SERVES 4

Combine lime juice, sugar, and mint in a medium bowl. Stir the mixture well, then stir in ½ cup rum and club soda. Taste, and if desired, add up to ½ cup additional rum. Fill four 8-ounce wine glasses with ice cubes, then pour the rum mixture over them. Garnish with a lime slice slit halfway so it fits over the rim of the glass. Serve immediately.

BACKYARD SANGRIA

1 750-milliliter bottle dry red wine, preferably a Spanish wine such as rioja

1½ cups fresh or bottled orange juice (not from concentrate)

¼ cup fresh lemon juice

3 tablespoons sugar

3 tablespoons brandy

1½ tablespoons orange liqueur such as Cointreau, curaçao, or Grand Marnier

1½ cups soda water

1 orange, sliced into thin rounds

1 lemon, sliced into thin rounds

1 peach, peeled and sliced (optional)

Sangria is one of those quintessentials. Like the little black dress, Cole Porter, or a VW Beetle, it never seems to go out of style, and we never tire of sipping it. The following is a classic version made with wine, brandy, oranges, and lemons, plus soda water. For an extra touch, try adding sliced fresh peaches, when in season, as part of the garnish.

SERVES **6 TO 8**; MAKES ABOUT 1¾ QUARTS

Combine wine, orange juice, lemon juice, sugar, brandy, and liqueur in a large non-reactive bowl. Stir well so that sugar is completely dissolved. Cover and refrigerate until chilled.

When ready to serve, transfer mixture to a large, glass pitcher, and add soda water, sliced orange and lemon, and sliced peach, if desired. Serve in wine glasses.

The red-wine-and-fruit-based drink sangria is named for its dark red color—it is derived from the word sangre, *which means "blood" in Spanish.*

HEAT OF SUMMER PIÑA COLADAS

A traditional piña colada (Spanish for strained pineapple) is made with three ingredients: pineapple juice, coconut cream, and rum. The addition of vanilla ice cream makes this version luxuriously smooth and rich. The pineapple juice, coconut cream, and ice cream can be mixed a day ahead and kept chilled in the refrigerator. At serving time, all that is necessary is to combine the pineapple base with crushed ice and rum and to transfer it to a pitcher. Fresh pineapple slices make an attractive and edible garnish for each serving.

3 cups pineapple juice

1 pint vanilla ice cream

6 tablespoons cream of coconut (not coconut milk)

3 cups ice cubes

1 cup plus 2 tablespoons light or dark rum, plus a little extra if desired (see note)

8 thin wedges fresh pineapple (optional)

SERVES 8

In a blender or food processor, combine pineapple juice, ice cream, and cream of coconut. Process until mixture is smooth. (This pineapple base can be prepared 1 day ahead; cover and refrigerate.)

When ready to finish piña coladas, combine half the ice, half the pineapple base, and half the rum in a food processor or blender and process until smooth. Transfer to a pitcher. Repeat with remaining ingredients and add to the pitcher. Taste the mixture and stir in additional rum if desired. Fill 8 large wine or tall glasses with the piña colada mixture. If desired, slit pineapple wedges halfway through and slip onto the rims of the glasses.

NOTE: Although rum is a traditional ingredient in piña coladas, you can omit it from this version if you like, and still have a delicious drink.

CHAPTER 7

RIBBON-WINNING

PIES, CAKES, AND FRUIT DESSERTS

My father had an endearing habit of eating his dessert with his main course. He would taste his steak, his chicken, or his meatloaf, then take a bite of whatever confection my mother had prepared. His philosophy was simple–he didn't want to fill up on his entrée and miss dessert. Although I have never engaged in this ritual, I have been tempted because dessert is my favorite course, too.

When I culled my files in search of ideas for this book, I discovered that I had created two distinctive folders for sweets: One was chock-full of recipes for pies, cakes, and fruit desserts, and the other included cookies, brownies, bars, and ice creams. I followed the same model in this book. This chapter gives due to luscious pies and cakes. More informal treats are the focus of the next chapter.

Glorious berries, cherries, plums, peaches, and nectarines arrive just in time for the backyard cook to use them imaginatively. They can be turned into fillings for perfectly gorgeous pies or baked in delectable crumbles, crisps, buckles, or kuchens. They're also spectacular folded into creamy parfaits or served plain, dusted with spiced sugar. There's no shortage of choices on the following pages. If you are in a pie-making mood, try the Cherry Almond Tart or the Upside-Down Lemon Meringue Pie with Raspberries. Desserts like Blueberry and Peach Crisp or Nectarine Almond Crumble are even simpler.

Cakes of all kinds–pound cakes, loaf cakes, cheesecakes, and layer cakes–are perfect endings to an open-air meal. Best made in advance, they don't require any last-minute fuss. The ones featured here are varied in their flavorings. For chocolate lovers, there's Chocolate Pound Cake as well as a dense Chocolate Toffee Brownie Cake. The refreshing taste of citrus shines through in Lemon Pecan Cake and in Daiquiri Cheesecake. Bananas and carrots get star billing in two all-time favorites, a dense banana nut loaf and a tall, rich carrot cake.

STRAWBERRY ICE-BOX PIE

I've always been a fan of ice-box pies made with graham cracker crusts like this one. Baked until crunchy and golden, this cookie-crust shell is filled with a crimson-hued mixture of strawberries. Chilled until set, the pie is garnished with whipped cream at serving time.

CRUST

6 tablespoons (¾ stick) unsalted butter, melted, plus extra for greasing pie plate

1 cup slivered blanched almonds, toasted (see page 15)

½ cup graham cracker crumbs

¼ cup sugar

FILLING

About 1½ quarts (6 cups) fresh strawberries

¼ cup cornstarch (see note)

1 cup sugar

2 tablespoons fresh lemon juice

2 teaspoons grated orange zest

1½ cups heavy cream

Arrange an oven rack at center position and preheat oven to 350 degrees F. Butter a 9-inch glass pie plate and set aside.

TO MAKE THE CRUST: Process almonds in a food processor, pulsing, until coarsely chopped. Add graham cracker crumbs and sugar and process until mixture resembles fine bread crumbs. Pour in melted butter and process 20 to 30 seconds or until mixture is moistened. Using the back of a tablespoon, press crumbs evenly onto the bottom of the pie plate and up to the edge of the rim. Bake crust until lightly browned, 12 to 15 minutes. Remove and set aside to cool completely.

TO MAKE THE FILLING: Hull and halve enough strawberries lengthwise (quarter any extra-large berries) to yield 5 cups. Save extra berries for another use. Place 2 cups of the berries in a large, heavy saucepan and mash with a potato masher until chunky.

Sift cornstarch and add it along with sugar and lemon juice to the saucepan. Stir well until sugar and cornstarch are completely dissolved. Place pan over medium-high heat, and whisk constantly until mixture begins to bubble. Cook about 1 minute more, until mixture thickens. (Be careful not to cook the mixture more than 1 to 2 minutes once it starts to bubble, or the cornstarch will lose its ability to thicken.)

Remove pan from heat and transfer mixture to a large nonreactive bowl. Cool to room temperature. Fold in the remaining 3 cups of berries and orange zest. Mound filling in the crust. Refrigerate until chilled and firm, 3 to 4 hours. For the best texture, serve the pie the day it is made.

Using an electric mixer, whip cream on high speed until stiff peaks form and place cream in a pastry bag fitted with a medium star tip. Pipe a lattice pattern over the top of the pie. Or, spread cream over berries and make a swirl pattern with a spatula.

NOTE: Strawberries, especially those that are not perfectly ripe, tend to be acidic. Berries that are high in acidity cause cornstarch to break down. Normally 4 tablespoons of cornstarch will work in this recipe, but if your berries are well on the underripe side, you could add another ½ tablespoon.

BLUEBERRY CREAM CHEESE PIE

This pie, with its cheesecake-like base and blueberry pie topping, could not be easier to make. There's no crust to fuss over. Instead, a lemon-scented cream cheese batter bakes in a pie plate and puffs up, then deflates slightly to form a shallow shell, which is filled with glazed blueberries. Dollops of sour cream and fresh mint garnish the tart.

Butter for greasing pie plate

CREAM CHEESE FILLING

12 ounces regular or reduced-fat (not nonfat) cream cheese

½ cup sugar

1½ tablespoons fresh lemon juice

1¼ teaspoons grated lemon zest

½ cup sour cream

2 large eggs

BLUEBERRY TOPPING

3 cups fresh blueberries, divided

½ cup sugar

2¼ teaspoons fresh lemon juice

6 teaspoons sour cream for garnish

6 mint sprigs for garnish

SERVES

Arrange an oven rack at center position and preheat oven to 350 degrees F. Butter a 9-inch Pyrex pie plate.

TO MAKE THE FILLING: With an electric mixer on medium speed, beat cream cheese until smooth, about 3 minutes, scraping down sides of bowl if necessary. Continue beating while gradually adding sugar in a thin stream. Beat in lemon juice and zest. Finally, add sour cream and eggs, and beat until incorporated, scraping down sides of bowl if necessary.

Pour batter into the prepared pie plate and bake until filling is set and a toothpick inserted in middle comes out clean, 25 to 30 minutes. As it bakes, the mixture will puff up. When done, remove pie from oven and cool to room temperature. The filling will deflate slightly as it cools, forming a shallow cavity.

TO MAKE THE TOPPING: Combine half of the blueberries, the sugar, and lemon juice in a medium saucepan over medium heat. Stir constantly. As the mixture cooks, the sugar will liquefy and the berries will cook down and release their juices. Bring to a boil and cook 1 minute. Remove from heat, and stir in remaining blueberries. Cool to room temperature.

When both filling and berries are cool, use a slotted spoon and spread berries evenly on top of pie. Reserve remaining sauce for serving with pie. Refrigerate pie until chilled, 2 hours or longer. (The pie can be prepared 1 day ahead; refrigerate pie and sauce separately. Reheat sauce just to liquefy so that it is easy to pour.)

To garnish pie, spoon 6 dollops of sour cream, evenly spaced, around edge of the blueberry topping. Tuck a mint sprig into each dollop. Serve each slice with a drizzle of reserved blueberry sauce.

BLUE RIBBON APPLE PIE

This dessert is based on my memory of an apple pie that won first place in an Ohio baking contest I judged many years ago. I remembered that the crust had been particularly flaky, and that the filling was perfectly balanced with sweet and tart flavors. However, it was the crunchy, streusel-like topping covering the apples that made the pie so distinctive and helped it garner the blue ribbon. After several attempts, my version came close to the original. The flaky crust is achieved by using shortening along with butter, and the filling works best with Golden Delicious apples, which hold their shape beautifully when baked. Both brown and white sugars blended with butter, flour, and pecans produce the golden topping.

Butter-Rich Sweet Pie Dough (page 19)

FILLING

⅔ cup granulated sugar

2 tablespoons all-purpose flour

½ teaspoon ground cinnamon

¼ teaspoon salt

4 to 5 large Golden Delicious apples

2 teaspoons fresh lemon juice

TOPPING

1 cup coarsely chopped pecans

½ cup all-purpose flour

¼ cup granulated sugar

2 tablespoons light brown sugar

8 tablespoons (1 stick) unsalted butter, chilled and diced

SERVES **6 TO 8**

Roll dough out on a lightly floured surface into a 12-inch round, then transfer it to a 9-inch pie plate. Fold in overhanging dough to form a high-rising border and flute the edges. Refrigerate dough while you prepare the filling and topping.

Arrange an oven rack at center position and preheat oven to 450 degrees F.

TO MAKE THE FILLING: Mix together sugar, flour, cinnamon, and salt in a large bowl. Peel, core, and cut apples into ¼-inch-thick slices to measure 5 cups. Toss apples with lemon juice, then add them to the bowl of dry ingredients and toss well to coat. Fill prepared pie shell with apple mixture, scraping the bowl well.

TO MAKE THE TOPPING: Combine nuts, flour, and sugars in a medium bowl. Sprinkle butter over them and rub into dry ingredients using your fingertips until mixture resembles pea-sized clumps. Sprinkle mixture over the apple filling.

Bake pie for 15 minutes, then reduce heat to 350 degrees F. Bake 20 minutes, then check and cover loosely with foil if the topping or crust is starting to brown too quickly. Continue baking until apples are tender and topping is golden and crisp, about 20 minutes more. Cool 15 minutes before slicing. Serve warm or at room temperature.

UPSIDE-DOWN LEMON MERINGUE PIE WITH RASPBERRIES

In this pie, meringue finds itself in a new role–on the bottom as the crust instead of as a topping. The sweetened egg-white mixture is baked to form the pie shell, which is then filled with a tart lemon cream. Each slice is garnished with fresh raspberries and drizzled with a sauce made of sweetened, puréed berries. Both the pie and the sauce can be prepared several hours ahead.

Butter for greasing pie plate

1 tablespoon unflavored dried bread crumbs

MERINGUE SHELL

½ cup egg whites (about 4 large eggs; save yolks for the filling) at room temperature

1 cup sugar

FILLING

3 large thick-skinned lemons

4 egg yolks

8 tablespoons sugar, divided

1 cup heavy cream

3 cups (1½ pints) fresh raspberries, divided

Arrange an oven rack at center position and preheat oven to 225 degrees F. Butter a 9-inch Pyrex pie plate and sprinkle the bottom with bread crumbs.

TO MAKE THE SHELL: With an electric mixer on medium speed, beat egg whites until soft peaks form. Increase speed to high and continue to beat. Slowly add sugar, 1 tablespoon at a time, until whites form very stiff peaks and are glossy, 7 to 9 minutes total.

With a rubber spatula, spread meringue evenly over the bottom and up the sides of the pie plate to form a shell. Using the back of a spoon, form a slight cavity. Remove any excess meringue from the top edges of the pie plate with a dampened paper towel. Place shell in oven and bake for 1½ to 2 hours, or until the top edges and the center of the meringue are very crisp. Remove and cool to room temperature.

TO MAKE THE FILLING: While shell is baking, grate enough lemons to yield 1 tablespoon zest and set aside. Juice lemons to yield ⅓ cup for the filling and an additional 1 tablespoon for the raspberry sauce.

Combine egg yolks, 6 tablespoons of the sugar, ⅓ cup lemon juice, and all of the lemon zest in a heavy, medium saucepan over medium-low heat. Whisk constantly until mixture coats the back of a spoon and is very thick, about 5 minutes. Transfer to a medium nonreactive bowl and cool to room temperature.

Using an electric mixer, whip cream on high speed until stiff peaks form. Remove ⅓ cup of the cream and fold into the lemon filling to lighten it. Fold remaining cream into the mixture. Spread filling in shell and refrigerate, uncovered, at least 2 to 3 hours until set and firm. (This can be made 1 day ahead, but is best when made and served the same day.)

Process 1 cup of the raspberries, the remaining sugar, and remaining lemon juice in a food processor until mixture is completely puréed, then strain through a fine-mesh strainer to make a smooth sauce.

Garnish each slice of pie with a sprinkle of some of the remaining raspberries and a drizzle of some raspberry sauce.

PEACH TART WITH ALMOND CRUST

A butter-rich nut crust, baked with a filling of fresh sliced peaches sprinkled with sugar and a little lemon zest, makes a tempting dessert to end an outdoor meal. The tart can be served warm soon after it comes from the oven or at room temperature. For an extra indulgence, serve each slice with a scoop of ice cream.

CRUST

6 tablespoons (¾ stick) unsalted butter, chilled and diced, plus extra for greasing tart pan

¾ cup sliced almonds

¾ cup all-purpose flour

6 tablespoons sugar

1 egg yolk, beaten

¼ teaspoon vanilla extract

FILLING

2 tablespoons peach preserves

6 tablespoons sliced almonds, divided

1½ pounds ripe peaches, peeled, cut into ½-inch-thick slices

3 tablespoons sugar

1½ teaspoons grated lemon zest

2 tablespoons unsalted butter, diced

1 pint Crème Fraîche Ice Cream (page 292) or best-quality vanilla ice cream (optional)

SERVES **6 TO 8**

TO MAKE THE CRUST: Butter a 9-inch tart pan with a removable bottom. Coarsely grind almonds in a food processor. Add flour and sugar and continue processing until nuts are finely ground. Add 6 tablespoons butter and pulse machine until mixture resembles coarse meal. Pour egg yolk and vanilla over flour mixture, and pulse again until mixture forms large moist clumps. Remove dough from food processor. Press dough evenly onto bottom and up sides of tart pan to form a crust. Cover and freeze 30 minutes.

When ready to bake pie, arrange an oven rack at center position and preheat oven to 375 degrees F. Bake crust until golden brown, piercing the bottom with a fork if crust bubbles, 20 minutes or longer. Remove, but maintain oven temperature. Cool crust 5 to 10 minutes.

TO MAKE THE FILLING: Spread preserves evenly over bottom of crust. Coarsely chop 4 tablespoons of the almonds and sprinkle over bottom of tart shell. Arrange peaches in an overlapping spiral pattern in shell, and sprinkle them with sugar, then with lemon zest. Dot with butter and sprinkle with remaining almonds. Bake until peaches are tender, about 35 minutes. Cool slightly.

Serve warm or at room temperature with ice cream, if desired.

CHERRY ALMOND TART
WITH A STREUSEL TOPPING

It took several tries one summer before I balanced the cherry and almond flavors in this pie. For the winning version, a precooked pastry shell is filled with a mixture of almond paste, eggs, lemon, and cherries, then baked with a streusel topping. Served with scoops of vanilla ice cream, this tart would make a fine ending to a grill or barbecue menu. Although the tart can be prepared early in the day and reheated, it is best when baked, cooled slightly, and served still warm.

Butter-Rich Sweet Pie Dough (page 19)

FILLING

4 ounces (½ cup) almond paste, crumbled (see note)

2 large eggs, lightly beaten

Pinch of salt

1½ tablespoons fresh lemon juice

2 teaspoons grated lemon zest (about 2 lemons)

3½ cups (about 1¼ pounds) sweet cherries, pitted

STREUSEL

¼ cup all-purpose flour

2½ tablespoons light brown sugar

2½ tablespoons unsalted butter, chilled and diced

1 pint best-quality vanilla ice cream or Burnt-Sugar Vanilla Ice Cream (page 291; optional)

The state fruit of Utah is the cherry.

Roll dough out on a lightly floured surface into a 12-inch round. Transfer to a 9-inch tart pan with a removable bottom. Trim overhanging dough to 1 inch. Fold overhanging dough in and press to form double-thick sides. Prick bottom of crust all over with the tines of a fork. Cover and freeze 30 minutes. Arrange an oven rack at center position and preheat oven to 400 degrees F.

Bake crust until golden brown, piercing the bottom with a fork if crust bubbles, about 20 minutes. Transfer crust to a cooling rack and reduce temperature to 375 degrees F.

TO MAKE THE FILLING: Combine almond paste and eggs in a food processor. Process until mixture is smooth, 15 to 20 seconds. Add salt, lemon juice, and lemon zest, and process 10 seconds more. Pour mixture into tart shell. Arrange cherries on top and press into filling.

TO MAKE THE STREUSEL: Mix together flour and sugar in a small bowl. Add butter and rub into dry ingredients using your fingertips, until mixture resembles pea-sized clumps. Pat over top of cherries. Bake tart until filling is set, 20 minutes or longer. Remove tart from oven and cool 20 minutes.

To serve, remove sides of tart pan. Cut into 6 to 8 servings and garnish each portion with a scoop of ice cream, if desired.

NOTE: Almond paste, which is usually sold in 7- or 8-ounce packages, is available in the baking section of the grocery. Unused almond paste can be wrapped tightly in plastic wrap, then in foil, and frozen for another use.

LEMON TART—PLAIN OR FANCY

This indulgent tart with its golden buttery crust and extra-tart lemon filling can be served plain and unadorned, or with any number of complementary toppings. I love to garnish it with a border of toasted walnuts or almonds. In season, you can encircle the tart with raspberries, blueberries, or strawberries, or a combination of all three.

CRUST

1½ cups all-purpose flour

8 tablespoons (1 stick) unsalted butter, chilled and diced

¼ teaspoon salt

3 tablespoons ice water, plus more if needed

1 large egg yolk, lightly beaten

FILLING

1 cup (2 sticks) unsalted butter

1 cup sugar

⅓ cup fresh lemon juice

1 tablespoon grated lemon zest

3 large eggs

3 large egg yolks

1½ teaspoons vanilla extract

TOPPINGS (OPTIONAL)

½ cup toasted sliced almonds or toasted coarsely chopped walnuts (see page 15)

½ pint fresh raspberries, blueberries, or strawberries tossed with 1 to 2 teaspoons sugar (if berries need sweetening)

SERVES 6 TO 8

TO MAKE THE CRUST: Combine flour, butter, and salt in a food processor. Pulse until mixture resembles coarse meal. Add ice water and egg yolk. Process until moist clumps form, adding more water by teaspoonfuls, if dough is dry. Gather into a ball and flatten into a disk. Wrap in plastic and chill 30 minutes. (Dough can be made 1 day ahead; keep chilled.)

Roll dough out on a lightly floured surface into a 12-inch circle. Carefully transfer dough to a 9-inch tart pan with removable bottom. Trim overhanging dough to 1 inch. Fold overhanging dough in and press to form double-thick sides. Prick bottom of crust all over with the tines of a fork. Cover and freeze 30 minutes. Arrange an oven rack at center position and preheat oven to 375 degrees F.

Bake crust until golden brown, piercing the bottom with a fork if crust bubbles, about 40 minutes. Transfer to a rack to cool.

TO MAKE THE FILLING: Melt butter in a medium saucepan over medium heat and remove from heat. Whisk in sugar, lemon juice and zest, eggs, yolks, and vanilla. Return to medium heat and cook, whisking constantly until mixture thickens, about 10 minutes. (Do not let mixture boil or eggs will curdle.) Reduce heat to low and whisk 2 minutes more. Pour hot filling into prepared shell. Chill, uncovered, until filling is set, 2 hours or longer.

Serve the tart plain or garnish the top with a border of toasted nuts or berries, if desired.

PLUM TART

SERVES **6 TO 8**

Butter-Rich Sweet Pie Dough (page 19)

FILLING

1 tablespoon red currant jelly or jam

1½ pounds (4 to 5 large) plums such as Santa Rosa

3½ tablespoons sugar

Scant ¼ teaspoon ground cinnamon

2½ tablespoons unsalted butter, divided

½ cup sliced almonds

1 pint Crème Fraîche Ice Cream (page 292) or best-quality vanilla ice cream (optional)

The rich, flaky crust of this tart is filled with a single layer of sliced plums that are sprinkled with cinnamon sugar and dotted with butter. A delectable topping of sliced almonds is added at the end of the baking time. The tart, which can be prepared several hours in advance, is good served at room temperature, but even better when quickly reheated and offered warm.

Roll dough out on a lightly floured surface into a 12-inch circle. Carefully transfer dough to a 9-inch tart pan with removable bottom. Trim overhanging dough to 1 inch. Fold overhanging dough in and press to form double-thick sides. Prick bottom of crust all over with the tines of a fork. Cover and freeze 30 minutes. Arrange an oven rack at center position and preheat oven to 400 degrees F.

Bake crust until golden brown, piercing the bottom with a fork if crust bubbles, about 20 minutes. Transfer crust to a cooling rack and reduce temperature to 375 degrees F.

TO MAKE THE FILLING: Spread red currant jelly over bottom of warm tart. Halve plums lengthwise, then cut into ¾-inch-thick slices. Spread plums in prepared shell. Stir sugar and cinnamon together in a small bowl and sprinkle over plums. Cut 1½ tablespoons of the butter into small pieces and dot plums with butter. Bake until plums are juicy and tender and crust is golden, 25 to 30 minutes. Remove from oven but retain oven temperature.

Heat remaining butter and almonds in a small saucepan until butter melts. Then with a spoon, spread the almond mixture in a border on top of tart. Return to oven and bake until nuts are golden, 10 to 15 minutes. Remove and cool slightly before slicing.

Serve warm or at room temperature with scoops of ice cream, if desired.

CARAMEL GLAZED BANANA NUT LOAF

6 tablespoons (¾ stick) unsalted butter at room temperature, plus extra for greasing pan

1⅓ cups all-purpose flour, plus extra for flouring pan

¾ teaspoon baking powder

¾ teaspoon baking soda

½ teaspoon salt

¾ cup sugar

1¼ cups (3 medium) mashed very ripe bananas

2 large eggs, lightly beaten

¾ cup pecans, coarsely chopped

Best Ever Caramel Sauce (page 332) room temperature

One of my earliest childhood memories is of my grandmother's deli-cious banana nut bread. I loved the dark golden loaves moistened with puréed fruit and studded with pecans. Like many of her gener-ation, she never wrote down recipes. "A pinch of this" and "a hand-ful of that" were typical directions she offered. After a week of baking, I finally reproduced a similar loaf and as an extra flourish, spread the top with a creamy caramel glaze. This dessert, which holds up well under refrigeration for several days, would make a fine ending to a backyard picnic, or you could offer slices as an afternoon treat along with iced coffee or tea.

SERVES 6 to 8

Arrange a rack in the lower third of the oven and preheat oven to 350 degrees F. Butter and flour an 8-by-4-inch loaf pan.

Sift together flour, baking powder, baking soda, and salt into a medium bowl and set aside.

With an electric mixer on medium-high speed, cream butter until smooth, about 1 minute. Gradually add sugar and beat until dissolved, 2 to 3 minutes. Lower speed and add dry ingredients. When blended, add bananas and eggs, and beat just until incorporated. Remove from mixer, and fold in nuts.

Pour batter into prepared pan, and spread evenly with a spatula. Bake until a cake tester comes out clean, 55 to 60 minutes. Cool in pan 10 minutes, then unmold onto a cooling rack.

Using an icing spatula or table knife, spread enough of the caramel sauce over the top of the banana loaf to coat evenly. Heat any extra sauce and serve drizzled over slices of banana loaf. (The banana loaf can be stored in an airtight container in the refrigerator for up to 5 days. Bring to room temperature before serving.)

KENTUCKY BOURBON CAKE WITH FRESH BERRIES

This pound cake, made with the traditional ingredients of butter, flour, sugar, and eggs, calls for two extra additions. A sprinkling of chopped pecans is spread on the bottom of the pan before baking, and as the cake's name implies there is bourbon in the batter, which imparts a mellow flavor. This tall cake, which easily serves twenty, is even more glorious when garnished with fresh berries. A native Kentuckian, who always serves this large cake at her Derby Day parties, shared the recipe with me.

- **1** pound (4 sticks) unsalted butter at room temperature, divided
- **3** cups all-purpose flour, divided
- **½** cup chopped pecans
- **3** cups granulated sugar, divided
- **8** large eggs, separated
- **⅔** cup bourbon
- **2** teaspoons vanilla extract
- **2** teaspoons almond extract
  Confectioners' sugar for garnish
- **1** quart fresh strawberries, hulled and halved lengthwise for garnish
- **1** quart fresh blueberries for garnish
  Mint sprigs for garnish

Arrange an oven rack at center position and preheat oven to 350 degrees F.

Use 1 tablespoon of the butter and 2 tablespoons of the flour to grease and flour a 10-inch tube or angel-food cake pan. (A nonstick pan would work particularly well in this recipe, but would still need to be buttered and floured.) Tap out excess flour. Sprinkle chopped pecans in bottom of pan.

With an electric mixer on medium-high speed, cream remaining butter until smooth. Gradually beat in 2 cups of granulated sugar. Add egg yolks, 1 at a time, beating well after each addition.

Combine bourbon, vanilla, and almond extract in a small bowl. Alternately beat ⅓ of the remaining flour and ⅓ of the bourbon mixture into butter mixture. Continue until flour and liquids are all added.

With clean beaters, beat egg whites in a separate bowl on medium-high speed until soft peaks form. Increase speed and gradually add remaining cup of granulated sugar. Fold whites into cake batter in 3 additions. Spoon batter into prepared pan, smoothing top.

Bake cake until a tester inserted in center comes out clean, 1¼ to 1½ hours. Remove pan from oven and set on rack to cool completely. Run knife around inside edges of pan to loosen cake. Invert pan and remove cake to a platter. (Cake can be made 2 days ahead. Store in an airtight container at room temperature.)

To serve, arrange cake, bottom-side up, on a serving platter and dust lightly with confectioners' sugar. Garnish the center and the sides of cake with berries and with several sprigs of mint.

CHOCOLATE POUND CAKE WITH COFFEE ICE CREAM AND WARM CHOCOLATE SAUCE

This is a dessert for those who love chocolate. The easy, make-ahead loaf gets a double dose of chocolate flavoring from cocoa powder and chocolate chips. The cake is delicious plain, but if you want to gild the lily, serve each slice with a scoop of coffee ice cream and a drizzle of Chocolate Coffee Sauce.

14 tablespoons (1¾ sticks) unsalted butter at room temperature, plus extra for greasing pan

1½ cups sifted cake flour, plus extra for flouring pan

½ cup unsweetened cocoa powder

¾ teaspoon baking powder

¼ teaspoon salt

1 cup sugar

3 large eggs

⅓ cup whole milk

1 teaspoon vanilla extract

⅔ cup (about 4 ounces) chocolate chips

1 quart best-quality coffee ice cream
Chocolate Coffee Sauce (page 334)

6 to 8

SERVES

Arrange an oven rack at center position and preheat oven to 350 degrees F. Butter and flour an 8-by-4-inch loaf pan and shake out any excess flour.

Combine 1½ cups flour, cocoa powder, baking powder, and salt in a medium bowl and whisk to blend. Set aside.

With an electric mixer on medium-high speed, cream butter until smooth, 1 minute. Gradually add sugar and beat until mixture is light and fluffy, about 4 minutes. Add eggs 1 at a time, beating well after each addition and stopping to scrape down sides of bowl with a spatula if necessary.

Reduce speed to low. Alternately add dry ingredients and milk, beginning and ending with dry ingredients. Stop and scrape down sides of bowl if necessary. Beat in vanilla. Remove from mixer and fold in chocolate chips. Pour batter into prepared pan and spread evenly with a spatula.

Bake until a cake tester comes out clean, 55 to 60 minutes. Cover top of cake with a sheet of buttered aluminum foil after 35 minutes to prevent top of cake from browning too much. When done, remove and cool 20 minutes. Remove cake from pan. (Cake can be prepared 2 days ahead; cool and store in an airtight container at room temperature.)

To serve, cut cake into ¾-inch-thick slices and arrange on dessert plates. Garnish each portion with a scoop of ice cream and drizzle with Chocolate Coffee Sauce.

Pound cake is so called because the original recipe called for 1 pound each of butter, sugar, flour, and eggs.

LEMON PECAN CAKE WITH LEMON SAUCE

8 tablespoons (1 stick) unsalted butter at room temperature, plus extra for greasing pan

½ cup all-purpose flour, plus extra for flouring pan

1 cup sugar

3 large eggs

1 cup (4 ounces) pecans, finely ground, plus 6 pecan halves for garnish

¼ cup unflavored dried bread crumbs

2 tablespoons fresh lemon juice

1 teaspoon grated lemon zest

Warm Lemon Sauce (page 336)

This delectable, single-layer cake, baked with a small amount of flour and a generous addition of ground nuts, is extra moist. Glazed with a tart, translucent lemon sauce and decorated with pecan halves, the cake can be served plain or garnished with fresh strawberries, blueberries, or raspberries.

SERVES 6 TO 8

Arrange an oven rack at center position and preheat oven to 375 degrees F. Butter and flour an 8-inch round cake pan. Line the pan with a circle of waxed paper cut to fit the bottom of the pan; butter and flour the paper. Tap out excess flour.

With an electric mixer on medium-high speed, cream butter until smooth, 1 minute. Gradually add sugar and beat until mixture is light and fluffy, 3 to 4 minutes. Add eggs, 1 at a time, beating well after each addition and stopping to scrape down sides of bowl with a spatula, if necessary. Lower speed and add ground pecans, flour, and bread crumbs, mixing until well blended. Add lemon juice and zest, and mix well.

Pour the batter into the prepared pan and spread evenly with a spatula. Bake until the cake is golden on top and a tester inserted in the center comes out clean, 25 to 30 minutes. Cool 10 minutes. Run a knife around edges and invert onto a cake rack. Remove waxed paper.

To serve, heat Warm Lemon Sauce until just warm. Pour ¼ to ⅓ cup over the top of the cake and swirl lightly so sauce just covers top of cake. Arrange pecan halves evenly around the edge as a border. Serve each slice with some of the remaining Warm Lemon Sauce. (The cake can be baked, glazed, and decorated 1 day in advance. Place in an airtight container and refrigerate. Bring to room temperature an hour before serving.)

ORANGE ALMOND CAKE WITH ORANGE SAUCE AND ICE CREAM

8 tablespoons (1 stick) unsalted butter at room temperature, plus extra for greasing pan

½ cup all-purpose flour, plus extra for flouring pan

3 large eggs

¾ cup granulated sugar

1 cup almonds, toasted, finely ground (see page 15)

2 tablespoons fresh orange juice

1 tablespoon grated orange zest

½ teaspoon ground coriander

Pinch of salt

Confectioners' sugar

Fresh Orange Sauce (page 335)

1 pint best-quality vanilla ice cream

This airy cake, with almond and orange flavorings, makes a light but satisfying ending to an outdoor meal. For serving, the single-layer torte is cut into slices that are garnished with scoops of vanilla ice cream and drizzled with a refreshing orange sauce.

SERVES 6

Arrange an oven rack at center position and preheat oven to 375 degrees F. Butter an 8-inch springform pan. Line bottom of pan with parchment paper cut to fit the pan. Butter and flour parchment, tapping out excess.

Leave 1 egg whole, but separate the remaining 2 eggs.

With an electric mixer on medium-high speed, cream butter until smooth, 1 minute. Gradually add granulated sugar and beat until mixture is light and fluffy, 3 to 4 minutes. Beat in whole egg, then yolks, 1 at a time, beating well after each addition. Reduce speed to low and beat in almonds, flour, orange juice and zest, coriander, and salt. Stop machine and scrape down the sides of bowl with a spatula, if necessary.

With clean dry beater on medium speed, beat whites in a medium bowl until soft peaks form. Increase speed and beat until stiff but not dry. Fold whites into batter in 2 additions. Transfer to prepared pan.

Bake cake until top is golden and tester inserted into center comes out clean, 30 to 35 minutes. Cool cake in pan on a rack. (Cake can be made 1 day ahead. Keep in an airtight container at room temperature.)

Dust cake with confectioners' sugar. Cut cake into wedges and serve with Fresh Orange Sauce and ice cream.

CARROT CAKE WITH MAPLE CREAM CHEESE ICING

There's nothing better to end an outdoor feast than a stately, moist carrot cake covered with a rich cream cheese icing. This version gets a gentle update with the addition of freshly grated ginger in the cake batter and some maple syrup in the icing.

CAKE

Butter for greasing pan

2 cups all-purpose flour, plus extra for flouring pan

2 teaspoons baking soda

1 teaspoon salt

1 teaspoon ground cinnamon

2 cups sugar

1¼ cups canola oil

4 large eggs

3 cups grated peeled carrots

1¼ cups coarsely chopped walnuts

2 tablespoons minced peeled fresh ginger

ICING

10 ounces cream cheese at room temperature

5 tablespoons unsalted butter at room temperature

2½ cups confectioners' sugar

¼ cup pure maple syrup

12 walnut halves for garnish

Arrange an oven rack at center position and preheat oven to 350 degrees F. Butter two 9-inch cake pans. Line bottom of pans with waxed paper cut to fit. Butter and flour paper; tap out excess flour.

TO MAKE THE CAKE: Whisk flour, baking soda, salt, and cinnamon in a medium bowl to blend. Whisk sugar and oil in a separate large bowl until well blended. Whisk eggs into sugar, 1 at a time. Add flour mixture and stir until blended. Stir in carrots, walnuts, and ginger. Divide batter between prepared pans.

Bake cakes until a tester inserted into center comes out clean, about 40 minutes. Cool cakes in pans 15 minutes. Turn out onto racks. Peel off waxed paper and cool cakes completely.

TO MAKE THE ICING: Using an electric mixer on medium speed, beat cream cheese and butter in a large bowl until light and fluffy. Add confectioners' sugar and beat on low speed until well blended. Beat in maple syrup. Chill until just firm enough to spread, about 30 minutes.

To assemble, place a cake layer on a cake plate or platter. Spread with ¾ cup icing. Top with second layer and spread remaining icing over entire cake. Arrange walnut halves evenly around top edge of cake. (Cake can be made 1 day ahead. Store in an air-tight container; chill. Let stand at room temperature 30 minutes before serving.)

ALMOND GINGER CAKE WITH STRAWBERRIES AND GINGER CREAM

This light, airy cake, made in the French genoise style, is seasoned with both powdered and crystallized ginger and with both toasted almonds and almond extract. For this classic preparation, sugar is slowly beaten with gently warmed eggs until the volume is tripled. Then dry ingredients and melted butter are folded in. Although the batter requires a few extra minutes of beating time, the resulting cake, which is moist and tender, is well worth the effort. Sliced and filled with ginger-scented whipped cream and surrounded with a border of strawberries, this is a cake to serve for special occasions.

CAKE

6 tablespoons unsalted butter, melted, plus extra for greasing pan

1 cup cake flour, plus extra for flouring pan

1 tablespoon ground ginger

¾ cup whole unblanched almonds, toasted and coarsely ground (see page 15)

2 tablespoons very finely chopped crystallized ginger

6 large eggs

½ teaspoon almond extract

1 cup sugar

GINGER CREAM

1½ cups heavy cream

2½ tablespoons confectioners' sugar, plus extra for dusting top of cake

¼ teaspoon almond extract

1½ tablespoons finely chopped crystallized ginger

1 quart fresh strawberries, sliced

1 tablespoon sugar, plus more if needed

Arrange an oven rack at center position and preheat oven to 350 degrees F. Butter a 9-inch springform pan, and line the bottom with parchment paper cut to fit the pan. Butter and flour parchment, tapping out excess.

TO MAKE THE CAKE: Sift flour and ground ginger into a medium bowl. Combine almonds and crystallized ginger in another bowl. Whisk eggs in the bowl of an electric mixer, then place bowl over a pan of simmering water, and stir until eggs are just warm to the touch, a minute or less. Remove from the heat, and with an electric mixer on high speed, beat eggs 2 minutes. Add almond extract, and gradually add sugar, beating until egg mixture is light, has tripled in volume, and is the consistency of softly whipped cream. This should take 4 to 5 minutes in a heavy-duty mixer with a whisk attachment and up to 15 minutes with a hand-held electric mixer. Sift ⅓ of the flour mixture and ⅓ of the nut mixture over the beaten eggs and using a rubber spatula, fold into the eggs. Repeat 2 more times with remaining flour and nuts. Fold in butter in 3 equal additions.

Scrape the batter into prepared pan, and bake until cake is golden brown on top and springs back when lightly pressed, 30 to 35 minutes. Cool in pan 25 minutes. Run a knife around edges to loosen and remove rim. Invert cake onto a rack, remove paper, and cool completely.

TO MAKE THE GINGER CREAM: Using an electric mixer on high speed, whip cream until soft peaks form. Gradually add 2½ tablespoons confectioners' sugar and beat until stiff peaks form. Fold in almond extract and crystallized ginger.

With a serrated knife, cut cake in half horizontally. Place a layer, cut-side up, on a platter, and spread 1½ cups of the Ginger Cream evenly over it. Cover cake with second layer, cut-side down. Cover with plastic wrap and refrigerate at least 2 hours or up to 6 hours to firm filling.

To serve, toss strawberries with 1 tablespoon of sugar; taste and sprinkle with additional sugar if needed. Surround cake with berries. Dust cake with confectioners' sugar. Serve remaining whipped cream in a small bowl.

CHOCOLATE TOFFEE BROWNIE CAKE

Chocolate chips, pecans, and bits of toffee are special additions that are folded into the batter of this seductive chocolate cake. Coated with a dark chocolate glaze, the dense, moist cake, which easily serves ten, can be made a day in advance.

CAKE

8 tablespoons (1 stick) unsalted butter, plus extra for greasing pan

3½ tablespoons unsweetened cocoa powder, divided

¾ cup all-purpose flour

½ teaspoon baking powder

¼ teaspoon salt

2 large eggs

⅔ cup sugar

1¾ cups (about 7 ounces) pecans, coarsely ground

½ cup (about 3 ounces) English toffee bits (see note)

½ cup (about 3 ounces) semisweet chocolate chips

GLAZE

4 ounces bittersweet (not unsweetened) or semisweet chocolate, chopped

3 tablespoons unsalted butter

1 tablespoon honey

¼ cup chopped pecans

½ cup (about 3 ounces) English toffee bits

Arrange an oven rack at center position and preheat oven to 350 degrees F. Butter a 9-inch cake pan with 2-inch sides. Dust bottom and sides of pan with ½ tablespoon cocoa powder, tapping out excess.

TO MAKE THE CAKE: Mix flour, baking powder, and salt in a small bowl and set aside.

Stir butter and remaining 3 tablespoons cocoa powder in a small, heavy saucepan over medium-low heat until butter melts and the mixture is smooth. Remove from heat.

With an electric mixer on medium-high speed, beat eggs and sugar in a large bowl until thick and fluffy, 2 to 3 minutes. On low speed, beat in ¼ cup hot water and the cocoa mixture, then beat in flour mixture. By hand, stir in pecans, toffee bits, and chocolate chips.

Transfer batter to the prepared pan, and smooth the top with a spatula. Bake cake until top is firm and a tester inserted into the center comes out with moist crumbs still attached, about 25 minutes.

Cool cake in pan on a cooling rack 15 minutes. Run a sharp knife around pan sides to loosen the cake. Turn cake out onto a platter. Cool to room temperature.

TO MAKE THE GLAZE: Stir chocolate, butter, and honey in a small saucepan over low heat until chocolate and butter have melted and mixture is smooth. Cool until mixture thickens slightly but is still liquid enough to be poured, about 10 minutes.

With the cake on the platter, pour glaze over top of cake, allowing some to run down the sides. Spread glaze over the top and sides of the cake. Mix together pecan and toffee bits and arrange them in a border on top of the cake. Wipe any chocolate glaze from the cake platter. Chill until glaze is set, about 1 hour. (The cake can be made 1 day ahead. Keep chilled. Let stand at room temperature 15 minutes before serving.)

NOTE: Hershey's Skor English Toffee Bits and Heath Bits of Brickle are two good products, which are available in the baking section of most supermarkets.

DAIQUIRI CHEESECAKE

It took several attempts to get this dessert perfected, but the final results yielded a smooth, creamy cheesecake, finely balanced in both sweet and tart notes with a crisp bottom crust. This splendid cake flavored with lime, lemon, and rum is better when made a day ahead, and would be ideal for a large gathering since it easily serves twelve.

CRUST

4 tablespoons (½ stick) unsalted butter, melted, plus extra for greasing pan

1 cup graham cracker crumbs

2½ tablespoons sugar

FILLING

4 to **5** limes

2 to **3** lemons

2 pounds regular or reduced-fat (not nonfat) cream cheese at room temperature

1 cup, plus 1 ½ tablespoons sugar, divided

3 tablespoons light rum

1 tablespoon cornstarch

4 large eggs

½ cup regular or reduced-fat (not nonfat) sour cream

⅓ cup chopped unsalted pistachios (optional; see note)

Arrange an oven rack at center position and preheat oven to 350 degrees F. Butter a 9-inch springform pan.

TO MAKE THE CRUST: Stir crumbs and sugar in the prepared pan. Add melted butter, and mix well with 2 forks. Press firmly onto bottom of pan. Bake 8 minutes. Remove and cool, but retain oven temperature.

TO MAKE THE FILLING: Grate enough peel from the limes to yield 2 teaspoons zest and juice them to yield 3 tablespoons. Grate enough peel from the lemons to yield 2 teaspoons and juice them to yield 3 tablespoons. Set aside.

Beat cream cheese in the bowl of an electric mixer on medium-high speed while gradually adding 1 cup of the sugar. Beat until well blended, then lower speed and add 1½ teaspoons each of the lime and lemon zests. Add all but 1 teaspoon each of the lime and lemon juices. Add rum, then cornstarch. Add eggs, 1 at a time, beating well after each addition. Pour the batter into the prepared pan. Bake until a tester inserted into the middle comes out almost clean, about 45 minutes. Turn oven off and remove cheesecake.

In a small bowl, whisk together sour cream, remaining 1½ tablespoons sugar, and the remaining lime and lemon zests and juices. Spread mixture evenly over top of cheesecake. Return cheesecake to turned-off oven and close door. Leave in oven for 45 minutes.

Remove cheesecake from oven, cool to room temperature, cover, and refrigerate 4 to 6 hours. (The cheesecake can be prepared 1 day ahead; keep refrigerated.) To serve, run a small knife around inside edges of pan, then remove sides from pan and transfer cake to a serving plate. Make a 1-inch border on top of cake with chopped pistachios, if desired.

NOTE: In place of the pistachio garnish, you could slice any remaining lemons or limes into paper-thin rounds. Halve the rounds and arrange them in an alternating, slightly overlapping border on top of the cake.

NO-BAKE LEMON CHEESECAKE
WITH **WARM BLUEBERRY SAUCE**

This cheesecake, which is a snap to assemble, is perfect for when you need a delicious dessert but have little time for cooking. The crust, made with shortbread cookie crumbs, gets baked for less than 10 minutes. A filling of cream cheese blended with purchased lemon curd (bound with gelatin) is added. Then the cake goes straight to the refrigerator, bypassing the oven. At serving time, the cheesecake is sliced and drizzled with warm blueberry sauce.

CRUST

1 5- to 5.3-ounce package pure-butter shortbread cookies (see note)

FILLING

¼ cup half-and-half

1 packet (2 teaspoons) unflavored gelatin

24 ounces regular or reduced-fat (not nonfat) cream cheese at room temperature

1 cup purchased lemon curd

2 teaspoons grated lemon zest

Warm Blueberry Sauce (page 337)

Arrange an oven rack at center position and preheat oven to 350 degrees F.

TO MAKE THE CRUST: Process shortbread cookies in the bowl of a food processor until finely ground. Press into an 8-inch springform pan in an even layer on the bottom and about ¾ inch up the sides. Bake until crumbs are lightly browned, 7 to 8 minutes. Cool completely.

TO MAKE THE FILLING: Pour half-and-half into a small saucepan, and sprinkle gelatin over it. Let stand for 1 minute. Place saucepan over low heat and whisk constantly until gelatin dissolves, 1 to 2 minutes. Remove from heat and cool.

With an electric mixer on medium-high speed, whip cream cheese until fluffy. Add lemon curd and beat until blended completely with cream cheese. Stop mixer and scrape down sides of bowl as necessary. Beat in lemon zest. Lower speed, pour in half-and-half mixture, and beat just until blended. Pour batter into prepared crust and spread evenly with a spatula. Cover with plastic wrap and refrigerate until completely set, 4 hours or overnight.

To serve, bring cheesecake to room temperature for 45 minutes. Run a small knife around inside edges of pan, then remove sides from pan and transfer cake to a serving plate. Serve slices of cheesecake with Warm Blueberry Sauce.

NOTE: Be sure to use pure-butter shortbread cookies. They contain enough butter so that you don't need to add melted butter to the crumbs for the crust. I like Walker's Shortbread Cookies, available in many groceries.

BLUEBERRY AND PEACH CRISP

Butter for greasing baking dish

FRUIT FILLING

½ cup plus 2 tablespoons lightly packed light brown sugar

6 tablespoons all-purpose flour

1½ teaspoons ground cinnamon

½ teaspoon ground ginger

4 pounds ripe, but not mushy, peaches

3 cups fresh blueberries

STREUSEL TOPPING

¾ cup all-purpose flour

¾ cup lightly packed light brown sugar

½ teaspoon ground cinnamon

1⅓ cups pecans, coarsely chopped

9 tablespoons unsalted butter, chilled and diced

1 quart Crème Fraîche Ice Cream (page 292) or best-quality vanilla ice cream (optional)

Baked until the topping is golden brown and the fruit filling beneath is bubbling hot, this crisp, which serves ten, is ideal for a crowd. The crisp can be baked ahead and reheated so there is no last minute fuss.

SERVES 10

Arrange an oven rack at center position and preheat oven to 375 degrees F. Butter a shallow, 3-quart, ovenproof baking dish.

TO MAKE THE FILLING: Mix together sugar, flour, cinnamon, and ginger in a large bowl. Peel peaches, halve, and cut them into ½-inch-thick wedges. Add them and blueberries to the bowl with flour mixture. Toss well to coat. Spoon the mixture and any loose remaining seasonings into the prepared baking dish. Spread evenly.

TO MAKE THE TOPPING: Mix together flour, sugar, and cinnamon in a medium bowl. Add pecans and butter and rub into dry ingredients using your fingertips until mixture resembles pea-sized clumps. Scatter streusel mixture evenly over the fruit in the baking dish.

Bake the crisp until the fruit is tender and bubbling and the topping well browned, 35 to 40 minutes. Remove and cool 10 minutes. (The crisp can be prepared 3 to 4 hours ahead; leave at room temperature. Reheat in a preheated 350-degree F oven 15 minutes or longer before serving.)

Serve each portion of the crisp with a scoop of ice cream, if desired.

NECTARINE ALMOND CRUMBLE

Butter for greasing baking dish

FRUIT FILLING

2 pounds nectarines

1½ tablespoons fresh lemon juice

2 tablespoons sugar, plus more if needed

¼ teaspoon ground cinnamon

¼ teaspoon ground ginger

TOPPING

⅓ cup light brown sugar

⅓ cup all-purpose flour

⅓ cup quick or regular oatmeal

⅓ cup sliced almonds

3 tablespoons unsalted butter, chilled and diced

Burnt-Sugar Vanilla Ice Cream (page 291) or best-quality vanilla ice cream (optional)

Sliced nectarines, sweetened and spiced, are topped with a crumbled mixture of butter and flour mixed with oats, nuts, and sugar. When pulled from the oven, the warm and juicy fruit slices are covered with a crisp, golden coating. The warm crumble is even better when garnished with scoops of ice cream.

SERVES 6

Arrange an oven rack at center position and preheat oven to 375 degrees F. Butter a shallow, 2-quart, ovenproof baking dish.

TO MAKE THE FILLING: Peel and halve nectarines, then cut into ½-inch-thick wedges. Place the slices in the prepared baking dish and drizzle with lemon juice. In a small bowl, mix together 2 tablespoons sugar, cinnamon, and ginger and toss with the nectarine slices. Taste and, if needed, sprinkle with a little additional sugar.

TO MAKE THE TOPPING: Mix together sugar, flour, oatmeal, and almonds in a medium bowl. Add butter and rub into dry ingredients using your fingertips, until mixture resembles pea-sized clumps. Pat mixture evenly over the fruit.

Bake until the fruit is tender and bubbling and the topping well browned, 45 to 50 minutes. Cool 10 minutes. (The crumble can be prepared 3 to 4 hours ahead; leave uncovered at room temperature. Reheat in a preheated 350-degree F oven to warm, 15 minutes or longer.)

Serve each portion of the crumble with a scoop of ice cream, if desired.

STOVERS' BLUEBERRY BUCKLE

Blueberries are nestled into a rich cake batter and baked under a golden topping of butter, flour, brown sugar, and cinnamon in this old-fashioned dessert. The contrast of textures–the soft luscious cake with the juicy berries covered with the crisp streusel–is what makes this confection so irresistible. The recipe came to me from Ohio cooking teacher and lawyer Steve Stover, whose mother, Virginia, has served this buckle for over 50 years.

BATTER

4   tablespoons unsalted butter at room temperature, plus extra for greasing baking dish

1   cup sifted all-purpose flour, divided

2   cups fresh blueberries

1   teaspoon baking powder

¼   teaspoon salt

½   cup sugar

1   large egg, beaten

½   teaspoon vanilla extract

⅓   cup whole milk

TOPPING

¾   cup light brown sugar

½   cup all-purpose flour

5   tablespoons unsalted butter, chilled and diced

1   teaspoon ground cinnamon

1   pint Crème Fraîche Ice Cream (page 292) or best-quality vanilla ice cream (optional)

Arrange an oven rack at center position and preheat oven to 375 degrees F. Butter a shallow 2-quart baking dish or a 9-inch square baking dish.

TO MAKE THE BATTER: Toss 2 tablespoons of the flour with the blueberries in a bowl and reserve. Stir remaining flour, baking powder, and salt together and set aside.

With an electric mixer on medium-high speed, cream butter and sugar until smooth, 2 to 3 minutes, stopping machine and scraping down the sides of the bowl as necessary. Beat in egg and vanilla and mix well to blend. Beat in half of the dry ingredients, then milk, and finally the remaining dry ingredients, mixing well after each addition.

Remove from mixer and gently fold in the floured blueberries. Scrape any flour remaining in the bowl into the batter. Spread the batter evenly in the prepared baking dish.

TO MAKE THE TOPPING: Combine sugar, flour, butter, and cinnamon in a food processor and pulse until mixture resembles pea-sized clumps. Scatter topping evenly over the batter.

Bake until topping is a rich golden brown, 40 to 45 minutes. Remove and cool 10 minutes. Serve warm with ice cream, if desired.

BETTY GORMAN'S RASPBERRY KUCHEN

This recipe was given to me many years ago by one of my students. Although called a kuchen, which is a German yeast-raised cake filled with fruit or cheese, this version does not include a yeasted batter. Instead, a rich pastry dough is baked in a springform pan, then spread with raspberry jam and topped with meringue. Cut into wedges and garnished with fresh raspberries, this dessert would make an attractive, yet simple, finale for any backyard meal.

16 tablespoons (2 sticks) unsalted butter at room temperature

½ cup confectioners' sugar

1 cup sifted all-purpose flour

2 large eggs, separated

½ cup sugar

¼ teaspoon ground cinnamon

½ cup coarsely chopped pecans

1 12-ounce jar seedless raspberry jam

1 pint fresh raspberries

Fresh mint sprigs for garnish

8 SERVES

Arrange an oven rack at center position and preheat oven to 350 degrees F. Use some of the butter to lightly grease the bottom of an 8-inch springform pan.

With an electric mixer on medium-high speed, cream remaining butter until smooth, 1 minute. Gradually add confectioners' sugar and beat until light and fluffy, 2 to 3 minutes. Add flour and egg yolks and beat until ingredients are well blended, 1 to 2 minutes.

Spread and flatten dough evenly onto the bottom of the prepared pan. Bake crust 15 minutes. While crust is baking, prepare meringue. Mix sugar and cinnamon together in a bowl. Beat egg whites in the bowl of an electric mixer on medium speed until soft peaks start to form. Increase speed to high and beat until whites start to expand and hold a shape. Gradually add sugar mixture, 1 tablespoon at a time, until whites are stiff and glossy, 7 to 9 minutes. Remove meringue from mixer and fold in pecans. Set aside.

When crust has baked 15 minutes, remove from oven but retain oven temperature. Spread jam evenly over the warm crust. Then use spatula to spread meringue evenly over jam layer.

Return kuchen to oven and bake until meringue is golden brown, 30 to 35 minutes more. Cool to room temperature. (Kuchen can be made 2 hours ahead. Cover loosely with foil and leave at cool room temperature.)

To serve, remove sides from pan. Place kuchen on a serving platter, and garnish top and sides with fresh raspberries and mint sprigs. Cut into 8 wedges.

CHILLED SUMMER CREAMS WITH FRESH BERRIES

1 package (2½ teaspoons) unflavored gelatin

2½ cups heavy cream

1 cup sugar

2 cups regular (not reduced-fat or nonfat) sour cream

1 teaspoon vanilla extract

1½ to **2** pints (3 to 4 cups) fresh strawberries, sliced, or half strawberries and half blueberries, divided

Mint leaves for garnish

This rich dessert made with both heavy and sour creams is an indulgence, but the taste is so luscious and the texture so velvety that it's worth it. Plan on 15 minutes to assemble the chilled creams, and then put them in the refrigerator several hours or, even better, overnight. Although strawberries and blueberries are my favorite choices to pair with these snowy white creams, raspberries work well, too.

SERVES **6**

Place gelatin in a small bowl and cover with ¼ cup cold water. Stir to dissolve. Set aside.

Combine heavy cream, sugar, and dissolved gelatin in a medium, heavy saucepan over medium heat. Stir until mixture is warm. Let cool to room temperature. Fold in sour cream and vanilla and ⅔ of the berries.

Divide the cream evenly among 6 medium to large wine glasses and refrigerate until firm, 1 to 2 hours or more. (The creams can be made 1 day ahead. Cover the tops of wine glasses with plastic wrap if refrigerating overnight.)

To serve, ladle a few of the remaining berries on top of each chilled cream and garnish each serving with a mint sprig.

CREAMY LEMON PARFAITS
WITH RASPBERRIES

When you don't have time to fuss over a dessert, this is a good recipe to call upon. Store-bought lemon curd (enhanced with some extra lemon juice and zest) is combined with whipped cream and raspberries. Served in large wine glasses with a garnish of fresh berries, these parfaits make a distinctive presentation and look as if they took far more effort than what is required.

1½ cups heavy cream

2 11-ounce jars lemon curd (see notes)

2½ tablespoons fresh lemon juice

2 tablespoons grated lemon zest

3 cups (about 1½ pints) fresh raspberries, divided (see notes)

6 fresh mint sprigs for garnish

6
SERVES

Using an electric mixer, whip cream on medium-high speed in a large bowl until stiff peaks form. Mix together lemon curd, lemon juice, and lemon zest in another large bowl. Fold in whipped cream, and then 2 cups of the raspberries.

Divide lemon mixture among 6 large wine glasses. Cover and chill until parfaits are cold, at least 30 minutes or longer. (Parfaits can be made 1 day ahead. Keep covered and refrigerated.)

To serve, sprinkle remaining raspberries on top of the parfaits and garnish with mint sprigs.

NOTES: Robertson's lemon curd is widely available and works well in this recipe.

: You could substitute hulled, sliced strawberries or fresh blueberries for the raspberries.

STRATEGIES DUSTED WITH CARDAMOM SUGAR

Strawberries always taste good sprinkled with a little sugar. But try splashing the berries first in some Grand Marnier, then dusting them with sugar combined with ground cardamom for a more interesting dessert. The enticing hint of cardamom and the orange scent of the liqueur complement strawberries beautifully.

½ cup sugar

½ teaspoon ground cardamom (see note)

4 tablespoons Grand Marnier

4 pints fresh strawberries, hulled

Mint sprigs for garnish

SERVES 6

Combine sugar and cardamom in a small bowl and set aside. (Cardamom sugar can be made 2 to 3 days ahead. Cover and leave at room temperature.)

At serving time, pour Grand Marnier into a large bowl. Add strawberries and toss to coat well. Spread half the cardamom sugar on a dinner plate and roll half the berries in sugar to coat well. Divide berries among 3 wide-mouthed wine glasses or goblets. Coat remaining berries with cardamom sugar and place in 3 more glasses. Pour any remaining Grand Marnier in mixing bowl over berries in glasses. Garnish each serving with a mint sprig.

NOTE: Ground cardamom can vary in its aroma and taste. A new bottle of the spice will usually be extremely fragrant and very intense in flavor, while an opened bottle that has been on the shelf for a while might not be as aromatic. Taste the cardamom sugar and before using it, add more cardamom in very small quantities if needed.

A strawberry, on average, contains about 200 tiny seeds.

GINGER SHORTCAKES WITH PEACHES

These flaky shortcakes owe their distinctive taste to dried and candied ginger, both of which are used to season the dough. The warm biscuits, sliced and filled with fresh peaches, are served with dollops of sweetened whipped cream.

SHORTCAKES

- **2** cups all-purpose flour
- **¼** cup finely chopped crystallized ginger
- **2** tablespoons sugar
- **2½** teaspoons baking powder
- **1** teaspoon ground ginger
- **¾** teaspoon salt
- **6** tablespoons unsalted butter, chilled and diced
- **¾** cup half-and-half

PEACHES AND CREAM

- **2** pounds ripe yellow peaches (see note)
- **1** large lemon
- **2** to **3** teaspoons granulated sugar
- **1½** cups heavy cream
- **¼** cup confectioners' sugar, plus extra for garnish

  Mint leaves for garnish (optional)

Plant City, Florida, produced a strawberry shortcake that weighed 6,000 pounds and made the Guinness Book of World Records *in 1999.*

SERVES 6

Arrange an oven rack at center position and preheat oven to 400 degrees F. Have ready an ungreased baking sheet.

TO MAKE THE SHORTCAKES: Whisk together flour, crystallized ginger, sugar, baking powder, ground ginger, and salt in a medium bowl. Add butter, and rub it into the dry ingredients with your fingertips until mixture resembles pea-sized clumps. Add half-and-half and stir gently, just until all dry ingredients are moistened and blended. Do not overmix. With floured hands, gather the dough into a ball and lightly knead it about 8 to 10 times against the sides of the bowl, just to incorporate any loose bits of dough.

On a floured work surface, roll out dough into a ¾-inch-thick circle and using a 3-inch-round cutter, cut out 6 pieces. Gather dough scraps together and roll again to get an additional 1 to 2 rounds (these will not be quite as picture perfect as the earlier ones). Place rounds on the baking sheet with several inches between each, and bake until golden, 12 to 15 minutes. Remove to a rack to cool. (The shortcakes can be prepared 4 to 5 hours ahead. Cool, place in an airtight container, and leave at room temperature.)

TO MAKE THE PEACHES AND CREAM: When ready to serve, peel and halve peaches lengthwise. Cut into ½-inch slices and place in a bowl. Grate the lemon to get ¼ teaspoon zest and set aside, then juice the lemon to yield 2 teaspoons. Sprinkle lemon juice and granulated sugar over peaches and toss to mix.

Using an electric mixer, whip cream on medium-high speed in a large bowl just until soft peaks form, then beat in confectioners' sugar and lemon zest. Split and lightly toast 6 of the shortcakes. (Save extras for snacking.) Place bottoms on 6 dessert plates and divide and mound peaches on top of them. Ladle ½ cup whipped cream on top of each and cover with shortcake tops. Dust shortcakes with confectioners' sugar, and garnish each with a mint sprig, if desired. Serve immediately.

NOTE: You can substitute 1 to 1½ quarts strawberries. Hull and halve them. Season with sugar and lemon to taste.

HOMEMADE

8

COOKIES, BROWNIES, CUPCAKES, AND ICE CREAMS

What could be more comforting than a plate of sweet nibbles and scoops of homemade ice cream to end a delicious outdoor meal or to star in an afternoon tea party? Cookies, brownies, cupcakes, and those little bars and squares with luscious toppings are what I think of as little pick-ups. Even though they are decadently rich, we can eat them without guilt because they are mere mouthfuls.

In this chapter, you'll find a dozens of recipes for both sweet bites and ice-cream confections. You can opt for serving the little pick-ups and the ice creams separately, since they can easily stand on their own as a finale to a meal. But you can also have fun pairing a cookie or a cupcake with an ice cream or sorbet for an extra-special ending.

Chocolate figures prominently in many of these confections. Chocolate Chip Maple Pecan Cookies (made with extra-rich dark chocolate), Chocolate Heaven Cookies so grand that they needed a celestial name, Mini Chocolate Almond Cupcakes, Chocolate Mint Brownies, and Chocolate Cardamom Ice Cream should satisfy your cravings.

If Americans were to compose a list of their favorite warm-weather desserts, there's no doubt ice creams would be right up there at the top. Two vanilla ice creams get new spins. One is made with "burnt," or caramelized, sugar, which provides a fresh dimension of flavor, while another is prepared with crème fraîche. A crunchy almond praline powder permeates one variety, while coconut milk adds its distinctive taste to another home-churned creation. Strawberry, grapefruit, and banana lend their assertive flavors to refreshing sorbets. Other creations include sundaes and a memorable ice-cream sandwich. And, if you don't have an ice cream maker, you might want to consider getting one of the new, modestly priced electric models that make ice-cream making a breeze.

CHOCOLATE CHIP MAPLE PECAN COOKIES

It was in London that I came upon this version of the all-American cookie. On a visit to England's capital, I stopped by the bakery at Clarke's Restaurant, a favorite culinary haunt of mine, and picked up a package of chocolate chip maple pecan cookies. One bite and I was addicted! I called the owner, Sally Clarke, who was willing to share the ingredients and a few tips about assembling the dough. The secret to these sublime cookies lies in using high-quality dark bittersweet chocolate in place of chips, in baking with unbleached flour, which produces a darker-crusted cookie, and in adding maple syrup for a special sweet accent.

1½ cups unbleached all-purpose flour

1½ teaspoons baking powder

¾ teaspoon baking soda

¾ teaspoon salt

5 ounces best-quality dark bittersweet or semisweet chocolate (see note)

12 tablespoons (1½ sticks) unsalted butter, chilled and diced

¾ cup sugar

2½ tablespoons pure maple syrup

1 cup chopped pecans, plus about 20 pecan halves for garnish

Massachusetts is the home of the chocolate chip cookie (also known as the Toll House cookie), created in 1930 at the Toll House Restaurant near Whitman, Massachusetts, by Ruth Graves Wakefield.

Arrange an oven rack at center position and preheat oven to 375 degrees F. Line 2 large baking sheets with aluminum foil and set aside.

Sift flour, baking powder, baking soda, and salt into a medium bowl. Set aside.

Place chocolate on a work surface and chop finely with a sharp knife.

With an electric mixer on medium-high speed, cream together butter and sugar until light and fluffy, 3 to 4 minutes. Pour in maple syrup, then reduce speed to low, and gradually add sifted dry ingredients, beating to combine. Mixture will be somewhat lumpy, rather than smooth. If necessary, stop mixer and scrape down sides of bowl with a rubber spatula.

Remove from mixer and stir in chopped chocolate and chopped pecans with a wooden spoon. Gather the dough into a mass and shape into a ball. Cover with plastic wrap and refrigerate 30 minutes to chill and firm dough.

Divide dough in half. Pinch off 10 pieces (about 2 to 2½ tablespoons each) from half and roll each into a golf-ball shape. Place balls on 1 of the baking sheets, leaving at least 2 inches around each. Flatten balls with your fingers so they are about ½ inch thick and then press a pecan in the center of each. Repeat with remaining dough to fill second baking sheet.

Put 1 baking sheet in refrigerator. Place the other in preheated oven and bake until cookies are brown around the edges, about 14 minutes. Remove and cool 3 minutes on baking sheet, then remove cookies with a spatula and cool completely on a rack. Bake second sheet of cookies in same way and cool. Store in an airtight container at room temperature. (Cookies can be prepared 5 days ahead.)

NOTE: A dark, high-quality chocolate with 70% cocoa works best in this recipe. Callebaut, Valrhona, or Scharffen Berger are good brands and are available in some supermarkets and in specialty food stores.

MAKES 20 COOKIES

CHUNKY PEANUT BUTTER COOKIES

1½ cups all-purpose flour

½ teaspoon baking soda

¼ teaspoon salt

8 tablespoons (1 stick) unsalted butter at room temperature

½ cup smooth peanut butter

½ cup sugar

½ cup lightly packed light brown sugar

1 large egg, lightly beaten

½ teaspoon vanilla extract

½ cup unsalted dry-roasted peanuts, chopped

Made with both peanut butter and coarsely chopped peanuts, these golden cookies are moist and have a delectably crunchy texture. It takes only a few minutes to assemble and bake these cookies, which will keep well for several days when stored in an airtight container.

MAKES **36 TO 40** COOKIES

Arrange an oven rack at center position and preheat oven to 350 degrees F. Have ready 2 large ungreased baking sheets.

Sift flour, baking soda, and salt into a small bowl and set aside.

With an electric mixer on medium-high speed, cream butter and peanut butter together until smooth, 2 to 3 minutes. Gradually add both sugars, beating until dissolved, 2 to 3 minutes. Add egg and vanilla and beat just to incorporate. Reduce speed to low and add dry ingredients, beating until flour is blended into the dough, 1 minute or less. Remove and stir in chopped peanuts.

Form dough into balls that are 1 inch in diameter. Place balls 2 inches apart on the cookie sheets. With the tines of a fork, press down on each, making a criss-cross pattern and flattening the cookies so they are about 1¾ inches round.

Bake 1 sheet at a time until cookies are browned around the edges, 9 to 11 minutes. Halfway during baking, reverse the sheet front to back so that cookies brown evenly. Cool on baking sheet 1 to 2 minutes. Using a spatula, transfer cookies to a rack to cool to room temperature. Store in an airtight container at room temperature. (Cookies can be prepared 3 days ahead.)

PECAN SHORTBREAD COOKIES

A generous amount of butter, plus ground nuts, is what makes these cookies so rich and special. Baked until golden brown and crisp, these delectable little cakes could be served accompanied simply by glasses of iced coffee for dessert or offered as a garnish to sorbets or ice creams or sliced watermelon.

1 cup all-purpose flour, plus extra for dusting

⅛ teaspoon baking soda

Pinch of salt

8 tablespoons (1 stick) unsalted butter, chilled and diced

½ cup pecans, toasted (see page 15) and coarsely ground, plus 16 pecan halves, untoasted, for garnish

¼ cup sugar

1 teaspoon vanilla extract

MAKES 16 COOKIES

Arrange an oven rack at center position and preheat oven to 325 degrees F. Have ready 1 or 2 large ungreased baking sheets.

Sift 1 cup flour, baking soda, and salt into a medium bowl. Add butter and cut in with a pastry blender or 2 table knives until butter is coated with flour but still in chunks. Rub butter into dry ingredients with fingertips, until mixture resembles pea-sized clumps.

Add ground pecans, sugar, and vanilla to bowl and mix well. Gather dough into a mass, and then knead on a work surface several times until smooth. Shape into a ball and flatten into a disk. Place a large sheet of waxed paper on a work surface and flour lightly. Place dough in center and cover with another large sheet of waxed paper. Roll dough into a circle ¼ to ⅜ inch thick. Using a 2-inch fluted or plain cookie cutter, cut out as many rounds as you can and transfer to the ungreased baking sheet. Reshape and roll out dough again to same thickness, and cut out more cookies. Continue until all the dough is used. You should get 16 cookies. Press a pecan half in the center of each cookie top.

Cover cookies on baking sheet with plastic wrap and refrigerate until firm, 10 to 15 minutes. Remove plastic wrap and bake until cookies are lightly browned on bottom and top, 25 to 28 minutes. Transfer cookies to a rack to cool completely. Store in an airtight container. (Cookies can be baked 2 days ahead.)

CHOCOLATE HEAVEN COOKIES

A small amount of flour and a very short baking time are what make these cookies unique and worthy of their name. Only ½ cup of flour is called for, and the cookies are in the oven for just 10 minutes. This yields cookies with firm, crackly exteriors and moist, fudgy centers that taste, as the name implies, "heavenly." Serve these addictive morsels alone or offer them as a garnish to fresh berries or ice cream.

½ cup all-purpose flour

½ teaspoon baking powder

¼ teaspoon salt

6 ounces semisweet chocolate, broken into chunks

4 tablespoons (½ stick) unsalted butter, diced

2 large eggs

1 teaspoon instant coffee powder or crystals

1 cup sugar

½ cup (about 3 ounces) semisweet chocolate chips

½ cup chopped walnuts or pecans

"Cookie" comes from the Dutch word kookje, *a diminutive form of* koek, *which means cake.*

MAKES ABOUT **36** COOKIES

Arrange an oven rack at lower position and preheat oven to 325 degrees F. Line 2 baking sheets with parchment paper. (Do not omit the parchment paper, which is essential to this recipe to keep the cookies from sticking.)

Sift flour, baking powder, and salt into a bowl and set aside.

In the top of a double boiler (or in a heat-proof bowl) set over but not touching simmering water, stir chocolate and butter constantly until mixture is smooth and shiny, 2 to 3 minutes. Remove from heat and set aside.

In a large bowl, beat eggs and powdered coffee with an electric mixer on medium speed for 30 seconds. Gradually add sugar and beat until sugar is dissolved and mixture is thick and pale yellow in color, about 2 minutes. With mixer on low speed, beat in melted chocolate mixture, then flour mixture. Remove from mixer and stir in chocolate chips and walnuts by hand.

Drop the batter by generous teaspoonfuls 2 inches apart onto the baking sheets. Bake, 1 sheet at a time, 9 to 10 minutes. Cookies will look cracked and shiny on the outside and may not appear to be set. Remove from oven and let cookies cool to room temperature, 5 to 10 minutes. Using a spatula, transfer to racks to cool completely. Repeat until all cookies are baked.

Store cookies in an airtight container at cool room temperature. (They can be prepared 2 days ahead.)

DEB BARRETT'S CHOCOLATE ORANGE BISCOTTI

Several years ago at the end of a cooking class I taught in New Jersey, an assistant, Deb Barrett, gave me a small bag of homemade biscotti. I took one bite and knew I was in for a treat. The Italian word biscotti *translates as "twice cooked," and these delectable cookies—a blend of crisp, golden baked dough studded with bits of chocolate, pecans, and orange peel—are baked two times, once in log shapes, then in slices. They are especially good served with ice creams or sorbets. Stored in an airtight container, they keep well for several days.*

8 tablespoons (1 stick) unsalted butter at room temperature

¾ cup sugar

2 large eggs

2 tablespoons Grand Marnier

1 tablespoon grated orange zest

2 cups plus 2 tablespoons all-purpose flour

1½ teaspoons baking powder

¼ teaspoon salt

1 cup lightly toasted pecans, coarsely chopped (see page 15)

6 ounces best-quality bittersweet chocolate, chopped

Arrange an oven rack at center position and preheat oven to 350 degrees F. Line a large baking sheet with parchment paper and set aside.

With an electric mixer on medium-high speed, cream butter and sugar until light and fluffy, 3 to 4 minutes. Stop and scrape down the sides of the bowl as necessary. Beat in eggs, 1 at a time, then beat in orange liqueur and zest.

In a separate bowl, sift together flour, baking powder, and salt. On low speed, add flour mixture to egg mixture, and beat until flour is incorporated. Remove and stir in pecans and chocolate by hand. Divide dough in half and place both halves on a plate. Freeze uncovered, 15 to 20 minutes, until chilled.

Place half of the dough on the baking sheet. With lightly floured hands, shape the dough into a log 14 inches long, 2½ inches wide, and ¾ inch thick. Repeat with other half of dough, leaving 2 inches or more between the logs.

Bake logs until lightly browned, about 25 minutes. Remove and transfer logs, still on parchment, from baking sheet to a rack. Cool 20 minutes. Lower oven temperature to 300 degrees F.

When cool, place logs on a cutting board and return parchment to baking sheet. With a serrated knife, cut each log diagonally into slices ½ inch thick. Place slices upright on the baking sheet, leaving ½-inch spaces between them. Bake 20 to 23 minutes more to dry biscotti slightly. Cool biscotti on racks.

Store biscotti in an airtight container at room temperature. (Biscotti can be prepared 2 days ahead.)

CONGO BARS

A neighbor shared the recipe for these bars with me and also offered some of the history surrounding these golden blonde brownies studded with chocolate chips. She explained that in the Boston area, these little confections were often brought to potluck suppers at the First Congregational Church, thus the "Congo" in the name. There are many variations of these bars. Sometimes the chocolate chips are used as a glaze on top, and occasionally chopped nuts are added to the batter. The recipe that follows is among the simplest and best I have encountered.

10 tablespoons (1 stick plus 2 tablespoons) unsalted butter, diced, plus extra for greasing pan

2 ¼ cups all-purpose flour, plus extra for flouring baking pan

2 teaspoons baking powder

⅛ teaspoon salt

1 16-ounce box light brown sugar

3 large eggs

12 ounces best-quality semisweet chocolate chips (see note)

MAKES **32** BARS

Arrange an oven rack at center position and preheat oven to 350 degrees F. Butter a 9-by-13-inch baking pan generously, then dust with flour. Shake out any excess.

Sift together flour, baking powder, and salt and set aside.

Melt butter in a large, heavy saucepan over medium heat. Remove from heat and add sugar, stirring until dissolved and mixture is smooth. Let mixture cool 3 to 4 minutes, then stir in eggs, 1 at a time. Stir in dry ingredients and finally chocolate chips. The chips may start to melt slightly; that is okay. Scrape batter into prepared pan and use a spatula to smooth the top.

Bake until a tester comes out clean, 20 to 30 minutes. Cool to room temperature.

Cut into 32 squares. Store bars in an airtight container at room temperature. (Bars can be prepared 3 days ahead.)

NOTE: Ghirardelli's Double Dark Chocolate Chips, available in many supermarkets, are particularly good in these bars. They are intensely chocolate in flavor and slightly larger than regular chips.

CARAMEL ALMOND SQUARES

CRUST

8 tablespoons (1 stick) unsalted butter, chilled and diced, plus extra for greasing baking pan

1 cup all-purpose flour

3 tablespoons confectioners' sugar

TOPPING

2 ounces regular or reduced-fat (not nonfat) cream cheese at room temperature

¼ cup heavy cream

¾ cup sugar

3 tablespoons unsalted butter

1¾ cups slivered almonds, toasted (see page 15)

These rich nut-laden squares are composed of a buttery baked crust that is topped with a toasted almond caramel mixture. The almond squares can easily stand on their own as a backyard dessert or they could be offered as a garnish to bowls of vanilla or peach ice cream.

MAKES 16 SQUARES

Arrange an oven rack at center position and preheat oven to 375 degrees F. Butter an 8-inch square baking pan generously and set aside.

TO MAKE THE CRUST: Combine flour and confectioners' sugar in a food processor. Add butter, then pulse until mixture resembles coarse meal. (Alternatively, by hand, cut butter into dry ingredients using a pastry blender or 2 table knives.) Remove mixture from processor and knead gently until it holds together and forms a solid mass. Press dough into an even layer in the prepared pan.

Bake until crust is golden brown, 20 to 25 minutes. Cool to room temperature.

TO MAKE THE FILLING: Whisk together cream cheese and cream in a small bowl until smooth and blended, and set aside. Combine sugar and 6 tablespoons water in a heavy, medium saucepan over medium heat, swirling pan occasionally until sugar dissolves. Increase heat and boil, without stirring, until syrup turns a rich golden brown color, about 8 minutes. Remove pan from heat and stir in cream cheese and cream. Be very careful, since mixture will bubble vigorously. Whisk in butter, then mix in almonds. Pour filling over crust. Spread evenly with a metal spatula or table knife. Let stand at room temperature until cool and set, at least 1 hour.

When set, cut into 16 squares. Store in an airtight container. (Squares can be prepared 2 days ahead.)

BITTERSWEET CHOCOLATE TOFFEE SQUARES

These tempting little pick-ups are simple to prepare. A sweet butter crust is spread with a thin layer of dark chocolate, sprinkled with chopped pecans and toffee bits, then baked, and cut into squares. No last-minute work is involved since these chocolate-nut confections can be made up to 3 days in advance.

16 tablespoons (2 sticks) unsalted butter at room temperature

1 cup packed light brown sugar

1 large egg yolk

1 teaspoon vanilla extract
   Generous ¼ teaspoon salt

2 cups all-purpose flour, sifted

8 ounces bittersweet chocolate, broken into chunks

2 tablespoons whole milk

¾ cup toffee bits (see note)

¾ cup coarsely chopped pecans

MAKES **24** SQUARES

Arrange an oven rack at center position and preheat oven to 375 degrees F. Use some of the butter to grease a 10-by-15-inch jelly-roll pan.

With an electric mixer on medium-high speed, cream butter until smooth, 1 minute. Gradually add sugar, and beat until mixture is light and fluffy, 3 to 4 minutes. Stop and scrape down sides of bowl if necessary. On medium speed, beat in egg yolk, vanilla, and salt. Lower speed, and add flour. Beat just until mixture holds together well. Pat dough in an even layer into prepared pan.

Place chocolate in top of double boiler (or in a heat-proof bowl) set over but not touching simmering water. Stir until chocolate is smooth and shiny, 2 to 3 minutes. Remove 2 tablespoons of the chocolate to a small microwaveable bowl and whisk in milk. Set aside.

With a metal spatula or dinner knife, spread remaining melted chocolate over dough in pan. Sprinkle toffee bits, then pecans, over chocolate. Bake until toffee melts and nuts are slightly toasted, about 18 minutes. Transfer pan to a wire rack.

Reheat reserved chocolate mixture in microwave or place bowl in a skillet filled with about 1 inch of simmering water. Stir until smooth. Using a teaspoon, drizzle chocolate over the baked crust. Cool until chocolate glaze is set, about 1 hour. Using a sharp knife, cut into 24 squares. (Squares can be prepared 3 days ahead. Store in an airtight container at cool room temperature.)

NOTE: Hershey's Skor brand Bits o' Brickle work well in this recipe. Do not use chocolate-coated toffee bits.

COCONUT CUPCAKES WITH CREAM CHEESE ICING

These tender yellow cupcakes, moistened generously with butter and flavored with coconut, are covered with a cream cheese icing, then sprinkled with toasted coconut flakes. They make scrumptious partners to bowls of fresh strawberries or raspberries to end a casual meal.

CUPCAKES

6 tablespoons (¾ stick) unsalted butter at room temperature, plus extra for greasing pan

1 cup plus 2 tablespoons cake flour, plus extra for flouring pan

1⅛ teaspoon baking powder

¼ teaspoon salt

¾ cup sugar

2 large eggs

½ teaspoon almond extract

⅓ cup whole milk

⅔ cup sweetened flaked coconut

ICING

3 ounces regular or reduced-fat (not nonfat) cream cheese

1½ tablespoons unsalted butter at room temperature

½ cup confectioners' sugar

¼ cup regular or reduced-fat (not nonfat) sour cream

1 teaspoon grated lemon zest

¾ cup sweetened flaked coconut, toasted (see page 15)

MAKES **12** CUPCAKES

Arrange an oven rack at center position and preheat oven to 425 degrees F. Butter and flour a standard 12-cup muffin pan. Tap out excess flour.

TO MAKE THE CUPCAKES: Sift together flour, baking powder, and salt and set aside. With an electric mixer on medium-high speed, cream butter until smooth, 1 minute. Add sugar gradually and beat until mixture is light and fluffy, 3 to 4 minutes. Stop machine and scrape down sides of bowl if necessary. Add eggs 1 at a time, beating well after each addition. Add almond extract, reduce speed to low, and add dry ingredients alternately with milk, beginning and ending with dry ingredients. Stir in coconut by hand.

Spoon batter into molds, filling them about ⅔ full.

Bake until cupcakes are golden brown on top, 16 to 18 minutes. Remove from oven. Use a small knife to loosen cupcakes if necessary. Remove and cool on a wire rack.

TO MAKE THE ICING: With an electric mixer on medium speed, cream the cream cheese and butter until blended, 2 to 3 minutes. Gradually beat in sugar, then lower speed and beat in sour cream and lemon zest.

With an icing spatula or table knife, spread icing over tops of cupcakes. Sprinkle each cupcake generously with toasted coconut flakes. Let cupcakes sit at room temperature until icing is set. Store in an airtight container at cool room temperature or in refrigerator. Bring to room temperature 30 minutes before serving. (Cupcakes can be prepared 1 day ahead.)

The term "cupcakes" appeared in the early 19th-century in the United States. They were so named either because they were made in cups or because their ingredients were measured in cups.

MINI CHOCOLATE ALMOND CUPCAKES

These intensely chocolate-flavored cupcakes, baked with a small amount of flour but with a generous amount of ground nuts, are dense and moist. A silken-smooth, dark chocolate glaze coats the baked cakes.

CUPCAKES

8 tablespoons (1 stick) unsalted butter at room temperature, plus extra for greasing pan

¼ cup all-purpose flour, plus extra for flouring pan

4 ounces semisweet chocolate, broken or cut into small chunks

½ teaspoon instant coffee powder or crystals

⅔ cup sugar

3 large eggs

1 cup slivered or sliced almonds, finely ground

GLAZE

4 ounces semisweet chocolate, broken or cut into small chunks

¼ cup heavy cream

2 tablespoons unsalted butter

2 teaspoons instant coffee powder or crystals

30 slivered or sliced almonds for garnish

MINI-CUPCAKES

30 TO 32

MAKES

Arrange an oven rack at center position, and preheat oven to 375 degrees F. Butter and flour generously 3 mini-muffin tins, each with 12 cups about 1¾ inches in diameter. (If you don't have 3 pans, butter and flour as many as you have and bake the cupcakes in batches.) Tap out excess flour.

TO MAKE THE CUPCAKES: Melt chocolate in top of a double boiler (or in a heat-proof bowl) set over but not touching simmering water in a saucepan. Stir until melted and smooth. Stir in coffee powder until dissolved. Remove pan from heat and cool 5 minutes.

With an electric mixer on medium-high speed, cream butter in a medium bowl until smooth, 1 minute. Add sugar gradually, beating until mixture is light and fluffy, 3 to 4 minutes. Stop and scrape down sides of bowl if necessary. Lower speed, and add eggs 1 at a time, beating well after each addition. Beat in melted chocolate, ground almonds, and flour.

Spoon mixture evenly into prepared cupcake tins. Do not fill tins more than ¾ full. (Mini-cupcake molds vary in size, so depending on your pans, you should get 30 to 32 cupcakes.)

Bake cupcakes until a tester inserted into middle comes out clean, about 15 minutes. Run a knife around inside edges of molds to loosen. Cool cupcakes in molds for 10 to 15 minutes, then unmold.

TO MAKE THE GLAZE: Combine chocolate, cream, butter, and coffee powder in top of a double boiler (or in a heat-proof bowl) set over but not touching simmering water in a saucepan. Stir until melted and smooth. Cool 10 minutes.

With an icing spatula, spread glaze over tops of cupcakes and garnish each with an almond sliver. Cool until glaze is set and firm, about 30 minutes. Store in an airtight container and refrigerate. (Cupcakes can be prepared 2 days ahead. Bring to room temperature before serving.)

NOTE: If you are using 3 pans and do not have enough batter to fill all of the molds of one of the pans, fill the empty molds with water to prevent the butter and flour from sticking to the pan.

CHOCOLATE MINT BROWNIES

These unusual brownies are composed of three layers—a dense chocolate cake-like layer, a peppermint-scented white chocolate icing, and a dark chocolate glaze. With their unmistakable, refreshing mint taste, these brownies are perfect to offer after a filling meal. They take a little longer to prepare than those whose batters are simply mixed and poured into a pan, but the extra effort yields special little morsels, which keep well for several days when refrigerated.

CAKE

8 tablespoons (1 stick) unsalted butter at room temperature, plus extra for greasing pan

½ cup all-purpose flour, plus extra for flouring pan

2 ounces unsweetened chocolate, coarsely chopped

1 cup sugar

2 large eggs

1 teaspoon vanilla extract

¼ teaspoon ground cinnamon

ICING

6 ounces white chocolate, coarsely chopped

3 tablespoons heavy cream

¾ teaspoon peppermint extract

GLAZE

4 ounces semisweet chocolate, coarsely chopped

¼ cup heavy cream

Arrange an oven rack at center position and preheat oven to 325 degrees F. Butter and flour an 8-inch square baking pan, tapping out excess. Line the pan with a sheet of parchment paper, cut so it extends 2 to 3 inches over 2 sides of the pan. Butter and flour the parchment paper, tapping out excess.

TO MAKE THE CAKE: Melt chocolate in the top of a double boiler (or in a heat-proof bowl) set over but not touching simmering water. Stir until melted and smooth. Set aside.

With an electric mixer on medium-high speed, cream butter in a medium bowl until smooth, 1 minute. Add sugar gradually, beating until mixture is light and fluffy, 3 to 4 minutes. Stop mixer and scrape down sides of bowl with a spatula if necessary. Lower speed and add eggs 1 at a time, beating well after each addition. Beat in melted chocolate and vanilla. Add flour and cinnamon and beat just until incorporated, stopping machine to scrape down sides of bowl if necessary.

Pour batter into pan and spread evenly with a spatula. Bake until a tester comes out clean, 25 to 30 minutes. Cool to room temperature.

TO MAKE THE ICING: Melt chocolate and cream in the top of a double boiler (or in a heat-proof bowl) set over but not touching simmering water. Stir until melted and smooth. Stir in peppermint extract. Spread icing over cake layer. Refrigerate until cool and set, about 30 minutes.

TO MAKE THE GLAZE: Melt chocolate and cream in top of a double boiler (or in a heat-proof bowl) set over but not touching simmering water. Stir until melted and smooth. Spread over white chocolate layer. Refrigerate until glaze is set, 30 minutes or longer.

Run a knife around the edges of pan to loosen brownies. Then, using the parchment paper extending over the sides of pan as an aid, lift the brownies from the pan. Cut into 16 squares. Store brownies in an airtight container in the refrigerator. Bring to room temperature 15 minutes before serving. (Brownies can be made 5 days ahead.)

MAKES **16** BROWNIES

DARK CHOCOLATE BROWNIES WITH CHERRIES AND ALMONDS

½ cup dried sour cherries

8 tablespoons (1 stick) unsalted butter, plus extra for greasing pan

½ cup all-purpose flour, plus extra for flouring pan

2 ounces unsweetened chocolate, coarsely chopped

1 cup sugar

¼ teaspoon almond extract

2 large eggs

Pinch of salt

½ cup slivered or sliced almonds, toasted (see page 15)

Confectioners' sugar for dusting

The trio of cherries, almonds, and chocolate is a winning combination in Black Forest cake and works equally well in brownies. Tart sour cherries and toasted almond slivers are mixed into a classic brownie batter in the following recipe. These dense, moist brownies would make a fine addition to a picnic menu or could be served as a tempting garnish to bowls of vanilla ice cream.

MAKES 16 SMALL BROWNIES

Place cherries in a small mixing bowl and cover with ½ cup hot water. Soak until softened, 15 to 20 minutes, then drain and pat dry.

Adjust an oven rack at lower third of oven, and preheat oven to 350 degrees F. Butter and flour an 8-inch square baking pan, tapping out excess flour. Line pan with a piece of parchment paper cut to fit bottom of pan, and butter and flour paper, tapping out excess.

Combine butter and chocolate in the top of a double boiler (or in a heat-proof bowl) set over but not touching simmering water. Stir until chocolate and butter are melted and smooth. Cool 5 minutes, then stir in sugar and almond extract. Add eggs 1 at a time, stirring well after each addition. Next, add flour and salt, then stir in cherries and almonds.

Spread batter in the prepared pan and smooth top with a spatula. Bake until a tester inserted into center comes out clean, 25 to 30 minutes. The top of the brownies will be shiny and cracked and the inside moist and somewhat soft. Do not overbake.

Cool brownies to room temperature. With a small knife, loosen edges of brownies from baking pan. Gently invert brownies onto a work surface and peel off parchment paper. Invert again and cut into 16 squares. Store in an airtight container at cool room temperature. (The brownies can be prepared 5 days ahead.)

To serve, arrange brownies in a napkin-lined basket or stack on an attractive platter and dust with a little confectioners' sugar.

BURNT-SUGAR VANILLA ICE CREAM WITH **WARM CHOCOLATE SAUCE**

My friend Tom Johnson, a talented Ohio chef, created this special vanilla ice cream. What distinguishes it from others is that the sugar is "burnt" or caramelized, before being added to the other ingredients. Made with heavy cream infused with a vanilla bean and seasoned with a hint of freshly grated nutmeg, the finished product is incredibly smooth and beautifully balanced in flavorings. A warm dark chocolate sauce drizzled over icy cold scoops is a further indulgence.

1 vanilla bean

4 cups heavy cream

Pinch of salt

¾ cup sugar

Pinch of freshly grated nutmeg

Extra-Rich Chocolate Sauce (page 333)

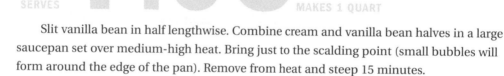

SERVES 4 TO 5   MAKES 1 QUART

Slit vanilla bean in half lengthwise. Combine cream and vanilla bean halves in a large saucepan set over medium-high heat. Bring just to the scalding point (small bubbles will form around the edge of the pan). Remove from heat and steep 15 minutes.

Remove vanilla bean halves and with a small, sharp knife, scrape out pulp and seeds from each half. Stir the scrapings into the cream and mix well. Discard the vanilla bean shells. Season cream with salt and reserve.

Combine sugar and 2 tablespoons water in a medium, heavy skillet and place over medium-high heat. Stir the mixture until sugar dissolves completely and starts to liquefy. Cook, without stirring, until mixture caramelizes, 3 to 4 minutes. Remove from heat, pour carefully (because mixture is hot) into cream mixture, and stir. If the caramel solidifies instead of dissolving, place pan over low heat and stir until caramel is completely dissolved in cream, several minutes. Stir in nutmeg. Chill mixture thoroughly.

Place the chilled mixture in an ice-cream machine and process according to manufacturer's directions. Freeze resulting ice cream until needed. If ice cream is frozen solid, transfer it from freezer to refrigerator for 15 minutes to soften slightly before serving.

Serve scoops of the ice cream in bowls or ramekins drizzled generously with Extra-Rich Chocolate Sauce.

CRÈME FRAÎCHE ICE CREAM

Crème fraîche, a slightly acidic cream with origins in France, can be used to make excellent ice cream. In the following recipe, home-made crème fraîche, which needs to be started several hours ahead, is combined with a cooked egg custard mixture, then churned until creamy and smooth. Served with fresh seasonal berries, this delectable frozen dessert is perfect to offer on days when temperatures soar.

4 cups heavy cream, divided

1⅓ cups sour cream

4 large egg yolks

¾ cup sugar

½ teaspoon vanilla extract

1 pint fresh blueberries, raspberries, or hulled strawberries (optional)

SERVES **6 TO 7** : MAKES ABOUT 1½ QUARTS

To prepare crème fraîche, whisk together 2 cups of the heavy cream with sour cream in a nonreactive bowl. Leave uncovered at room temperature to thicken, 6 hours or overnight.

When ready to prepare ice cream, whisk together egg yolks and sugar in a medium bowl until well blended. Mixture will be quite thick.

Heat remaining 2 cups heavy cream in a medium, heavy saucepan over medium heat until scalded. (Small bubbles will form around the edge of the pan.) Very slowly, whisk the scalded cream into the egg yolk mixture, then return this mixture to the saucepan and place over medium heat. Stir constantly until mixture thickens and coats the back of a spoon, about 5 minutes.

Pour the egg and cream mixture back into the mixing bowl and whisk in the crème fraîche and vanilla. Refrigerate until chilled, at least 1 hour.

Place the chilled mixture in an ice-cream machine and process according to manufacturer's directions. Freeze resulting ice cream until needed. If ice cream is frozen solid, transfer it from freezer to refrigerator for 15 minutes to soften slightly before serving.

Serve scoops of the ice cream with a garnish of fresh berries, if desired.

JANE HORNUNG'S CHOCOLATE CARDAMOM ICE CREAM

A student, who overheard me raving about my new ice-cream maker, shared her recipe for chocolate ice cream scented with crushed cardamom seeds. I was surprised at how exquisitely this aromatic spice complements the flavor of chocolate. When combined, the two ingredients produce a refreshing taste redolent of mint.

2 cups heavy cream

2 cups whole milk

⅓ cup sugar

1 teaspoon ground cardamom (see note)

½ vanilla bean (cut the bean in half crosswise so that all the pulp remains enclosed in the pod)

8 ounces semisweet chocolate, coarsely chopped

SERVES 4 TO 5 ; MAKES ABOUT 1 QUART

Combine cream, milk, sugar, cardamom, and vanilla bean in a medium, heavy saucepan over medium-high heat. Stir to dissolve sugar and bring mixture to a simmer. Remove and let steep 10 minutes. Remove vanilla bean and split lengthwise with a paring knife. Then scrape out the pulp and seeds and add back to the cream mixture. Add chocolate and whisk or stir until it melts. If it doesn't melt completely, place pan over very low heat and stir until chocolate has dissolved. If some flecks of chocolate remain, that is okay. Refrigerate an hour or longer until chilled.

Place the chilled mixture in an ice-cream machine and process according to manufacturer's directions. Freeze resulting ice cream until needed. If ice cream is frozen solid, transfer it from freezer to refrigerator for 15 minutes to soften slightly before serving.

NOTE: Ground cardamom should have a fragrant, assertive aroma. If it doesn't, it is probably old and should be replaced.

COCONUT ICE CREAM

This homemade ice cream, prepared with coconut milk and cream, is rich and smooth and could easily be served unadorned. However, if you want to add some embellishments, sprinkle scoops with a garnish of toasted coconut flakes or drizzle them with warm Extra-Rich Chocolate Sauce (page 333).

1½ cups coconut milk (not cream of coconut)

1½ cups heavy cream

6 large egg yolks

½ cup sugar

Toasted coconut (optional; see page 15)

SERVES 4 TO 5; MAKES ABOUT 1 QUART

Heat coconut milk and cream in a medium, heavy saucepan over medium-high heat until scalded. (Small bubbles will form around the edge of the pan.) Remove from heat and set aside.

Whisk egg yolks in a large bowl until blended. Gradually whisk in sugar until very smooth. Very slowly, whisk the warm cream mixture into the egg yolks until blended. Return this mixture to the saucepan, and cook over medium heat, stirring constantly, until it thickens and coats the back of a spoon, 6 to 8 minutes. Transfer to a mixing bowl and refrigerate until chilled, at least 1 hour.

Place the chilled mixture in an ice-cream machine, and process according to manufacturer's instructions. Freeze resulting ice cream until needed. If ice cream is frozen solid, transfer it from freezer to refrigerator for 15 minutes to soften slightly before serving.

To serve, scoop ice cream into bowls and sprinkle with toasted coconut, if desired.

> *The ice-cream cone was invented in 1904 at the St. Louis World's Fair when an ice-cream vendor, who ran out of paper cups, is said to have asked a waffle booth to make some thin waffles he could roll up to hold his ice cream.*

ALMOND PRALINE ICE CREAM

Praline is a brittle mixture made with nuts and caramelized sugar. It can be broken into chunky pieces or ground and used as a powder. Almond praline powder is folded into this rich vanilla ice cream immediately after it is churned. The glistening little golden flecks add a delicious crunch to the velvety smooth ice cream.

ALMOND PRALINE

Vegetable oil for greasing baking sheet

1 cup blanched, slivered almonds

1 cup sugar

ICE CREAM

8 large egg yolks

¾ cup sugar

3 cups heavy cream

1 cup whole milk

1 teaspoon vanilla extract

SERVES 4 to 5 : MAKES ABOUT 1 QUART

TO MAKE ALMOND PRALINE: Grease a rimmed baking sheet with oil and set aside. Combine almonds and sugar in a medium saucepan over medium heat, and stir constantly until sugar dissolves. Continue cooking until sugar caramelizes and turns a golden brown, only a few minutes more. Carefully pour the hot mixture onto the oiled baking sheet. Spread evenly with an oiled metal spatula or knife. Cool completely. Break hardened caramel into chunks and place in a food processor. Process, pulsing, until mixture becomes a very coarse powder. Remove and store in an airtight container in refrigerator. (Praline powder can be made 1 week ahead.)

TO MAKE ICE CREAM: Whisk egg yolks and sugar in a medium bowl until well blended. Mixture will be quite thick. Heat cream and milk in a medium saucepan over medium heat until scalded. (Small bubbles will form around the edge of the pan.) Very slowly, whisk cream into the egg yolk mixture. Return this mixture to the saucepan, and cook over medium heat. Stir constantly until mixture thickens and coats the back of a spoon, about 5 minutes. Pour mixture back into the bowl and whisk in vanilla. Refrigerate until chilled, at least 1 hour.

Place chilled mixture in an ice-cream machine and process according to manufacturer's directions. When almost done, but while ice cream is still soft, remove from ice cream machine and stir in all but ¼ cup praline powder. Freeze resulting ice cream until needed. If ice cream is frozen solid, transfer it from freezer to refrigerator for 15 minutes to soften slightly before serving.

Serve scoops of the ice cream sprinkled with remaining praline powder.

PINK GRAPEFRUIT SORBET

This tart, soothing sorbet, made with fresh grapefruit juice, makes a light dessert to offer after a rich meal. Serve scoops of this icy cold sherbet with fresh strawberries, blueberries, or a combination of both.

1 cup sugar

1½ cups fresh or bottled pink grapefruit juice (not from concentrate)

2 tablespoons fresh lemon juice

Fresh mint sprigs

SERVES **3 TO 4**; MAKES ABOUT 1½ PINTS

Combine sugar and 1 cup water in a medium saucepan over medium-high heat. Stir until sugar dissolves, then simmer 5 minutes. Cool, then cover and refrigerate until chilled, at least 1 hour.

Combine the cooled sugar syrup, grapefruit juice, and lemon juice in an ice-cream machine and process according to manufacturer's directions. Freeze resulting sorbet until needed. If sorbet is frozen solid, transfer it from freezer to refrigerator for 15 minutes to soften slightly before serving.

Serve scoops of the sorbet in wine glasses and garnish with mint sprigs.

BANANA DAIQUIRI SORBET

3 ripe bananas

1 cup sugar

⅔ cup fresh orange juice (about 2 oranges)

½ cup fresh lemon juice (2 to 3 lemons)

¼ cup dark rum

Unlike most sorbets, this one is made without assembling a sugar syrup. The ingredients are blended in a food processor, then added to an ice-cream machine. Citrus accents of orange and lemon and a splash of rum complement this icy cold banana ice.

SERVES **4 TO 5** ; MAKES ABOUT 1 QUART

Peel bananas and cut 1 of them into ½-inch dice. Combine remaining 2 bananas in the bowl of a food processor, and add sugar, orange juice, and lemon juice. Process, pulsing, until mixture is smooth. Remove and place in a medium bowl. Stir in ¾ cup water, rum, and diced banana. Refrigerate mixture until chilled.

Place chilled mixture in an ice-cream machine and process according to manufacturer's directions. Freeze resulting sorbet until needed. If sorbet is frozen solid, transfer it from freezer to refrigerator for 15 minutes to soften slightly before serving.

FRESH STRAWBERRY SORBET

The taste of fresh strawberries shines through in this icy cold, hot pink sorbet. Both lemon and orange juices accentuate the flavor of the berries. Scoops of the sorbet can be served alone or with a sprinkling of strawberries.

1   cup sugar

1   quart fresh strawberries, hulled

⅓   cup fresh orange juice (about 1 orange)

⅓   cup fresh lemon juice (about 1 lemon)

SERVES **4 TO 5**; MAKES ABOUT 1 QUART

Combine 2 cups water and the sugar in a medium saucepan over high heat. Stir just until sugar is dissolved. Bring mixture to a boil and boil 5 minutes. Transfer to a medium bowl and refrigerate until chilled, at least 1 hour.

Purée strawberries in small quantities in a food processor or blender until all the berries have been puréed. Add puréed berries to the cooled sugar syrup along with the orange and lemon juices. Stir to mix well.

Process mixture in an ice-cream machine according to manufacturer's instructions. Freeze resulting sorbet until needed. If sorbet is frozen solid, transfer it from freezer to refrigerator for 15 minutes to soften slightly before serving.

California produces enough strawberries in a single year that, laid berry to berry, there would be enough to wrap around the world 15 times.

HONEY PEACH SUNDAES

Peaches and cream are a dessert match made in heaven. Add a honey caramel sauce to this duo and the resulting confection is even more enticing. For these sundaes, scoops of vanilla ice cream are topped with warm caramel sauce and sliced peaches. Serve the sundaes as a refreshing finale at a barbecue or offer them as the pièce de résistance along with iced coffee at a backyard dessert party.

⅔ cup sugar

3 tablespoons honey

2½ tablespoons fresh lemon juice

8 medium (about 2 pounds) yellow peaches, ripe but not too soft

1 quart best-quality vanilla ice cream (see note)

½ cup toasted walnuts, chopped (see page 15)

Fresh mint sprigs for garnish

Combine sugar, honey, and lemon juice in a medium saucepan over medium heat and stir until sugar dissolves. Continue to cook, without stirring, until mixture caramelizes and becomes a rich, golden brown, about 2 minutes. (If not using sauce immediately, remove from heat and let cool. Leave at room temperature for up to 3 hours. The sauce will thicken and harden. Reheat, stirring over very low heat until hot.)

When ready to serve, peel peaches, halve them, and slice into ½-inch-thick wedges and place in a medium bowl. Add peaches and any juices collected in the bowl to the warm caramel honey sauce, and cook 1 to 2 minutes more just to warm fruit. Remove from heat.

Place 2 large scoops of ice cream in each of 6 dessert bowls or compotes. Ladle a generous amount of sauce and peaches over ice cream in each dish. Garnish each serving with a sprinkle of chopped nuts and a mint sprig. Serve immediately.

NOTE: You can substitute vanilla frozen yogurt for the ice cream in this recipe. The slight acidity of the yogurt works well with the sweet caramel sauce.

RUM CARAMEL PECAN SUNDAES

Scoops of vanilla ice cream coated with warm homemade caramel sauce and sprinkled with toasted pecans are an irresistible treat. The sauce can be made several days ahead so that the sundaes take only minutes to assemble.

Best Ever Caramel Sauce (page 332)

2 tablespoons dark rum

1 quart best-quality vanilla ice cream or Burnt-Sugar Vanilla Ice Cream (page 291)

¾ cup pecan halves, toasted and coarsely chopped (see page 15)

SERVES 4

Stir caramel sauce in a small saucepan over medium heat until hot. Remove and whisk in rum.

Place a generous scoop of ice cream in each of 4 sundae glasses or in wide-mouthed wine glasses. Drizzle each with 1 tablespoon of the warm sauce and sprinkle with 1 tablespoon of pecans. Make 2 more layers in each glass. If desired, drizzle the sundaes with any extra caramel sauce. Serve immediately.

Sundaes, invented in the late 19th century, are so spelled because religious Americans believed that it was sacrilegious to name a dish after the Sabbath.

PLUM SUNDAES

2 pounds medium, just ripe dark red or purple plums

4 tablespoons unsalted butter

⅓ cup sugar, plus more if needed

¼ teaspoon ground cinnamon, plus more if needed

¼ teaspoon ground ginger

1 quart best-quality vanilla ice cream or Burnt-Sugar Vanilla Ice Cream (page 291)

4 fresh mint sprigs

Fresh plums, cooked in sugar and spices until glazed and syrupy, make a scrumptious topping for ice cream sundaes. The plums can be prepared several hours ahead and left at room temperature until needed.

SERVES 4

Halve plums lengthwise, and slice each half into ½-inch-thick wedges.

Melt butter in a large, heavy skillet over medium-high heat until hot. Add plums and sprinkle with ⅓ cup sugar. Stir constantly and cook until sugar dissolves and becomes syrupy and plums are tender when pierced with a knife, 6 to 8 minutes. After several minutes the glaze will become a crimson color. Watch carefully, and do not overcook, or plums will become mushy. Remove from heat and stir in ¼ teaspoon cinnamon and ginger. Taste and add more sugar and an extra pinch of cinnamon, if needed. Cool cooked plums 5 minutes. (The plums can be prepared 4 hours ahead. Leave at cool room temperature. Reheat, stirring, over medium heat.)

To assemble sundaes, place a generous scoop of ice cream in each of 4 sundae glasses or in wide-mouthed wine glasses. Ladle about ¼ cup of the warm plums over the ice cream. Make 2 more layers in each glass. Spoon any remaining plums over sundaes. Garnish each sundae with a fresh mint sprig. Serve immediately.

BLUEBERRY SUNDAES

Warm Blueberry Sauce (page 337)

Warm, thick blueberry sauce ladled over scoops of tart lemon sorbet is the simple concept for these sundaes. The sauce can be made several days ahead and reheated when needed.

3 tablespoons dry red wine

1 quart best-quality lemon sorbet

4 fresh mint sprigs

Stir blueberry sauce in a medium, heavy saucepan over medium heat until warm. Stir in red wine, then cool 5 minutes.

Place a generous scoop of sorbet in each of 4 sundae glasses or in wide-mouthed wine glasses. Drizzle each with 2 tablespoons of the warm sauce. Make 2 more layers in each glass. Drizzle sundaes with any extra sauce, or save for another use. Garnish each sundae with a fresh mint sprig. Serve immediately.

EXTRA-SPECIAL ICE CREAM SANDWICHES

For this creation, scoops of vanilla ice cream are sandwiched between homemade Chocolate Chip Maple Pecan cookies, then pressed together into sandwiches. The cookies can be baked a day or two ahead so that only a quick assembly is necessary at serving time.

8 Chocolate Chip Maple Pecan Cookies (page 272)

1 pint best quality vanilla ice cream or ½ recipe Burnt-Sugar Vanilla Ice Cream (page 291), slightly softened

SERVES 4

To make sandwiches, place a cookie on a work surface (flat/bottom-side up). Top with about ⅓ cup ice cream. Place another cookie (flat/bottom-side down) on top of ice cream and press gently to form sandwich. Repeat to make 3 more sandwiches. Freeze the ice cream sandwiches on a baking sheet until ice cream is firm, 30 minutes or longer. Serve ice-cream sandwiches with paper napkins.

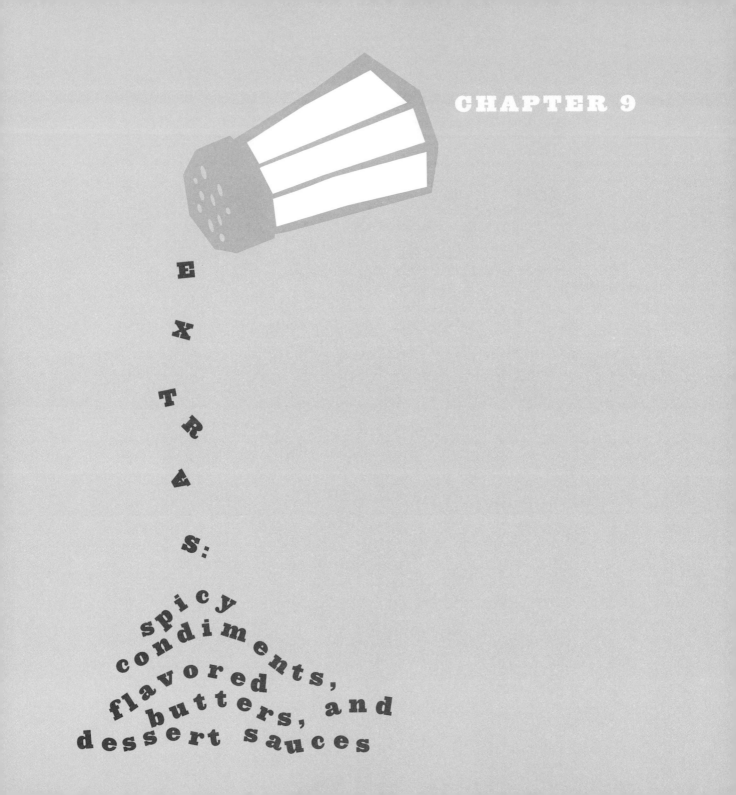

CHAPTER 9

EXTRAS:

spicy condiments, flavored butters, and dessert sauces

The Creole word *lagniappe* means a "little something extra." In Louisiana, where the term originated, you hear it all the time. It's a bonus—an unexpected gratuity. Merchants routinely surprise their customers with *lagniappe*, as a way of showing their appreciation. I think of the extras in this book—piquant condiments, seasoned butters, and scrumptious dessert sauces—as *lagniappe*. They are those unexpected extras that surprise and please palates, and let your guests know that you have put heart and soul into a preparation.

There are dozens of salsas, relishes, butters, mayonnaises, and chutneys in this chapter that will dress up a plain chicken, enliven a burger, or add pizzazz to chops or steaks. A taste of sweet, hot, or piquant definitely gets your attention and transforms ordinary dishes into memorable ones. Easy homemade chutneys like the crimson-hued Plum Chutney or the tart Rhubarb Chutney can reside for days in the refrigerator, ready to add bursts of flavor to your dishes. Colorful salsas, made with all manner of fruits or vegetables, are perfect partners to just about anything cooked on the grill. Chunky Guacamole Salsa is irresistible on juicy sirloins or mounded atop a thick burger, and festive Tomato Orange Salsa makes swordfish unforgettable. Relishes, distinguished by both sweet and tart notes, are make-ahead accents that give zing to grilled sausages or to a plate of cold cuts. Pats of seasoned butter are instant flavor boosters, too. Blue Cheese Walnut Butter, when spread on piping hot grilled steaks, melts instantly to form a luxurious sauce. Similarly, Lime Cilantro Butter invigorates grilled fish or chicken fillets. And mayonnaise and mustard, two familiar standbys, are even better when enhanced with herbs or spices, then used in condiment roles.

Desserts need extras, too. Maybe it's gilding the lily, but for me less is *not* more when it comes to the sweet course. Best Ever Caramel Sauce, Chocolate Coffee Sauce, or Warm Blueberry Sauce make already good things even better! Consider it just a little *lagniappe*.

CHUNKY GUACAMOLE SALSA

Homemade guacamole far surpasses store-bought varieties. In this enticing version, coarsely chopped avocados and plum tomatoes are tossed in lime juice and sprinkled with cilantro. Hot peppers and shallots add heat and texture. The salsa makes a delicious garnish for juicy hamburgers (page 38), or it can be used as a dip with crispy tortilla chips. You could scoop out summer tomatoes, fill them with this guacamole, then serve them as a side dish. Or, you might like to top soft flour tortillas with grilled shrimp, shredded lettuce, and some guacamole before rolling them into burritos.

2 ripe avocados, soft but not mushy

2 large (about 6 ounces) ripe plum tomatoes

1 3-inch-long jalapeño pepper, minced (see page 17)

2 tablespoons fresh lime juice

2 tablespoons chopped shallots

2 tablespoons chopped fresh cilantro

1½ teaspoons ground cumin

½ teaspoon salt

2 tablespoons olive or vegetable oil

MAKES 2½ CUPS

Halve, seed, and peel avocados, then cut into ½-inch dice. Place in a medium non-reactive bowl. Halve tomatoes, seed them, and cut into ½-inch dice. Add to medium bowl along with minced jalapeño.

In a small bowl, mix together lime juice, shallots, cilantro, cumin, and salt. Whisk in oil. Pour over the avocados and tomatoes and mix gently so that avocados do not get mashed. Taste and add more salt, if needed. Serve immediately or cover with plastic wrap and leave at room temperature for up to 1 hour. (The salsa can also be covered and refrigerated for 4 hours. Bring to room temperature 30 minutes before serving.)

The jalapeño pepper gets its name form Jalapa, the capital of Veracruz, Mexico.

MANGO LIME SALSA

1 large, ripe mango

¼ cup chopped red onion

1 tablespoon fresh lime juice, plus more if needed

½ teaspoon grated lime zest

2 teaspoons chopped fresh cilantro

1 teaspoon finely minced serrano chile pepper (see note; also see page 17)

Salt

Freshly ground black pepper

This salsa, like most, is a study in contrasts. The mango's flesh is silken smooth compared to the crisp texture of the onions. This fruit is naturally sweet and is complemented by the tart lime. Both fresh serrano peppers and black pepper add piquancy. The colorful mélange makes a tempting garnish to grilled fish or chicken.

MAKES ABOUT 1 1/3 CUPS

Peel the mango, then cut the flesh away from the large flat seed. Cut flesh into ½-inch dice so that you have about 1 cup. Place diced mango in a medium nonreactive bowl.

Add onion, 1 tablespoon lime juice, lime zest, cilantro, and serrano to the mango and mix well. Taste and season the salsa with salt and pepper and with a little extra lime juice, if desired. Serve immediately, or cover and refrigerate. (The salsa can be prepared 6 hours ahead; bring to room temperature 15 minutes before serving.)

NOTE: A serrano chile is a small 1½-inch-long, slightly pointed pepper with a very hot taste. As it matures, its smooth dark green skin becomes orange, then yellow. I like the green serrano peppers, but you could substitute another hot pepper, adding it gradually in small amounts and tasting until you have the degree of hot seasoning you like.

TOMATO-ORANGE SALSA

3 medium navel oranges

1½ cups chopped, seeded tomatoes

¼ cup minced red onion

¼ cup chopped fresh flat-leaf parsley

2 tablespoons fresh orange juice

2 teaspoons minced garlic

2 teaspoons balsamic vinegar

1 teaspoon minced peeled fresh ginger

⅛ teaspoon cayenne pepper

Salt

Freshly ground black pepper

This salsa, with its burst of orange and red hues, makes a perfect garnish to grilled swordfish (page 92) or other grilled seafood. It is also a tempting condiment to serve with grilled pork or chicken.

MAKES ABOUT **4** CUPS

Peel oranges, cutting away all the white pith beneath the skin. Cut out segments, then cut segments into ½-inch dice and place in a large nonreactive bowl. Add tomatoes, onion, parsley, orange juice, garlic, vinegar, ginger, and cayenne. Mix well, then taste and season with salt and pepper. Let salsa stand at least 1 hour. (Salsa can be prepared 4 hours ahead. Cover and refrigerate. Bring to room temperature before using.)

MANGO, TOMATO, AND KIWI SALSA

2 ripe (but not mushy) mangoes (see note)

3 ripe (but not mushy) kiwis

2 jalapeño peppers, minced (see page 17)

2 plum tomatoes

3 tablespoons fresh lime juice

Kosher salt

⅓ cup chopped fresh cilantro

This tri-colored salsa, which tastes best when made a few hours in advance, makes an excellent condiment to serve with grilled chicken, fish, or pork. Or, you could use it as a garnish to pita pocket sandwiches filled with thinly sliced roasted turkey or chicken.

MAKES ABOUT 4 CUPS

Peel mangoes, then cut the flesh away from the large flat seed. Cut flesh into ½-inch dice, and put into a medium nonreactive bowl. Peel kiwis and cut into ½-inch dice and add to bowl along with jalapeños. Halve tomatoes lengthwise and scoop out and discard seeds and membranes. Cut tomatoes into ½-inch dice and add to the bowl. Add lime juice and mix well. Taste and season with salt. (Salsa can be made 4 hours ahead; cover and refrigerate, and bring to room temperature 30 minutes before using.) At serving time, stir in the cilantro.

NOTE: You can substitute 2 cups peeled, diced peaches or nectarines for the mangoes in this recipe.

QUICK ROASTED RED PEPPER RELISH

4 7-ounce jars roasted red bell peppers

3 tablespoons olive oil

1½ cups chopped yellow onions

1 tablespoon minced garlic

4½ tablespoons cider vinegar

3 tablespoons sugar

¼ teaspoon dry mustard

¼ teaspoon cayenne pepper

Salt

Purchased roasted red bell peppers work beautifully in this relish and are a great time saver. They are chopped and sautéed with onions and garlic, then seasoned with vinegar, sugar, and spices. This delicious condiment makes a fine garnish for turkey, beef, or lamb burgers.

MAKES ABOUT **2½** CUPS

Rinse, drain, and pat roasted bell peppers dry, then chop them. Heat oil in a large, heavy skillet over medium-high heat until hot. Add bell peppers and sauté, stirring, 2 minutes. Add onions and garlic, and cook, stirring, until onions are soft, 3 to 5 minutes.

Whisk vinegar and sugar together in a small bowl and add to pepper and onion mixture in the skillet. Stir in mustard, cayenne, and ¼ teaspoon salt. Continue cooking, stirring often, until all the liquid has evaporated, about 5 minutes more. Cool to room temperature. Taste and season with more salt, if needed. (The relish can be prepared 1 day ahead; cover and refrigerate. Bring to room temperature before using.)

RED AND YELLOW PEPPER RELISH

2 tablespoons unsalted butter

2 tablespoons olive oil

1 large yellow onion, halved lengthwise and thinly sliced

1 red bell pepper, cut into ½-inch dice

1 yellow bell pepper, cut into ½-inch dice

⅓ cup coarsely chopped pitted kalamata olives

1 tablespoon Dijon mustard

1 large clove garlic, peeled and chopped

Salt

Freshly ground black pepper

A sauté of sweet bell peppers, onions, and kalamata olives are the primary ingredients in this colorful relish, which has many uses and which can be prepared two days ahead. It is delicious served on grilled burgers, steaks, lamb, or chicken, but would also make a fine topping for crostini.

MAKES **2** CUPS

Combine butter and oil in a large, heavy skillet over medium-high heat. When hot, add onion and cook, stirring, until softened and golden, about 5 minutes. Add bell peppers and sauté, stirring, until just tender, about 3 minutes. Add olives, mustard, and garlic and stir 1 minute. Remove from heat, taste, and season with salt and pepper. Transfer relish to a bowl and cool. If not using immediately, cover and refrigerate. Bring to room temperature before serving. (Relish can be prepared 2 days ahead.)

CUCUMBER WATERCRESS RELISH

MAKES ABOUT **3** CUPS

This slightly sweet, fresh relish, which can be prepared a few hours in advance, is delicious served with such grilled mild fish as trout, Arctic char, or Chilean sea bass. It is particularly good with Salmon Fillets with Fresh Tarragon and Crushed Fennel (page 87).

2   teaspoons yellow mustard seeds

¾   teaspoon fennel seeds

¼   cup white wine vinegar

2   tablespoons olive oil

1   tablespoon sugar

   Salt

   Freshly ground black pepper

2   cups peeled, seeded, and finely diced (¼ inch) cucumber

1   cup chopped red onion

½   cup stemmed, coarsely chopped watercress leaves

Stir mustard seeds and fennel seeds in a small, heavy skillet over medium heat and cook until mustard seeds start to pop, about 3 minutes. Remove from heat and put in a medium nonreactive bowl.

Add vinegar, oil, sugar, 1 teaspoon salt, and several grinds of pepper to the bowl and whisk well to combine. Add cucumber and onion and stir to mix. Let relish marinate for 30 minutes. (Relish can stay at cool room temperature for up to 2 hours.)

At serving time, stir in watercress, then taste and add more salt and pepper, if needed.

Cucumbers maintain an internal temperature that is several degrees cooler than that outside—perhaps giving validity to the phrase "cool as a cucumber."

TOMATO MUSTARD RELISH

2 tablespoons olive oil

1 tablespoon minced garlic

2 pounds ripe plum (Roma) tomatoes, seeded and cut into ½-inch dice

2 tablespoons whole-grain mustard

1 teaspoon dried thyme

½ teaspoon dried rosemary, crushed

Salt

⅛ teaspoon cayenne pepper

Sugar (optional)

This fresh tomato relish, which can be prepared a day ahead, makes a spicy addition to grilled sausages or burgers. Use it also as a garnish to pita pockets filled with thin slices of grilled flank steak or lamb.

MAKES ABOUT **2** CUPS

Heat oil in a heavy, medium skillet over medium heat. Add the garlic and sauté for a few seconds. Add tomatoes and stir well. Stir in mustard, thyme, rosemary, ½ teaspoon salt, and cayenne. Cook and stir only 1 minute more or tomatoes will get mushy.

Remove from heat, taste, and season with more salt, if needed. If mixture seems too acidic, stir in a pinch of sugar. (The relish can be made 1 day ahead. Cover and refrigerate. Either reheat sauce just to warm or bring to room temperature when ready to use.)

HOT SPICY TOMATO RELISH

¾ pound ripe (but not soft) plum (Roma) tomatoes

1 tablespoon olive oil

¾ cup (about 1 large) cleaned, chopped leek, white parts only

½ teaspoon dried rosemary, crushed, plus more if needed

Salt

¼ teaspoon dried thyme

¼ teaspoon red pepper flakes

1 teaspoon grated orange zest

1 teaspoon balsamic vinegar

This cooked relish, which can be prepared several hours ahead, is good served warm or at room temperature. I like to mound it on grilled beef steaks, especially tenderloins (page 30). The flavors are also a good match for grilled lamb chops or grilled butterflied leg of lamb.

MAKES ABOUT 1 CUP

Halve tomatoes lengthwise and scoop out seeds and membranes. Cut halves into ½-inch dice. Drain tomatoes in a colander while you make the relish.

Heat oil in a medium, heavy skillet over medium heat. When hot, add leeks and cook, stirring, until softened, about 3 minutes. Add ½ teaspoon rosemary, scant ½ teaspoon salt, thyme, and red pepper flakes and cook and stir 30 seconds more. Remove from heat and stir in tomatoes, orange zest, and balsamic vinegar. Taste and add more crushed rosemary and salt, if needed. (The relish can be prepared 2 hours ahead. Leave at room temperature.) Serve relish warm or at room temperature.

California produces nearly all of the United States' fresh artichokes.

ARTICHOKE, RED PEPPER, AND OLIVE CONFETTI

¾ cup pitted kalamata olives

1 large (8-ounce) red bell pepper

1 9-ounce package frozen artichoke hearts, thawed and dried

4 ounces small button mushrooms, cleaned

¼ cup thinly sliced yellow onion

½ cup olive oil

2 tablespoons red wine vinegar

1½ tablespoons chopped fresh basil, plus 5 to 6 additional leaves for garnish

1 tablespoon chopped fresh flat-leaf parsley

1½ teaspoons minced garlic

½ teaspoon whole-grain Dijon mustard

Salt

Freshly ground black pepper

This colorful mélange of marinated vegetables bursts with flavor and is delicious served with a platter of assorted Italian cold cuts (page 109). It also makes a fine condiment to offer with a grilled leg of lamb or with grilled juicy beef steaks. The vegetables can be prepared a day in advance.

MAKES ABOUT 4 CUPS

Quarter olives lengthwise. Slice bell pepper lengthwise into paper-thin slices. Cut artichoke hearts lengthwise into thin slices. Halve mushrooms through stems. In a large bowl, mix together olives, bell pepper, artichoke hearts, mushrooms, and onion.

In a medium bowl, whisk together olive oil, vinegar, chopped basil, parsley, garlic, mustard, ½ teaspoon salt, and ⅛ teaspoon pepper until thickened. Pour over vegetable mixture and stir to coat well. Cover and let sit at room temperature 1 hour for flavors to blend. The olives and vegetables can be prepared 1 day ahead; cover and refrigerate. Bring to room temperature 30 minutes before serving.

To serve, taste, and add more salt and pepper, if needed. Arrange the marinated olives and vegetables in a bowl. Julienne remaining basil leaves and sprinkle over olive and vegetable mixture.

TOMATO FENNEL CONFETTI

3 slices (2 to 3 ounces) smoked bacon

3 tablespoons minced shallots

3 tablespoons minced fennel bulb (see note)

½ teaspoon minced garlic

1½ cups grape tomatoes, cut into ¼-inch dice

¼ cup dry white wine

Freshly ground black pepper

Salt

1½ teaspoons chopped fresh tarragon

1 teaspoon chopped fresh flat-leaf parsley

This colorful combination, made with sweet little grape tomatoes, diced fennel, and fresh herbs, makes a distinctive topping to use with grilled oysters (page 96) or with grilled salmon. It would be equally tempting as a garnish for a platter of steamed green beans. The key to this recipe is to cook the tomatoes no more than one minute so that they retain their shape and do not become mushy.

MAKES 1½ CUPS

In a medium, heavy skillet set over medium heat, sauté bacon until browned and crisp. Remove and drain on paper towels. Crumble and set aside.

Pour off and discard all but a thin film of the bacon drippings in skillet. Heat skillet over medium heat and add shallots, fennel, and garlic. Sauté and stir to soften, about 1½ minutes. Stir in tomatoes, wine, ¼ teaspoon pepper, and ⅛ teaspoon salt. Cook, stirring, only 1 minute more. Transfer to a nonreactive serving bowl. (The tomato-fennel mixture can be prepared 2 hours ahead; leave at room temperature.) When ready to serve, stir in tarragon, parsley, and crumbled bacon. Taste and season with more salt and pepper, if needed.

NOTE: To mince fennel, remove and discard the long lacy stems from the bulb. Halve the bulb lengthwise, then cut out and discard the tough inner core from each half. Then chop the bulb finely to yield 3 tablespoons.

PLUM CHUTNEY

MAKES **2** GENEROUS CUPS

I love the deep crimson color of this chutney, which makes a lively complement to grilled lamb, pork, or chicken. It is also appealing as a garnish for turkey burgers or ham sandwiches. The chutney keeps well in the refrigerator for several days.

4 to **5** (about 1¼ pounds) red plums, ripe but still firm

1 large Granny Smith apple

⅔ cup sugar

6 tablespoons red wine vinegar (see note)

1 tablespoon minced peeled fresh ginger

1 teaspoon chopped garlic

2 teaspoons grated orange zest

¼ teaspoon ground cinnamon

Halve plums and cut each half into ½-inch dice to yield 3 cups. (You may not need to use all the plums.) Set aside. Halve lengthwise and core apple without peeling. Cut into ½-inch dice to yield 1 cup.

Combine 1 cup water and the sugar in a large, heavy saucepan over high heat. Stir to dissolve sugar and then bring to a boil without stirring. Add vinegar, ginger, garlic, half of the diced plums, and the diced apple. Bring mixture to a boil and boil for 5 minutes. Add remaining plums, orange zest, and cinnamon. Bring to a gentle boil and cook until thick and syrupy, about 10 minutes. Remove and cool. (Chutney can be prepared 5 days ahead. Cover and refrigerate. Bring to room temperature before using.) Serve chutney at room temperature.

NOTE: Plums seem to vary in their sweetness. If this chutney doesn't seem tart enough when finished, you can add a little more vinegar (1 to 2 teaspoons at a time) and cook a few minutes more to evaporate until the sweet/tart tastes are balanced.

RHUBARB CHUTNEY

MAKES ABOUT **3** CUPS

1 cup lightly packed brown sugar

½ cup balsamic vinegar

4 teaspoons minced peeled fresh ginger

1 3-inch cinnamon stick, broken in half

1 teaspoon grated orange zest plus several julienned strips for garnish (optional)

¼ teaspoon ground cardamom

About 1 ¼ pounds rhubarb

⅔ cup (about 1 bunch) chopped green onions including 2 inches of green stems

½ cup currants

Rhubarb, the tart vegetable that appears in the spring, is most often used as a dessert ingredient. But it is also delicious when combined with sugar, spices, and vinegar and turned into a chutney. Rhubarb chutney can be used as a garnish to grilled pork or lamb and would be attractive mounded atop grilled turkey or chicken burgers. A bowl of the chutney could also be served with a platter of cold, sliced baked ham.

Combine sugar, vinegar, ginger, cinnamon, orange zest, and cardamom in a large, heavy saucepan set over medium heat. Cook, stirring, until sugar dissolves and mixture just comes to a simmer.

Trim rhubarb and cut into ½-inch slices to yield 4 cups. Add rhubarb, onions, and currants to saucepan and increase heat to medium-high. Cook until rhubarb is tender and mixture thickens slightly, about 5 minutes. (Do not overcook or rhubarb will become mushy.) Cool to room temperature. Remove the cinnamon stick halves and discard. Refrigerate chutney to set. (Chutney can be prepared 5 days ahead. Bring to room temperature 30 minutes before serving.)

Serve chutney in an attractive bowl garnished with some julienned orange peel in the center, if desired.

BALSAMIC ONION MARMALADE

While teaching in the Perigord, an area in southwestern France, I bought a jar of onion marmalade in one of the region's outdoor food markets and brought it home to savor. The sweet and tart accents of this condiment were so appealing that I decided to try re-creating it in my own kitchen. I sautéed onions in butter and sugar, then added balsamic vinegar, red wine, and dark raisins to the pan. When the mixture cooked until it was glistening and syrupy, I added crushed black pepper. The onions would be excellent with grilled chicken breasts or pork chops or as a garnish to turkey burgers (page 44).

1½ tablespoons unsalted butter

2 cups (1 large) chopped yellow onion

1 tablespoon sugar, plus 1 to 1½ teaspoons extra, if needed

½ cup balsamic vinegar

¼ cup dry red wine

3 tablespoons dark raisins

Coarsely ground black pepper

Salt

MAKES ABOUT 2/3 CUP

Heat butter in a medium, heavy saucepan until hot and add onion. Cook, stirring, 5 minutes. Sprinkle with 1 tablespoon sugar, and continue to cook until onion is very soft and browned, 8 to 10 minutes more. Add vinegar, wine, and raisins, and simmer until almost all of the liquids have evaporated and onion mixture is glistening and syrupy, about 5 minutes.

Stir in ¼ teaspoon pepper and ⅛ teaspoon salt. Taste, and if you would like marmalade slightly sweeter, stir in 1 to 1½ teaspoons extra sugar. (Marmalade can be prepared 3 days ahead; cover and refrigerate. Bring to room temperature before using.)

CHIMICHURRI SAUCE

1 cup very tightly packed fresh flat-leaf parsley leaves

½ cup olive oil

⅓ cup red wine vinegar

2 medium cloves garlic, peeled

¾ teaspoon red pepper flakes

½ teaspoon salt

½ teaspoon ground cumin

Parsley, vinegar, and oil are the basic ingredients in vibrant green-hued chimichurri sauce from Argentina. It takes just minutes to assemble the sauce, which is traditionally used as an accompaniment to beef steaks. It is also good on grilled chicken.

MAKES ABOUT **1** CUP

Combine all ingredients in the bowl of a food processor fitted with a metal blade, and process, pulsing machine, until mixture is puréed. (The sauce can rest at room temperature 3 hours before being used.)

CREAMY HORSERADISH SAUCE

1 cup sour cream

¼ cup minced unpeeled Granny Smith or other tart apple

2 tablespoons prepared horseradish (not horseradish sauce)

1 teaspoon caraway seeds, crushed (see page 15)

Quickly assembled, this creamy sauce gets its zing from a generous seasoning of horseradish, while crushed caraway seeds and minced tart apple enliven it even more. Try it as a garnish to Bratwursts on Toasted Rolls with Caramelized Onions (page 50) or as a spread for corned beef sandwiches on rye.

MAKES ABOUT **1¼** CUPS

Mix all ingredients together in a small bowl. Cover and refrigerate sauce until ready to use. (The sauce can be prepared 2 days ahead.)

WHIPPED HORSERADISH CREAM

MAKES ABOUT 1²/₃ CUPS

½ cup heavy cream

½ cup sour cream

¼ cup prepared horseradish (not horseradish sauce), drained, plus more if needed

¼ cup chopped green onions including 2 inches of green stems

2 tablespoons capers, drained and coarsely chopped

1½ tablespoons chopped fresh chives, divided

1 teaspoon Dijon mustard

Salt

Freshly ground black pepper

Whipped cream adds a light touch to this piquant condiment made with sour cream, horseradish, and mustard. Green onions, capers, and chives add even more flavor. This sauce is delicious on grilled beef steaks (page 31) or with grilled sausages.

Using an electric mixer, whip heavy cream on medium-high speed until stiff peaks form. Set aside.

In a medium nonreactive bowl, whisk together sour cream, horseradish, onions, capers, 1 tablespoon of the chives, mustard, ¼ teaspoon salt, and ¼ teaspoon pepper. Gently fold in the whipped cream. Taste, and if needed, add more salt and pepper. If you want the sauce to be more spicy, add ½ to 1 teaspoon additional drained horseradish sauce.

Transfer mixture to a small serving bowl and cover and refrigerate for up to 3 hours. Remove from the refrigerator 10 minutes before serving and sprinkle with remaining chives.

DEEP SOUTH BARBECUE SAUCE

8 tablespoons (1 stick) unsalted butter

¾ cup chopped yellow onion

5 medium cloves garlic, chopped

1 cup cider vinegar

½ cup chili sauce

½ cup ketchup

1 tablespoon light brown sugar

1 teaspoon dry mustard, preferably Coleman's

1½ teaspoons salt

½ teaspoon black pepper

¼ teaspoon cayenne powder

1 lemon

This barbecue sauce is an old family recipe that I discovered by accident when sorting through a stack of old folders in the back of a filing cabinet. There on a tattered and yellowed index card I found directions handwritten by my late father-in-law (who grew up in western Louisiana, near the Texas border) for the celebrated barbecue sauce he slathered on his ribs. This sauce, which is slightly tart and has no smokiness, is different from most commercial ones, which are sweet with smokey undertones. It's delicious on ribs (page 110) or mixed with chopped beef for burgers (page 40).

MAKES ABOUT 1 1/2 CUPS

Melt butter in a medium, heavy saucepan over medium heat. When hot, add onion and garlic and cook, stirring, until just softened, 3 to 4 minutes. Add 2½ cups water, the vinegar, chili sauce, ketchup, sugar, mustard, salt, black pepper, and cayenne. Stir well to blend. Mixture will be quite thin.

Halve lemon and juice it. Add juice and one of the juiced halves to the saucepan. Bring sauce to a simmer, lower heat, and cook, uncovered, at a brisk simmer, until sauce has thickened and reduced to about 1½ cups, about 1 hour. (The sauce can take up to 2 hours or more to reduce; it will depend on whether your saucepan is wide or narrow and the intensity of the heat from your burner.) Remove from heat when done and discard the lemon half. Cool, cover, and refrigerate. (Sauce can be prepared 1 week ahead. The sauce can also be put in an airtight container and frozen for up to 1 month.)

WARM CITRUS BUTTER

⅔ cup fresh orange juice

2 tablespoons plus 2 teaspoons fresh lemon juice

12 tablespoons (1½ sticks) unsalted butter

2 teaspoons grated orange zest

2 teaspoons hot (spicy) sesame oil

Salt

This quickly made butter is seasoned with bright splashes of lemon and orange, along with a dash of heat from some hot sesame oil. It makes an admirable dipping sauce for shrimp and lobster.

MAKES ABOUT 1⅓ CUPS

Combine orange and lemon juices in a small nonreactive pan set over medium-high heat. Reduce liquids to ½ cup, about 2 to 3 minutes. Add butter, orange zest, sesame oil, and scant ¼ teaspoon salt. Whisk until butter is melted. Taste, and season with more salt, if needed. (The butter can be prepared 1 day ahead; cool, cover, and refrigerate. Reheat, stirring, in a medium saucepan over low heat.)

CURRY BUTTER

8 tablespoons (1 stick) unsalted butter at room temperature

1 teaspoon curry powder

½ teaspoon dried thyme

½ teaspoon cayenne pepper

½ teaspoon ground cumin

¼ teaspoon salt

Curry powder is blended with hints of thyme, cayenne, and cumin to season this butter. It can be spread on hot ears of corn on the cob (page 136) or used to season grilled chicken or lamb.

MAKES ABOUT ½ CUP

Blend all the ingredients together and shape into a log 1 inch in diameter. Cover with plastic wrap and chill until firm. (The log can be prepared 2 days ahead. Bring to room temperature to soften before serving.)

LIME CILANTRO BUTTER

The clean, bracing taste of lime pairs well with fresh chopped cilantro in this seasoned butter. It's delicious used on corn on the cob (page 136), works wells as a garnish to grilled swordfish (page 90), and would be good tossed with cooked green beans.

8 tablespoons (1 stick) unsalted butter at room temperature

2 teaspoons fresh lime juice

2 teaspoons finely chopped fresh cilantro

1 teaspoon grated lime zest

1 teaspoon minced garlic

¼ teaspoon salt

MAKES ABOUT 1/2 CUP

Blend all the ingredients together and shape into a log 1 inch in diameter. Cover with plastic wrap and chill until firm. (The log can be prepared 2 days ahead. Bring to room temperature to soften before serving.)

RED BELL PEPPER BASIL BUTTER

MAKES ABOUT 1/2 CUP

8 tablespoons (1 stick) unsalted butter at room temperature

3½ tablespoons minced red bell pepper

1 to 1½ tablespoons finely julienned fresh basil

1 teaspoon minced garlic

¼ teaspoon salt

Diced red bell peppers, minced garlic, and chopped basil are the simple but assertive seasonings for this butter. It's good slathered on corn on the cob (page 136), on slices of crusty bread, or spread over grilled salmon or halibut fillets.

Blend all the ingredients together and shape into a log 1 inch in diameter. Cover with plastic wrap and chill until firm. (The log can be prepared 2 days ahead. Bring to room temperature to soften before serving.)

BLUE CHEESE WALNUT BUTTER

Crumbled blue cheese and toasted walnuts are the star ingredients in this seasoned butter, while rosemary and chopped fresh parsley are colorful accents. The butter, which can be prepared 2 days in advance, is delicious on grilled beef steaks (page 26) and lamb chops. It also makes a tempting topping for baked potatoes.

6 ounces blue cheese, crumbled

4 tablespoons (½ stick) unsalted butter at room temperature

3 tablespoons chopped fresh flat-leaf parsley

¾ teaspoon dried, crushed rosemary

¼ cup (about 1 ounce) toasted walnuts (see page 15)

Salt, if needed

MAKES ABOUT 2 CUPS

Combine cheese, butter, parsley, and rosemary in a medium nonreactive bowl. Stir to blend well. Mix in walnuts. Taste and add salt, if needed; the blue cheese is quite salty, so you will probably not need any salt. (Blue cheese butter can be prepared 2 days ahead; cover and refrigerate. Bring butter to room temperature before using.)

HOT APRICOT MUSTARD

This quickly assembled mustard sauce scented with apricot preserves and fresh rosemary is a fine accompaniment to grilled sausages (page 53) or a delectable garnish to slices of baked ham served at room temperature. The sauce can be made a day ahead and reheated when needed.

½ cup apricot preserves

¼ cup hot mustard (see note)

2 teaspoons chopped fresh rosemary

MAKES ABOUT 3/4 CUP

Place apricot preserves in a small, heavy nonreactive saucepan. With kitchen scissors or a small, sharp knife, chop up any large pieces of apricot. Set pan over medium heat and whisk constantly until liquefied, 1 minute or less. Whisk in mustard and continue to cook until mixture becomes almost translucent and starts to simmer, 1 minute or less. Remove from heat and stir in chopped rosemary. (The glaze can be prepared 1 day ahead. Cool, cover, and refrigerate. Reheat, stirring, over low heat.)

NOTE: Hot Mister Mustard, available in most groceries, works particularly well in this recipe.

GREEN MUSTARD SAUCE

Several years ago I was seduced by a delicious green mustard sauce served with roasted chicken at Carole Peck's Good News Café in Woodbury, Connecticut. I liked the sauce so well that I tried to reproduce it in my own kitchen. I found that grainy Dijon mustard, whole cloves of garlic, and chopped fresh spinach and arugula leaves could quickly be whirled together with sour cream and light cream in a food processor to produce the verdant sauce. This condiment is especially good with grilled salmon (page 88) or chicken.

⅔ cup coarsely chopped spinach leaves

⅔ cup coarsely chopped arugula leaves

¼ cup sour cream

¼ cup light cream

2 tablespoons whole-grain Dijon mustard

2 medium cloves garlic, peeled

MAKES ABOUT 3/4 CUP

Combine all ingredients in the bowl of a food processor or in a blender and process 30 seconds or longer until greens and garlic are chopped finely and blended into other ingredients.

If not using immediately, place in a nonreactive bowl. Cover and refrigerate. (The mustard sauce can be made 1 day ahead; bring to room temperature 30 minutes before using.)

BASIL MAYONNAISE

This basil-scented spread, made with store-bought mayonnaise, fresh basil, and garlic, takes no more than 10 minutes to prepare. It's a great addition to BLTs (page 120) and would be good on sandwiches made with grilled or roasted chicken or lamb.

½ cup regular or reduced-fat (not nonfat) mayonnaise

½ cup loosely packed chopped fresh basil leaves

1 clove garlic, coarsely chopped

MAKES ABOUT **2/3** CUP

Combine all ingredients in the bowl of a food processor and pulse 1 minute or less, until the basil and garlic are minced and blended into the mayonnaise. (The mayonnaise can be prepared 1 day ahead; cover and refrigerate.)

CUMIN MAYONNAISE

MAKES ABOUT **1** CUP

This mayonnaise, which takes only minutes to assemble, makes a distinctive and easy accompaniment to grilled pork chops. It also makes an excellent garnish for grilled turkey burgers or could be used as a dipping sauce for shrimp.

4 teaspoons ground cumin

1 cup regular or reduced-fat (not nonfat) mayonnaise

3 tablespoons chopped fresh cilantro

2 teaspoons fresh lime juice

Heat a small skillet over medium heat and when hot, add ground cumin. Cook, stirring for 1 minute, to develop the flavor of the spice. Set aside.

In a nonreactive bowl, whisk together mayonnaise, cilantro, lime juice, and toasted cumin. Cover and refrigerate. (The mayonnaise can be prepared 2 hours ahead.)

SESAME ORANGE MAYONNAISE

This sauce, made by whisking sesame oil, rice wine vinegar, and seasonings of orange juice and zest into store-bought mayonnaise, takes only a few minutes to assemble and holds up beautifully refrigerated for several hours. The strong accents of sesame and orange make it an excellent sauce to use with such shellfish as lobsters (page 128), shrimp, or scallops.

1 cup regular or reduced-fat (not nonfat) mayonnaise

2 to **4** teaspoons Asian sesame oil (see note)

2 teaspoons rice wine vinegar

2 teaspoons fresh orange juice

½ teaspoon grated orange zest

MAKES ABOUT 1 CUP

In a nonreactive bowl, whisk all ingredients together, using only 2 teaspoons of the sesame oil. Taste and add up to 2 more teaspoons of sesame oil, if desired. Cover and refrigerate until needed. (The mayonnaise can be made 4 hours ahead. Bring to room temperature 30 minutes before using.)

NOTE: Different brands of sesame oil seem to vary in their intensity, so add the oil gradually to taste.

CHUTNEY MAYONNAISE

Purchased mayonnaise can be easily enhanced by the addition of curry powder and mango chutney. The resulting spicy spread has many uses. Try making chicken salad with it, spread it atop grilled turkey burgers, or use it as a sauce for drizzling over pita pockets filled with sliced ham and Cheddar.

½ cup regular or reduced-fat (not nonfat) mayonnaise

2½ tablespoons mango chutney (chop any large pieces of mango coarsely)

¾ teaspoon curry powder

Stir together all ingredients in a small bowl. Cover and refrigerate. (Chutney mayonnaise can be prepared 1 day ahead.)

MAKES ABOUT 2/3 CUP

WASABI MAYONNAISE

Wasabi powder, which is made with ground, dried Japanese horse-radish, has a sharp, fiery, pungent flavor. When mixed with water to form a paste, this mixture can be stirred into purchased mayonnaise to make a piquant condiment. The mayonnaise is good served with grilled tuna or salmon or on Tuna Burgers with Pickled Ginger (page 48).

2 tablespoons wasabi powder

½ cup regular or reduced-fat (not nonfat) mayonnaise

In a small bowl, combine wasabi powder with 1 tablespoon water and stir to mix with a fork. Add mayonnaise and stir well to blend. Cover and refrigerate until needed. (Mayonnaise can be prepared 1 day ahead.)

MAKES ABOUT 1/2 CUP

QUICK TARTAR SAUCE

1 cup regular or reduced-fat (not nonfat) mayonnaise

6 tablespoons chopped dill pickle

¼ cup chopped fresh flat-leaf parsley

2 tablespoons minced yellow onion

2 tablespoons drained, chopped capers

2 teaspoons Dijon mustard

2 teaspoons fresh lemon juice, plus more if needed

This mayonnaise-based sauce is a time-honored classic to serve with fish. This version, made with purchased mayonnaise, takes only minutes to assemble and is delectable spread on Cape Cod Fried Scallop Rolls (page 126).

MAKES ABOUT **1½** CUPS

Combine all ingredients in a medium nonreactive bowl and stir to mix. Taste, and if you want a tarter taste, add a little additional lemon juice. Cover and refrigerate. (Tartar sauce can be prepared 1 day ahead.)

BEST EVER CARAMEL SAUCE

What distinguishes this caramel sauce from others is the addition of a small amount of cream cheese, which provides a slightly salty accent. The sauce can be made in advance and kept refrigerated several days until needed. It is good drizzled warm over scoops of vanilla ice cream to make Rum Caramel Pecan Sundaes (page 300) or used for Caramel Iced Coffee (page 213).

2 ounces cream cheese at room temperature

¼ cup light cream

¾ cup sugar

3 tablespoons unsalted butter, diced

MAKES ABOUT 3/4 CUP

Whisk together cream cheese and cream in a small bowl until smooth and set aside.

Combine sugar and 6 tablespoons water in a heavy, medium saucepan over low heat, swirling pan occasionally until sugar dissolves. Increase heat and boil until syrup turns a light golden brown color, 6 to 8 minutes. Remove pan from heat and stir in cream cheese and cream. Be very careful, as mixture will bubble vigorously. Whisk in butter. Use warm as a sauce or let cool to room temperature to use as a glaze or icing. (Caramel sauce can be prepared 5 days ahead. Keep covered and refrigerated.)

EXTRA-RICH CHOCOLATE SAUCE

Equal amounts of chocolate and cream, thinned with some water, make this a classic ganache sauce. Prepared with dark bittersweet chocolate, this indulgent accompaniment (which would make just about anything taste better!) is best served warm. It's a perfect partner for Burnt-Sugar Vanilla Ice Cream (page 291) and would be good with the Kentucky Bourbon Cake (page 244).

¾ cup heavy cream

6 ounces bittersweet chocolate, coarsely chopped

1 teaspoon bourbon (optional)

MAKES ABOUT 1¼ CUPS

Combine cream and 6 tablespoons water in a medium, heavy saucepan over medium-high heat. Bring to a boil. Remove from heat and add chocolate. Whisk until mixture is smooth and shiny. Stir in bourbon, if desired. (Chocolate sauce can be prepared 5 days ahead. Cool, cover, and refrigerate. Reheat, stirring, over medium-low heat.)

CHOCOLATE COFFEE SAUCE

1 cup light cream

1 tablespoon unsalted butter

1 tablespoon sugar

6 ounces semisweet chocolate, coarsely chopped

2 tablespoons coffee liqueur, such as Kahlúa

Chocolate and coffee make good partners in this dark, rich dessert sauce. The sauce, which keeps well for several days when refrigerated, can be reheated quickly when needed. It is delectable ladled over scoops of vanilla, coffee, or chocolate ice cream. Try it, too, with the Chocolate Pound Cake (page 246).

MAKES ABOUT 1½ CUPS

Combine cream, butter, and sugar in a heavy, medium saucepan over medium heat, and stir until mixture comes to a boil. Remove from heat and add chocolate. Whisk until chocolate has melted and sauce is smooth. Whisk in coffee liqueur. (Sauce can be made 4 days ahead; cool, cover, and refrigerate. Reheat, stirring, over low heat.)

FRESH ORANGE SAUCE

This easy, refreshing sauce, made with fresh orange juice, can be prepared a couple of days in advance. Try it drizzled over scoops of vanilla ice cream or over slices of pound cake garnished with strawberries.

1 cup fresh orange juice

1½ tablespoons cornstarch

2 tablespoons unsalted butter

¼ cup sugar

1 tablespoon grated orange zest

MAKES ABOUT 1¼ CUPS

Whisk orange juice and cornstarch in a bowl until cornstarch dissolves. Melt butter in a small saucepan over medium heat. Whisk in sugar, orange zest, and orange juice mixture. Whisk until sauce comes to a simmer and thickens slightly, about 4 minutes. Remove from heat and cool. (Sauce can be made 2 days ahead. Cover and chill. Bring to room temperature before serving.)

WARM LEMON SAUCE

MAKES ABOUT **1** CUP

⅔ cup sugar

1½ tablespoons cornstarch

⅛ teaspoon salt

1 tablespoon unsalted butter

3 tablespoons fresh lemon juice

½ teaspoon grated lemon zest

1 egg yolk

This tangy sauce would be delicious spooned over slices of angel food cake or pound cake topped with fresh strawberries. It can be made in advance and reheated quickly at serving time.

Combine sugar, cornstarch, and salt in a heavy, nonreactive medium saucepan over medium heat. Stir in ⅔ cup water. Cook, stirring constantly with a whisk, until sauce is clear and thick, 2 to 3 minutes. Remove from heat and stir in butter, lemon juice, and lemon zest.

Put egg yolk in a small bowl and slowly whisk in ⅓ cup of the warm sauce. Whisk the egg mixture back into the pan with the warm sauce. Heat the sauce again, whisking constantly over low heat until it thickens, about 1 minute. (Sauce can be made 2 days ahead. Cool, cover, and refrigerate. Reheat over low heat, stirring constantly. If sauce seems too thick when reheated, thin with 1 to 2 tablespoons of water.)

WARM BLUEBERRY SAUCE

This simple and quick sauce, made with fresh blueberries, can be used to embellish a number of desserts. Serve it warm over scoops of vanilla ice cream or pair it with icy cold lemon sorbet. Or, ladle it over slices of pound cake garnished with sliced peaches.

⅔ cup sugar

¼ cup fresh lemon juice

2 tablespoons cornstarch

2 cups fresh blueberries

MAKES ABOUT 2 CUPS

Combine 1 cup water, the sugar, lemon juice, and cornstarch in a heavy, medium saucepan, and whisk until cornstarch is completely dissolved. Place over medium heat and stir for 1 minute. Add blueberries and continue to stir and cook until sauce has thickened, about 5 minutes. (If not using immediately, cool, cover, and refrigerate for up to 2 days. Reheat over low heat, stirring, when ready to use.)

The wild blueberry is the state berry of Maine

INDEX

BIBLIOGRAPHY

ELECTRONIC REFERENCES

A Day in the Life: Dinner is Served. 2003. Monticello: The Home of Thomas Jefferson. 30 March 2003. <http://www.monticello.org/jefferson/dayinlife/dining/at.html>

A is for Artichoke. 2003. California Farm Service Agency. 13 April 2003. <http://www.fsa.usda.gov/ca/a_is_for_artichoke.html>

An Abbreviated History of Peanut Butter. 2001. Groceries USA. 13 April 2003.<http://www.groceries-usa.com/pbknowl.html>

Brainteasing Barbecue Trivia. 28 March 2002. Hearth, Patio & Barbecue Association. 23 March 2003 <http://hpba.org/newsroom/barbecuetrivia.pdf>

California Strawberry Commission. 2001. California Strawberry Commission. 13 April 2003. <http://www.calstrawberry.com>

State Fruit, the Cherry. 2003. State of Utah. 30 March 2003. <http://pioneer.utah.gov/cherry.html>

Cool as a Cucumber. 27 March 2000. Fargo Public Schools. 13 April 2003. <http://www.fargo.k12.nd.us/schools/Washington/Schutz/cool_as_a_cucumber.htm>

Corn. 2003. West Central Wisconsin Community Webring. 13 April 2003. <http://www.wcwcw.com/feature63.htm>

Facts About Maine. 2003. Information Resource of Maine. 13 April 2003. <http://www.maine.gov/portal/facts_history/facts.html>

Food History: Barbecue. 2002. James T. Ehler. 23 March 2003. <http://www.foodreference.com/html/artbarbecue.html>

Fun Facts. 2003. Watermelon.org. 13 April 2003. <http://www.watermelon.org/index.asp?a=dsp&htype=funn&pid=32>

Idaho: the Gem of the Mountains. 22 November 2002. Geobopological Survey. 30 March 2003 <http://www.geobop.com/World/NA/US/ID/index.htm>

Hawaii: Fast Facts and Trivia. 2003. Pike Street Industries, Inc. 30 March 2003. <http://www.50states.com/facts/hawaii.htm>

The History of Chocolate Chip Cookies – Ruth Wakefield. 2003. Mary Bellis. 30 March 2003. <http://inventors.about.com/library/inventors/blchocolatechipcookies.htm>

History of the Teabag. 2003. Sue Cummings. 13 April 2003. <http://www.teamemories.com/Tea_Bag_History.htm>

Mosquito Trivia. 2000. Clark County Mosquito Control District. 30 March 2003. <http://pithaya9.com/mosquito/trivia.html>

The Mustard Legacy Begins. 2001. Reckitt Benckiser. 13 April 2003. <http://www.frenchs.net/foodservice/hist.htm>

Onion History. 2003. National Onion Association. 13 April 2003. <http://www.onions-usa.org/onion_tips_info/onion_history.htm

Picnic Ideas and Picnic Baskets. 2000. Merchants Passage/Picnic Ideas. 30 March 2003. < http://www.picnic-ideas.com/picnic-ideas-picnic-baskets-picnic_history1.htm >

America's Favorite Sweet Onion. 2002. Vidalia Onion Bros. 13 April 2003.<http://www.vidaliaonions.com/history.htm>

Vital Hot Dog Statistics. 1999. The American Meat Institute. 23 March 2003 <http://www.hot-dog.org/hd_vitalstats.htm>

World's Only Corn Palace. 2003. Mitchell Chamber of Commerce. 13 April 2003. <http://www.cornpalace.org/cornpalace.html>

BOOK REFERENCES

Ayto, John. *The Diner's Dictionary: Food and Drink From A to Z.* Oxford University Press, 1993.

Chalmers, Irena. *The Great Food Almanac: A Feast of Facts From A to Z.* Collins Publishers San Francisco, 1994.

Claiborne, Craig. *Craig Claiborne's The New York Times Food Encyclopedia.* Times Books, 1985.

Davidson, Alan. *The Oxford Companion to Food.* Oxford University Press, 1999.

Herbst, Sharon Tyler. *Food Lover's Companion.* Barron's Educational Series, Inc., 2001.

Lobel, Evan, and Leon, Stanley, and Mark Lobel. *Prime Time: The Lobels' Guide to Great Grilled Meats.* Macmillan, 1999.

Purviance, Jamie. *Weber's Art Of The Grill: Recipes for Outdoor Living.* Chronicle Books, 1999.

Raichlen, Steven. *The Barbecue Bible.* Workman Publishing, 1998.

Schlesinger, Chris, and John Willoughby. *The Thrill Of The Grill.* William Morrow and Company, Inc.,1990.

TABLE OF EQUIVALENTS

THE EXACT EQUIVALENTS IN THE FOLLOWING TABLES HAVE BEEN ROUNDED FOR CONVENIENCE.

LIQUID AND DRY MEASURES

U.S.	METRIC
¼ teaspoon	1.25 milliliters
½ teaspoon	2.5 milliliters
1 teaspoon	5 milliliters
1 tablespoon (3 teaspoons)	15 milliliters
1 fluid ounce (2 tablespoons)	30 milliliters
¼ cup	60 milliliters
⅓ cup	80 milliliters
1 cup	240 milliliters
1 pint (2 cups)	480 milliliters
1 quart (4 cups, 32 ounces)	960 milliliters
1 gallon (4 quarts)	3.84 liters
1 ounce (by weight)	28 grams
1 pound	454 grams
2.2 pounds	1 kilogram

LENGTH MEASURES

U.S.	METRIC
⅛ inch	3 millimeters
¼ inch	6 millimeters
½ inch	12 millimeters
1 inch	2.5 centimeters

OVEN TEMPERATURES

FAHRENHEIT	CELSIUS	GAS
250	120	½
275	140	1
300	150	2
325	160	3
350	180	4
375	190	5
400	200	6
425	220	7
450	230	8
475	240	9
500	260	10